P9-AOE-197

APR   1986

WINNETKA PUBLIC LIBRARY
WINNETKA, ILLINOIS

FIGHT FOR A CITY

Clubhouse of the Union League Club of Chicago

OPLC 83

11322

FIGHT
for a City

The Story of the

Union League Club of Chicago

and Its Times · 1880–1955

By BRUCE GRANT

Foreword by HERBERT HOOVER

RAND McNALLY & COMPANY
Chicago   ·   New York   ·   San Francisco

WINNETKA PUBLIC LIBRARY
WINNETKA, ILLINOIS
THIS BOOK WAS A GIFT TO THE LIBRARY

ACKNOWLEDGMENTS

The illustrations on the following pages are reproduced through the courtesy of the Chicago Historical Society: pp. 17, 21, 29, 31, 34, 42 (Bradwell and Hoyne), 46, 49, 52, 55, 57, 61, 63, 65, 70, 89, 92, 101, 111, 116 (banquet), 122, 125, 126, 127, 129, 133, 135, 142, 153, 159, 167, 169, 172 (Hobson), 187, 189, 195.

Acknowledgment is also gratefully made to Mrs. John T. McCutcheon for permission to reproduce the cartoons on pp. 187 and 195; to the Chicago *Tribune* for the cartoons on p. 233; to Marshall Field III for the photograph on p. 139; to Reilly & Lee Company for permission to reprint the selection from *That Man Dawes,* by Paul Leach, on p. 156; to G. P. Putnam's Sons and to the Edgar Lee Masters estate for permission to use the selection from *Tale of Chicago,* by Edgar Lee Masters, on p. 260; and to the New York *World-Telegram and Sun* for permission to reproduce the cartoon by Will E. Johnstone on p. 249.

Illustrations on the following pages are credited as follows: pp. 75, 119, 209 are by United Press; p. 151, Pacific and Atlantic Photos; p. 196, copyright by Harris & Ewing; p. 235, Chicago *Daily News;* p. 258, Underwood & Underwood; p. 266, International Newsreel.

977.31
G76

copy # 21

Copyright 1955 by The Union League Club of Chicago
All rights reserved
Printed in U.S.A.

First printing

Library of Congress Catalog Card Number 55-7143

PREFACE

THE UNION LEAGUE CLUB of Chicago was chartered in 1879, and held its first meeting early in 1880. Hence, 1955 marks the Club's 75th Anniversary.

In 1952 the Club decided to publish in 1955 a history of its seventy-five years of activity. A History Project Committee was appointed, consisting of Joseph A. Matter, chairman, John P. Ballman, and George H. Redding. This committee carried through to the completion of the project, and was assisted in its work by a similar committee appointed by the Union League Civic and Arts Foundation, consisting of E. J. Bullock, Allin K. Ingalls, and Frank C. Rathje.

The members of the Union League Club of Chicago know that the Club's activities over its life have been in substantial part non-social, and have involved active participation in public affairs, with particular emphasis on patriotic activities and the improvement of state and city government. Because of this, and because this emphasis is not as well known to the public at large as to its members, the Club thought it advisable to devote a substantial part of the history to the story of the Club's activities in behalf of public betterment, especially of its immediate community: hence the title of this book, FIGHT FOR A CITY.

The committee was fortunate in obtaining as its author Bruce Grant, whose long experience in research and in the writing of history made him eminently qualified for the task at hand. The resourcefulness and skill with which he developed his manuscript proved the wisdom of the choice. Space limitations of course made it impossible to write about everything of interest in which the Club had been engaged during its busy seventy-five years of

160820

activity. Mr. Grant was given almost complete freedom in the selection of the incidents and material to appear in the book; only in one or two instances did internal considerations cause the Club to suggest the selection of material.

The committee is grateful to many persons for active help in the preparation and publication of the book. Professor Ray A. Billington, W. W. Goodpasture, E. R. Gray, Henry Regnery, Franklin Meine, and Stanley Pargellis gave valuable preliminary advice. Edwin Balmer of New York City gave the committee the benefit of his experience in the publication of a similar history for the Union League Club of New York. Paul Angle, Director of the Chicago Historical Society, was of substantial assistance, both in the giving of helpful advice and in making available the research and illustrative material of the Society.

Throughout the project Mr. Grant had the close collaboration of the staff of the Club, whose personal experience was frequently of assistance in the collation and interpretation of materials. Various Chicago newspaper libraries made valuable data available, as did several members of the Club. Special acknowledgment is made to Vernon R. Loucks, Russell Peters, and Alex D. Bailey, during whose terms as president of the Club the project was conducted, for co-operation and encouragement.

To more than any other one person, credit for the successful fruition of the project is due to Edward M. Martin, Director of Public Affairs for the Club for the past thirty years. His long familiarity with the work of the Club, his years of editorial work on Club publications, his ready willingness to devote many weeks of work to the book while also carrying on his regular duties at the Club, and particularly his unflagging interest throughout the progress of the work, made his assistance invaluable.

JOSEPH A. MATTER

CONTENTS

FOREWORD

This history of the first seventy-five years of the Union League Club of Chicago speaks for itself.

It is seldom, in the shifting of forces in our country, that a civic organization is able to survive and above all maintain its virility over such a span of years.

All of which proves that its foundation, purposes, and its service to the community have been of the highest order. And with these foundations in purpose and service, the Union League Club of Chicago will live to celebrate its 150th Anniversary.

Herbert Hoover

FIGHT FOR A CITY

Chapter One

TO THWART THE DESIGN
OF TRAITORS

ON THE NIGHT OF JUNE 25, 1862, ELEVEN DETERMINED MEN gathered secretly on the third floor of a brick building in the little town of Pekin, Illinois, lifted their right hands, and took an oath on the Bible, the Declaration of Independence, and the Constitution of the United States, which had been placed upon the Stars and Stripes. The occasion was marked by gravity. The oath was impressive:

"I do solemnly swear in the presence of God and these witnesses, that I have never voluntarily borne arms against the United States since I became a citizen thereof; that I will support, protect, and defend the Constitution and Government of the United States and the flag thereof against all enemies, foreign and domestic; that I will bear true faith and allegiance; and that I will also defend this state against any invasion, insurrection, or rebellion, to the extent of my ability. . . ."

These men had come together to form a new patriotic organization—the Union League of America. They dedicated themselves to the preservation of the Union. To their organization all loyal citizens could rally to stamp out treason. Their concern was immediacy; their solicitude was for all time. And so well were their patriotic foundations laid that Union League clubs throughout the nation were to survive them, and the movement was to sire in patriotic principle the present-day Union League Club of Chicago.

The oath these men swore was in grim earnest, for in this summer of 1862, slightly more than a year after canister and grape had rained on Fort Sumter to touch off the flames of civil strife, the lessons of war had at last begun to have their effect on the people of Illinois. It had been difficult at first for the northern states to come to a full realization of the conflict. Communities remote from the actual fighting were lulled into a feeling of confidence and security. Business went on as usual, and there was optimistic talk of industrial expansion.

But the fluctuating fortunes of war now brought a threat to the very existence of the Union. Disheartening rumors came from Vicksburg, and none too hopeful reports on Grant's movements near Memphis. McClellan had failed to take Richmond, and the South was jubilant at the prospect of an early victory. More threatening still was the news of Confederate raids into Indiana, creating a state of alarm all along the Ohio River. A spy was arrested in Chicago, and the city was said to be filled with Secessionists. "They are in the churches, schools, civic organizations. In some hotels it is fairly unsafe to proclaim oneself an unconditional Union man."

The presence of Southern sympathizers in the North had, of course, long been known and largely tolerated. Unchecked in their activities, they grew daily in boldness. Powerful subversive groups known variously as the Knights of the Golden Circle, the Sons of Liberty, or, in Illinois, the Sons of Illini, met openly to show their sympathy with the Rebel cause and to intimidate Union supporters. Spreading into the North from the border states, these groups occupied themselves in discouraging enlistments and encouraging desertions from the Union ranks. They resisted the draft and set up an espionage system. They even went so far as to smuggle arms, ammunition, medicine, and other supplies through the lines.

In Pekin, county seat of Tazewell County, Illinois, matters

The historic meeting place of the first Council of the Union League of America at Pekin, Illinois, is now marked by this tablet.

had come to such a state that the Secessionist element seemed to have the upper hand, while Union sympathizers spoke in whispers on the streets and were wary and afraid. Such a situation could not be endured. Patriotic citizens, stung by the ignominy of their position and roused by the danger of these hidden enemies in their midst, determined to take countermeasures. And thus it was that on that warm summer night of June 25, 1862, the first council of the Union League of America was formed—"for the purpose of organizing a pro-Union campaign AT HOME."

The moving spirit of this meeting was Major Richard Northcraft Cullom, one of Tazewell County's most respected citizens, an ex-legislator and long-time friend and political supporter of Abraham Lincoln. He had fought in the Blackhawk War and was active in Whig and Republican politics.

Present, too, was Dr. Daniel A. Cheever, recently conductor of an "underground railroad" to pass runaway slaves to Canada and freedom. Others were George H. Harlow, a clerk of the Circuit Court; John Glassgow, a justice of the peace; Jonathan

15

Merriam, a stock farmer; Hart Montgomery, the Pekin post-master; Levi Garrett, a Pekin merchant; Alexander Small, supervisor of Deer Creek township; Charles Turner, county attorney; and Henry Pratt, Delavan Township supervisor.

To Rev. W. M. Vernon, a Union refugee from Tennessee and pastor of Pekin's First Methodist Church, has been given the credit for planning and perfecting the procedure of the Union League of America, as the organization was called, taking as his model an earlier and similar organization in Tennessee.

Dr. Cheever was elected president of the Pekin Council of the League, with George Harlow as secretary. Rev. W. M. Vernon became "traveling agent," for it was hoped that the League would spread throughout the North.

And spread it did. As word of the League and its aims passed from town to town, new councils sprang up with amazing rapidity. Enoch Emery, editor and publisher of the Peoria *Transcript*, soon was a member, and on August 10 he journeyed to Chicago at the invitation of several prominent men who had heard of the League. After talking with him, some twelve or fifteen agreed to join the League and undertook to set up a Chicago council.

The time was propitious for such a step. Loyal citizens were becoming increasingly alarmed at the evidence of traitorous underground activities in their midst. Less than a month earlier, on July 23, ten thousand Confederate prisoners had attempted to break out of Camp Douglas, which was situated on the lake front between Thirty-second and Thirty-fifth streets. Intercepted letters showed that they had been in correspondence with citizens of Chicago. Some way must be found to combat the activities of the Secessionists and the more insidious Knights of the Golden Circle or Sons of Liberty. The Union League of America pointed the way.

On the night of August 19, the group of men who had talked

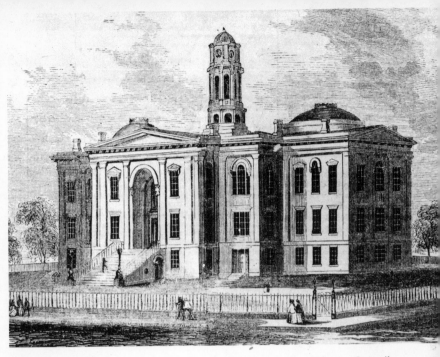

The Chicago Courthouse of Civil War days, where the Chicago Council of the Union League of America was organized.

to Enoch Emery met secretly in the chambers of Superior Judge Grant Goodrich in the Courthouse. Judge Goodrich, one of Chicago's first settlers, who some twenty years earlier had offered the then unknown Lincoln a place in his law office, explained that the newly formed League was an organization which could effectively support the Lincoln administration, counterbalance the treachery of the Sons of Liberty, and neutralize the "fire in the rear."

Others attending the meeting were Joseph Medill and Alfred Cowles, both part owners of the Chicago *Tribune;* Colonel F. A. Eastman, later to become postmaster of the city; Uriah R. Hawley, lawyer and clerk of the Court of Common Pleas; Ira Warren Buell, city attorney; Perkins Bass, former member of the school board; Jasper D. Ward, state senator and later United States district attorney; Peter Page, director of the Chicago Mutual Life Insurance Company and Internal Revenue assessor; and Josiah Bross. Senator Ward was elected president of the council, Josiah Bross treasurer, and Colonel Eastman secretary.

The existence of the organization was kept a strict secret, and meetings were at first held at night in Judge Goodrich's chambers. Membership increased so rapidly, however, that it soon became necessary to move into the larger courtroom of Superior Judge Van Hollis Higgins, and later to rent roomier quarters in Warner's Hall at Randolph and Clark streets. At the first meeting there it was resolved to call a state convention.

This convention was held at Bloomington, Illinois, on September 25, 1862, with thirty-four delegates from twelve counties. Joseph Medill, then managing editor of the Chicago *Tribune* and one of the founders of the Republican party, was chairman of the Executive Committee, a position which placed him virtually at the head of the Union League at the time. One of the first things done by his committee was to modify and revise the constitution and by-laws and write a new ritual, softening the original phraseology and making the obligation more attractive and impressive. New grips, signs, and passwords were adopted. Later these were accepted for the national organization and by other state organizations, to which many returned Union soldiers were to pledge their allegiance.

In its printed circulars the League stated: "The object of the Union League shall be to preserve Liberty and the Union of the United States, to maintain the Constitution thereof, and the Supremacy of the Laws; to put down the enemies of the Government and thwart the design of traitors and disloyalists; and to protect and strengthen all loyal men without regard to sect, condition, or party."

Specifically the councils of the League made it their business to keep track of the activities of the Sons of Liberty, noting its members and reporting their names to a central headquarters. They also encouraged enlistments, supported the prosecution of the war, and raised money and supplies for the sick and wounded.

The organization now had some 1,500 to 2,000 members in Illinois, including several smaller bodies known as Union Leagues or Union Clubs. All of these soon were absorbed by the Union League of America, and Medill and his associates set about to carry out their purpose of bringing into it every "reliable Union man in the State."

In Chicago the first council, known as the South Division Council, was drawing large and enthusiastic crowds at its meetings in Warner's Hall, and additional councils were being set up in various parts of the city, with a total membership of five hundred members. Medill also authorized John Wilson, ex-land commissioner for the Illinois Central Railroad, to organize councils anywhere in the United States.

Early in 1863, the Decatur *Gazette* commented on the organization of the League as "a safeguard to the public against the threats of the Knights of the Golden Circle." In ordinary times, the *Gazette* pointed out, secret political parties were to be disapproved, but "when evidence becomes so plain as to that now before the public concerning the designs of the Knights of the Golden Circle, it is perhaps the only salvation to our state that loyal men should hold meetings to consult upon the best plans for their own safety without their consultations being known to the tories." If the attempt were to be made to drag Illinois out of the Union, ". . . of which we hear many threats, we insist that the Union men should be prepared to resist the storm in whatever shape it may come."

The test was to come sooner than expected. When it did come in 1864, it was estimated that there were 1,300 councils of the Union League in Illinois with a total membership of 175,000. Throughout the nation there were some 2,000,000 members.

The average loyal citizen of Chicago in 1864 little realized that his city had been selected as the gathering place of conspirators and Southern agents to foment an uprising which the South hoped would result in the formation of a Northwest Confederacy.

The dream of a Northwest Confederacy, composed of the states of Illinois, Indiana, Wisconsin, Iowa, Kansas, Minnesota, and possibly Ohio, was not new. Even before the actual outbreak of the War between the States, the Southern Confederacy had hoped to induce the Northwest to join in secession. The argument was that the principal trade of the northwestern states was with the South. The Mississippi Valley had been a natural outlet for their livestock, produce, and manufactures. There was thus an inevitable economic bond between the Confederate States and those states which comprised the northwest section of the Union.

Now, in the third year of the war, violent means to attain this coalition were adopted by the South as an act of desperation. It was clear that mediation or intervention by Europe on behalf of the cotton grower would never come. And the South no longer underestimated the military qualities of the Northern soldiers, as it had at the beginning of the war. Worse still, the Confederate forces were feeling the ever-increasing pressure of the Union armies. Thus the South must place its hopes in the political influence of the Peace Democrats of the Northwest, or in crippling the Union by tearing from it the northwestern states.

Ready to aid the South in either scheme, or in any other sort of devilment that would harass or impair the Northern war effort, were the Knights of the Golden Circle or Sons of Liberty. In Illinois it was estimated that there were at this time 84,000 members of these pro-Southern groups, and throughout the North, all told, there were more than 300,000 members. Their Supreme Grand Commander was Clement Vallandigham of Ohio, who had been banished from the Union because of seditious utterances.

Loyal citizens also viewed with suspicion the so-called Peace Democrats, a Northern political group opposed to the prosecution of the war, who were termed "Copperheads" because of their practice of cutting the head of the Goddess of Liberty from a copper penny and wearing it in their coat lapels. Another popular belief derived the name from the deadly copperhead snake. Most Union sympathizers placed Copperheads and Sons of Liberty in the same class as subversive elements.

The first actual knowledge of the Chicago plot came just two weeks before the opening there of the National Democratic Convention in August, 1864. William Bross, part owner of the *Tribune* and its financial editor, learned that ten thousand stacks of arms were secreted in cellars and basements within four

"Copperheads" and other opponents of the North's war efforts were the subject of caustic cartoons.

HEADS OF THE DEMOCRACY.

blocks of the paper, presumably ready for a Rebel uprising. He at once communicated with Colonel B. J. Sweet, commandant of Camp Douglas.

At Camp Douglas, in a high-boarded enclosure of temporary barracks, some nine thousand Rebel prisoners were confined. One-third of these prisoners were former Texas Rangers and guerrillas who had served under Morgan, "wild, reckless characters, fonder of a fight than a dinner." Many others were genuine "Butternuts," so-called from their brown-dyed homespun clothes, "out at the toes, out at the elbows, out everywhere, in fact, and out of everything but their senses." The possibility of an outbreak of these desperate men was a constant threat to the city.

Colonel Sweet made his own investigation. "He verified some of our suspicions," Bross later recalled. "He had, subsequently, trusty men in every Golden Circle of Knights, and by ten o'clock the next day he knew what had occurred, and the plans that were made all over the city. Almost every leading rebel that had arrived from the South or from Canada was spotted and tracked to his den and could not move, even for the most trivial purpose if a leading man, but sharp loyal eyes were upon him."

The plot began to unfold. Weighing the information in his hands, Colonel Sweet communicated on August 12 with his superiors:

"I have the honor to respectfully report in addition to the supposed organization at Toronto, Canada, which was to come here in squads, then combine and attempt to rescue prisoners of war at Camp Douglas, that there is an armed organization in this city of five thousand men, and that the rescue of our prisoners would be a signal for a general insurrection in Indiana and Illinois."

Rescued prisoners, Confederate agents, and disloyal citizens would form an army of some twenty thousand men and "would be a nucleus about which conspirators in other parts of Illinois would gather; and being joined by prisoners liberated from other camps and members of the order [Sons of Liberty] from other states, would form an army of a hundred thousand strong."

The Union, it was surmised, could bring into the field no force capable of stopping the progress of such an army. The consequence would be that the whole character of the war would be changed, and its theater would be shifted from the border to the heart of the free states.

More details were forthcoming as time went on. The plot had originally been hatched in Canada, where the banished Vallandigham had taken refuge. Vallandigham himself had returned to the United States in June. He hoped the administration would arrest him, and this was to be the signal for the Sons of Liberty to rise in revolt.

However, when Vallandigham arrived in the United States his presence was ignored by the authorities. Despite his defiant speeches, he was allowed to rant and bluster, and he made his way without interference to the Democratic convention in Chicago. The revolt was now timed to come during the excitement of the convention.

In Chicago, Vallandigham found sentiment different than he had hoped. At his first public appearance, in Courthouse Square, he addressed a large group of citizens. John Wentworth, as police commissioner, assured him of protection, but when Vallandigham finished his tirade, "Long John" took the platform, raised his six-foot, six-inch frame to its full height, and in one of his most impassioned speeches, "full of patriotism, scathing sarcasm, and convincing argument," discredited Vallandigham and "inspired many citizens to efforts of renewed patriotism."

Meantime, Captains Thomas H. Hines and John B. Castleman, Confederate Army officers and one-time members of

Camp Douglas, on the outskirts of Chicago. An outbreak of the prisoners confined here was to touch off the Chicago uprising.

General Morgan's dashing cavalry raiders, had arrived in town with seventy-five Confederate soldiers, all in disguise. On August 28 and 29 Vallandigham called a meeting of some two hundred persons in Richmond House and read a proposed "peace platform" for the convention. Hines and Castleman here learned for the first time that there was to be no violence. The time was not right, it appeared.

The two Rebel agents had too much at stake to back down now. They arranged another meeting with Brigadier General Charles Walsh who, as head of the five thousand Sons of Liberty in Chicago, was to lead his men in the revolt. But the meeting was ill attended, and the Sons of Liberty apparently were not inclined to carry out their part in the uprising at this time. As Captain Hines later commented, "Their aggressive readiness was theoretical. They had not until now been brought to face the actualities of probable war."

The Sons of Liberty were further demoralized by the arrival of the 196th Pennsylvania Infantry and four companies of the 24th Ohio Battery—1,200 men in all—in response to the telegraphed request for reinforcements by Colonel Sweet.

Hines and Castleman now realized that it would be impossible to stage the uprising unless it were done with their seventy-five Confederate soldiers. Thus the entire project was abandoned, and peace and quiet reigned during the convention. The Peace Democrats nominated General George B. McClellan of New Jersey for President, and George H. Pendleton of Ohio for Vice-President. McClellan was nominated ostensibly as a "War Democrat," but the platform adopted was known as a "peace platform" and called for a cessation of hostilities.

The first attempt having failed, Captains Hines and Castleman, reinforced by several Confederate officers who had come down from Canada, sought as a last desperate effort to time the insurrection for the eve of the November election. But every move they made was being followed. On Monday, November 7, the *Tribune*, under the front-page headline, A GUERRILLA RAID ON CHICAGO, said: "Our military authorities were notified by telegraph yesterday of the presence of sixty mysterious persons in butternut uniforms on the Chicago, Alton, & St. Louis Railroad, holding tickets for Chicago."

Colonel Sweet acted promptly. By Tuesday morning, November 8, he had rounded up the leading conspirators, including Colonel George St. Leger Grenfell, Morgan's former adjutant general, and Brigadier General Walsh of the Sons of Liberty. In Walsh's home, Colonel Sweet's officers seized two cartloads of revolvers, loaded and capped, and two hundred muskets, as well as a large quantity of ammunition.

Captain Hines made a thrilling escape by concealing himself

in the boxsprings of a bed in the house where he was staying. Captain Castleman previously had been arrested in Sullivan, Indiana, where he had gone to meet with local Copperheads.

The great Chicago Conspiracy was at an end. But the *Tribune* was to bring home to Chicagoans the dangers they had escaped. Its edition of November 8 probably made many a coffee-cup hand tremble as some loyal citizen at breakfast read the following:

A shiver of genuine horror passed over Chicago yesterday. Thousands of citizens who awoke to the peril hanging over their property and their heads in the form of a stupendous foray upon the city from Camp Douglas, led by Rebel officers in disguise and Rebel guerrillas without disguise, and concocted by home Copperheads, whose houses had been converted into Rebel arsenals, were appalled as though an earthquake had opened at their feet. . . . Who can picture the horrors to follow the letting loose of nine thousand Rebel prisoners upon a sleeping city, all unconscious of the coming avalanche? With arms and ammunition stored at convenient locations, with confederates distributed here and there, ready for the signal of conflagation, the horrors of the scene could scarcely be paralleled in savage history. One hour of such a catastrophe would destroy the creations of a quarter of a century, and expose the homes of nearly two hundred thousand souls to every conceivable form of desecration.

There were happier events upon which to dwell. Lincoln was re-elected. Atlanta had fallen to Sherman. General Phil Sheridan had defeated Early and laid waste the Shenandoah Valley. Farragut had captured Mobile. Grant was weakening the Confederate forces by his stubborn investment of Richmond.

The Sons of Liberty were to vanish from the scene. The Union League of America was to perpetuate itself through a more permanent organization which would come down to modern times.

Chapter Two

TO DEFEND THE INTEGRITY
OF THE UNION

IT WAS THE AFTERNOON OF NOVEMBER 25, 1879. NINE MEN SAT around a table in the clubroom of Chicago's Sherman House to draw up the Articles of Association of a proposed new club, to be known first as the Chicago Club of the Union League of America, and later as the Union League Club of Chicago. Among these men were several who had met secretly in the old Courthouse, which had stood across the street in Civil War days, to form the first Chicago council of the old Union League of America. But on this present occasion there was no need for secrecy.

Ira Warren Buell, who had been one of the organizers of the first Chicago council of the Union League of America, read the Articles of Association and conditions of membership of the proposed organization to an attentive audience.

1. The condition of membership shall be absolute and unqualified loyalty to the Government of the United States.
2. The primary objects of this association shall be:
First, to encourage and promote by moral, social, and political influences, unconditional loyalty to the Federal Government, and to defend and protect the integrity and perpetuity of the nation.
Second, to inculcate a higher appreciation of the value and sacred obligations of American citizenship—to maintain the civil and political equality of all citizens in every section of our common country, and to aid in the enforcement of all laws enacted to preserve the purity of the ballot box.

Third, to resist and expose [later changed to "oppose"] corruption, and to promote economy in office, and to secure honesty and efficiency in the administration of National, State, and Municipal affairs.

Buell, as well as Long John Wentworth, Judge James B. Bradwell, and Orrin H. Salisbury, who were all present, could find in the preliminary objectives of the Club a parallel in spirit and sentiment to the oath or obligation of the old Union League of America: " . . . that I will support, protect, and defend the Constitution and Government of the United States and the flag thereof, against all enemies, foreign and domestic." This was to be the keynote of the new Union League, as it had been of the old.

Since those stirring days of the war years, in which the old League had played such a vital part, many changes had come about in Chicago, both material and cultural. The "wooden era" had ended with the disastrous fire of 1871, bringing about the destruction of what was termed "the largest frame-constructed city in the world." The new Chicago would be built on a more permanent basis. The word "fireproof" was heard whenever architects, contractors, and builders got together. Joseph Medill was swept into office as mayor on the "Fireproof Ticket.'

The period became one of social progress. The exigencies of the winter just after the fire had laid the foundations for a great transformation in civic society and social life. As a result of the disaster, the population had been reshuffled, and thousands of persons had been forced to move from one section of the city to another. Thus new ties and new associations were formed, to become the basis of social, cultural, and artistic organizations.

The development of club life, an almost neglected factor in Chicago's tumultuous early growth, was a significant feature of these times. By the late seventies, the anxieties consequent upon the re-establishment of business had subsided, and recovery

The great fire of 1871 destroyed most of the heart of Chicago. The Water Tower was one of the few landmarks to survive.

from the financial depression of 1874 had taken place. In the succeeding atmosphere of optimism and prosperity were organized most of the clubs which were to become so prominent in the affairs of the city. Among these were the Chicago Club, the most notable club organized prior to 1871; the Commercial Club, patterned after the Commercial Club of Boston; the Calumet Club and the Illinois Club, organized for social and cultural purposes; and the Iroquois Club, composed entirely of Democrats.

There was also at this time a nebulous but growing sentiment among leading Chicago Republicans for a strongly patriotic club, emphasizing Republican principles, such as those already established in New York and Philadelphia. This sentiment began to take definite form in an idea which originated with Orrin H. Salisbury, a local politician who had been a member of the old

Union League of America. The last Chicago council of the League had closed in 1877, having outlived its usefulness, and Salisbury undoubtedly wished to keep alive its ideals. He was imbued with the idea of a club which would have influence in the politics of the Northwest, particularly state and national politics.

Salisbury began canvassing for members in the summer of 1879. Among the first he approached was John Wentworth, big in physique and big in ideas, an astute politician, a student of early Chicago history, and what is more important, an ardent admirer of General Ulysses S. Grant.

A club, Republican in spirit, ready again to uphold the ideals of the Union as had the Union League of America during the fighting days of Grant, appealed to Wentworth at once. He visualized great political possibilities in such an organization. Grant had been spoken of as a candidate for a third term as President, and on this issue there were already controversial rumblings.

But not everyone interested in Salisbury's idea agreed with Wentworth. Fortunate it was for the future of the Club that more patriotic and social-minded individuals became interested in its creation. One such was Eliakim Raymond Bliss, a lawyer, who was to become the Club's first secretary.

Colonel Bliss, in later analyzing the origins of the Union League Club, was of the opinion that it "was not born of any spontaneous movement, nor was the idea received with any enthusiastic outburst. . . . In fact, its early organization moves rested under and were handicapped by a cloud of suspicion. There was an impression that the Club was to be selfishly political rather than broadly patriotic—in fact, not only political but factional in its purposes. It is of interest to record that the suspicion was that the Club was to be a factional instrument to aid in the attempt to nominate General U. S. Grant for a third term as President. . . . It was not until after the Chicago Republican National Convention of June, 1880, that the Club gained impetus for impressive growth." In other words, not until the more "broadly patriotic" and more social-minded element gained control.

Nevertheless, to have a beginning the Club needed the imposing personality of such a man as Wentworth. If Wentworth wanted it merely as a "marching club" to further the political interests of General Grant, he was at least a man who could bring men together for such a project. These men later could make of the Club what they wished.

John Wentworth was then sixty-four years old. His name and fame were not confined to Chicago. His great force of character, eminence in public life, and the many public services

"Long John" Wentworth, blunt, forthright, and uncompromising, was a dominating figure in Chicago's public life and in the formation of the Union League Club.

he had rendered were matters of more than local record. Born in New Hampshire, he later was graduated from Dartmouth College, and came to Chicago in 1836. His arrival in the frontier town was characteristic of the man. He walked barefoot through the swampy approaches to the city, carrying under his arms his boots and a jug of whiskey.

In his prime, Long John Wentworth was of imposing stature. He stood six feet six inches and weighed three hundred pounds. People paused in awe when he passed, attired in a black coat of square swallowtail cut and a broad-brimmed black slouch hat, and wielding a big black cane. He was blunt and forthright and of uncompromising principles. By 1879 he had a long and picturesque career behind him. He had been twice mayor of the city, police commissioner, and had served twelve years in Congress. He was a wealthy man. His farm of five thousand acres completely surrounded the town of Summit, Illinois.

At the Sherman House, where he lived weekdays, a huge sign was displayed: *John Wentworth's Card: Mr. Wentworth goes to his hotel to eat and sleep only and sees no one outside his office.* He dined at an enormous round table in his room, turning it as he finished one course after the other, thus literally "eating his way around the table." Once when a new manager took charge of the Sherman House and confronted Long John in the lobby and introduced himself, Long John glowered down at him and snapped: "I've been living at this hotel twenty years, young man. When I want you I'll call you, son."

If Wentworth conceived a club which would serve General Grant during peace as its prototype had served him during war, he was not the only one with such ideas. Certainly one of the most enthusiastic Grant men of that period was William Penn Nixon, who had assumed management of J. Young Scammon's Chicago *Inter Ocean* in 1875. The *Inter Ocean* announced itself as "Republican in Everything—Independent in Nothing." The paper favored Grant for a third term. Like Wentworth, Nixon was one of the founders of the Club.

How many others of the Club founders were ardent Grant men is difficult to determine. Yet most of them must have been of such political leanings to have made them acceptable to Wentworth, the dominating personality. In taking the initiative away from Salisbury, Wentworth suggested the advisability of holding a conference with some of his friends. He furnished the names of these friends, and they were invited to meet with him at the Sherman House clubroom. Those who accepted the invitation came as Wentworth's guests.

This first meeting was held in October, 1879. Besides Wentworth and Salisbury, there was Judge James B. Bradwell, former county judge and legislator; Philip A. Hoyne, United States commissioner for the District of Illinois; and Buell, Nixon, and Bliss. This gathering has been described as of a social nature, entirely informal, and "while the formation of a political club was the principal topic of conversation, no formal action was taken beyond agreeing to meet again the following week."

In fact, weekly conferences were held from that time until the first temporary organization was effected. Conversations were of a political-social order, but names were brought up of others who might be willing to join such a club if organized, and invitations were sent to these persons for later meetings.

Never more than eight or ten persons attended at one time. This was discouraging to Salisbury, who had hoped to get together at least seventy-five to start the club. But those who came to the meetings went away promising to join "when a club is started." They would wait until the club actually was formed.

About the middle of November, something happened to give new impetus to the club idea. General Grant, who had just returned from abroad, arrived in Chicago. During his enthusiastic

33

General Grant received a hero's welcome on his visit to Chicago in 1879.

reception there was much discussion of his intentions regarding his candidacy for the presidential nomination. Even the *Tribune* wavered in its opposition to a third term and conceded "there was no impropriety in his becoming a candidate *de novo*, after a period of retirement and instruction," such as the last four years had given the General.

Apparently timed to coincide with Grant's visit, a circular was sent out setting forth the plans and purposes of the proposed club, and announcing a decision to proceed with a temporary organization. This circular, carrying the signatures of twenty-six prominent Chicagoans, read as follows:

We the undersigned citizens of the United States, hereby agree to form ourselves into a *political club* to be denominated the Union League Club of Chicago, to be constituted of members who believe in the unity of the States and the supremacy of the United States Government, and pledge ourselves to aid in sustaining its authority against all enemies both at home and abroad, and to the furtherance of this end we agree to meet for the purpose of organization on Tuesday, the 18th inst. at 8 o'clock in the Grand Pacific clubroom.

With its belief in the "unity of the States" and the pledge to sustain the authority of the government "against all enemies both at home and abroad," this circular could have been taken from the files of the old Union League of America.

While the original call had been for the meeting in the Grand Pacific Hotel, this was changed and the temporary organization was effected several days later in the Sherman House clubroom. Less than half of those who had signed the circular were present. Lewis L. Coburn was selected as temporary chairman, and E. Raymond Bliss named temporary secretary. Philip A. Hoyne suggested "the necessity of having a committee on membership, to see that none but the right kind of men are admitted. Men are needed of character and standing who will pay their dues." William H. Bradley, clerk of the U. S. District Court, seemed the proper man to head this committee. Andrew Shuman, former lieutenant governor and editor of the Chicago *Evening Journal*, was named chairman of the temporary organization committee.

At the adjourned meeting five days later, Ira W. Buell read the proposed constitution, by-laws, and Articles of Association, which were at once adopted. Buell had been aided in drafting these measures by four others: William Penn Nixon, the newspaperman; Judge E. A. Otis, chancery lawyer, who had assisted in organizing the Republican party in Tennessee; Charles B. Farwell, Republican representative in Congress since 1870; and Jesse

35

Spalding, a former alderman. The name proposed, Union League Club of Chicago, had a gratifying precedent in the Union League clubs of New York and Philadelphia.

While there were some conflicting sentiments about the objects of the Chicago club from the start, the very name "Union League" denoted without doubt that, like the Union League clubs of the East, the local one was modeled to some extent upon the Civil War organization. The Articles of Association of the New York and Philadelphia clubs were very much like those of the Union League Club of Chicago. Colonel Bliss pointed out that "the object of the New York club is 'to promote absolute and unqualified loyalty to the Government of the United States, to discourage all disloyalty and every attempt against the integrity of the Nation.' To the same effect are the Articles of the Philadelphia club. The similarity in the objects and of the language used would seem to indicate a common prototype, and it is beyond question that all these clubs were modeled along the theoretical lines of the Union League of America."

It seems obvious that those who founded the Chicago Club of the Union League of America had much deeper motives in mind than merely to form an ephemeral organization to further the interests of one political candidate. The Articles of Association clearly indicate that the underlying motives of the Club were of a more permanent nature. Just as the Union League of America had backed Lincoln because its members thought him the best man for the job at the time, those who started the Chicago Club of the Union League of America gave their support to Grant for the same reason. Viewing the genesis of the Club through the perspective of time, it can also be considered fortunate that it was founded with a more serious purpose than just to become a downtown social or luncheon club, as some of the early members desired.

It had been hoped to incorporate under the name of "Union

The first meetings of the Union League Club were held in the Sherman House.

League Club of Chicago," but the founders learned upon investigation that a group headed by George M. Pullman, the "Palace Car King," had anticipated them. An organization by this name had been incorporated September 10, 1872. The existence of the older club, which had never been active, meant that another name must be selected. So the certificate of incorporation, dated December 19, 1879, carried the name "Chicago Club of the Union League of America."

By terms of the Illinois charter, the incorporators were to constitute the Board of Directors for the first year of the Club's existence. Only a handful of men actually attended the preliminary meetings. Colonel Bliss, who wrote from personal knowledge, reported years later:

"It was five or six weeks after the charter was obtained before the incorporators deemed it wise to proceed with the organization, lest they have on their hands a club without members. The plan was to have a list of names to submit to the club upon its organization, and not to begin until such a list was prepared. Having in mind offers previously made to join the club when it should start, an attempt was made to obtain the signatures of those persons and as many others as possible. A paper was prepared and several of the incorporators and others interested undertook to obtain signatures from their friends and acquaintances, but only a limited number of names were obtained."

On January 20, 1880, came the historic moment when the incorporators—seven in all—met together for the first time in the clubroom of the Sherman House. These men were: James B. Bradwell, John Wentworth, Philip A. Hoyne, Ira W. Buell, William Penn Nixon, E. G. Keith, and John H. Kedzie. The session was brief and the minute book simply states:

At a meeting of the persons named in the certificate of incorporation, comprising the Board of Directors for the first year of the Chicago Club of the Union League of America, a quorum being present, the following officers were elected for the ensuing year: James B. Bradwell, President; Philip A. Hoyne, Secretary.

Chapter Three

EARLY DAYS OF
THE UNION LEAGUE CLUB

As the first year of its existence, the year 1880 was to be a decisive one for the Union League Club. But in the early months of the year, the progress of the Club was overshadowed by the larger political issues of the day. This was a memorable year in national politics. Contemporary historians have recorded that the first six months of 1880 were marked by some of the bitterest political warfare ever waged in this country. The Republican party was torn with dissension over the "third term" issue for General Grant. Opposing Grant were the ardent supporters of James G. Blaine. Faction was pitted against faction, "each with positive and uncompromising convictions and grim determination to succeed."

In Chicago, now recognized as a great political center, party passions were at fever heat. The ample hall, hotel, railroad, and telegraph facilities offered by the Midwest metropolis made it the choice of the Republican National Committee for the Seventh National Convention of the Republican Party, to be known as "the greatest held by that party up to that time, with the possible exception of the historic convention which nominated Lincoln." Here the struggle for power within the Republican party came to its climax.

"For months prior to the meeting of the convention in this city on June 2nd, these factions were aligned in hostile array," records E. R. Bliss, first secretary of the Union League Club.

"Any movement made by the members of one faction was looked upon with disfavor by the others. One of these units, in the political parlance of today, would be denominated 'stand-patters.' To this latter class belonged a large majority of the incorporators of the Union League Club. The factional leanings of these men were not a matter of mere suspicion, but of fact. Not one of them hesitated to express his political preferences, and these sentiments were reflected in the editorials of the Republican newspaper (*Inter Ocean*) controlled by one of their number. It is no wonder, then, that there should have existed a suspicion that the Club was being organized in the interest of one of these factions, and that many of those offered membership should prefer to wait until the true character of the Club was disclosed."

It was in the midst of this political turmoil that the Board of Directors of the Chicago Club of the Union League of America met in the clubroom of the Sherman House on January 27, 1880. This was the second meeting of the board, and the matter before it was the election of nine additional members to the Club: Lewis L. Coburn, C. S. Squiers, W. H. Bradley, Luther Laflin Mills, O. H. Salisbury, Andrew Shuman, E. R. Bliss, Enos Ayres, and Jesse Spalding. With the seven members of the board, this brought the membership of the new club to sixteen, all of whom signed the constitution and by-laws, thus becoming the "founding fathers" of the Union League Club.

Of these sixteen original members, eight were lawyers, three held public office, two were newspapermen, one was an insurance man, one a real estate broker, and one a wholesale milliner. Their average age was fifty-three years, with Enos Ayres the oldest at sixty-six, and Luther Laflin Mills the youngest at thirty-two.

Ayres was in the real estate and brokerage business. Judge Bradwell, born in England, was a lawyer and former state legislator. William H. Bradley was clerk of the United States District Court. Ira Buell, a native of New York, practiced law. Bliss was

Chicago January 27 1880.

The Board of Directors of the Chicago Club of the Union League of America met pursuant to Call

Present James B Bradwell
John Wentworth
Ira W Buell
Philip A Hoyne

a quorum being present —

Upon Motion. The Constitution and By Laws as engrossed were adopted to take effect from and after the first Meeting of the Club to be Called by the Board of Directors

The following named gentlemen were then elected members of the Club all of whom signed the Constitution and By Laws to wit

Replica of a page of the minutes of the second meeting of the Union League Club's first Board of Directors.

Membership card No. 11, issued to Robert S. Critchell.

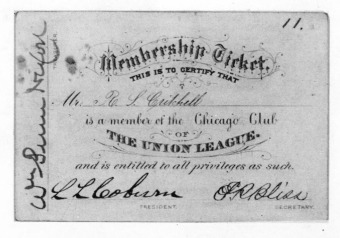

Membership Ticket.
THIS IS TO CERTIFY THAT
Mr. R S Critchell
is a member of the Chicago Club
OF
THE UNION LEAGUE.
and is entitled to all privileges as such.

L L Coburn
PRESIDENT.

R R Bliss
SECRETARY.

PHILIP A. HOYNE

JAMES B. BRADWELL

First officers of the Union League Club.

WILLIAM PENN NIXON

E. R. BLISS

LEWIS L. COBURN

a lawyer. L. L. Coburn was a patent attorney, described as "tall, courtly, and dignified." Phil Hoyne was United States Commissioner for Northern Illinois. John H. Kedzie was an insurance man. Elbridge G. Keith was in the wholesale millinery business. L. L. Mills, a graduate in law at the University of Michigan, was a man who "feels deeply and conceives vividly in language." William Penn Nixon was a lawyer and newspaper man. Orrin H. Salisbury was a politician. Andrew Shuman was editor of the Chicago *Evening Journal*. Jesse Spalding was an insurance man, lumber dealer, and politician. C. S. Squiers was assistant postmaster. John Wentworth was a lawyer, politician, and public figure.

During its first year the Club had two sets of officers. At the January 20 meeting, Judge Bradwell and Philip A. Hoyne were elected president and secretary respectively of the Board of Directors. At the January 27 meeting, on motion of John Wentworth, "the election of officers for the year ending the fourth Tuesday in January, 1881, was proceeded with and the following named gentlemen" were elected to their respective offices: L. L. Coburn, president; E. R. Bliss, secretary; O. H. Salisbury, assistant secretary, and William Penn Nixon, treasurer. The election of other officers was postponed to a future meeting of the Club.

Bradwell and Hoyne attested the minutes of meetings of the Board of Directors during 1880, and Coburn and Bliss attested the minutes of the meetings of the Club held during the same period. Hoyne is recorded in the minutes of the meeting of December 7, 1880, as signing a communication as " Secretary of the Board of Directors." At the first annual meeting on January 25, 1881, John C. Coonley was elected president, and Robert S. Critchell secretary. After that date Critchell signed the minutes of the meetings of both the board and the Club.

John Wentworth, as chairman of a temporary committee on

membership, presented a list containing eighty names, with the recommendation to the Club that they be elected to membership. While these members were duly elected, 40 per cent of them declined to join.

"There was little variation in the percentages of acceptances and declinations in the early months of the Club," wrote Secretary Bliss. "Taking the first 152 names elected, 49 per cent qualified and 51 per cent declined; and of the entire number elected prior to July 6, 103 of them, or 40 per cent, failed to qualify. It is a fact of record that every person elected to membership down to July 6, 1880, was recommended by Mr. Wentworth, and no objection was ever urged to any name so presented. The total of names presented by Mr. Wentworth and elected to membership was 267, all of whom, however, did not qualify."

Robert S. Critchell, a fire insurance man, later recalled: "In 1880, my friend Ira W. Buell, who was also my attorney, informed me that a new 'downtown' club might be started, and he was going into it and would like to have me join. From his description of the plan and the men who were to go in, I concluded that it was to be a rather high-toned Republican political club. I told Mr. Buell that I would be glad to put my name in, if the club would develop into a social club downtown, with a restaurant attached, to which he said that, of course, the club will develop into whatever its members might determine."

Of one of these meetings at the Sherman House, on February 10, the *Tribune* felt it had reason to complain.

"Before the meeting had been called to order," the story next day read, "Mr. John Wentworth, having silently nominated himself thereto, took possession of the chair, and singling out a *Tribune* reporter, who was present in his professional capacity, insolently ordered him to withdraw." The paper went on to say that "the Summit Farmer seems to have temporarily lost that

piano-polished urbanity for which he has a world-wide reputation. Doubtless he had been annoyed late in the afternoon by
a pressing invitation to subscribe to some worthy charity; otherwise he would have treated with more consideration a member
of the profession to which in the early days of this city he freely
contributed his greatness, if nothing else."

The *Tribune* took this occasion to state that the design of
the organization was to have a club of first-class businessmen
"with headquarters where commercial people from other points
may be entertained, and where views concerning matters of
State may be interchanged and discussed—in short, a politico-
social organization." Club members denied then that politics had
anything directly to do with the Club, and "it was asserted by
some of the members last night that no one will be admitted who
is known to be a candidate for office of any kind," to which the
Tribune, its dander up, added: ". . . although several well-known
aspirants for political honors appear upon the membership roll."

Meetings were continued in the clubroom of the Sherman
House, but on March 26 it was resolved to lease rooms in
the Honore Building, 202–204 Dearborn Street, where the
Marquette Building now stands, for a yearly rental not exceeding
$2,500. This business was transacted satisfactorily within four
days, and on March 30 a lease was signed giving the Club
possession of the rooms on May 1. Four months' rent was to be
paid in advance, and the Club was to have the privilege of renting
on the same terms for two more years.

The Board of Directors met for the first time in the new
rooms on May 22. The business in hand was permission for the
Furnishings Committee to purchase chairs from the Chicago Bar
Association, if "they could be got at $2.00 apiece." Also easy
chairs at $28 each, four tables at $100, and one at $55. The board
approved "the action of S. M. Moore, Esq. in relation to cur-
tains." William Penn Nixon moved that authorization for all

General view of the Republican National Convention in Chicago in 1880.

these expenditures be given, "if not to exceed $3,000." The purchase of a "body" Brussels carpet for the front room and reception room had been authorized at an earlier meeting, and additional furnishings were added from time to time in the course of the year.

On May 25, at the first meeting of the Club in its new quarters, upon motion of John Wentworth it was ordered that the Board of Directors keep the clubrooms open during the sitting of the Republican National Convention under such rules as it should decide. Wentworth, an ardent supporter of General Grant, was vice-president of this historic convention and a delegate from the First Illinois District.

With the close of the convention, after General Grant had been denied a candidacy for a third term and James A. Garfield had been nominated in a compromise move as the Republican choice for President, the intense and bitter factional feeling in the Union League Club appears to have subsided, and according to Bliss, "with it went, in a large measure, the suspicions entertained of the original purpose of the Club." At the meeting on June 14, the first held after the convention, nine persons were elected to membership in the Club, and for the first time everyone accepted. All was peace and harmony.

The financial condition of the Club was shown on this date when Treasurer Nixon reported having taken in $2,336.68, with disbursements of $1,410.73, leaving a balance of $925.95.

At this time, too, an embarrassing and somewhat ludicrous situation arose when it came time to ballot on an issue before the Club. Secretary Bliss set it down in the minutes thus:

Mr. Bradwell raised the point of order that no members of the Club who had not paid their semi-annual dues could vote, which point of order was sustained by the chair. Whereupon it appearing that only five members had paid their dues, the Club adjourned for two weeks.

At a meeting held on September 7, Ira Buell made a motion that the Board of Directors recommend to the Club the election of General U. S. Grant, President Rutherford B. Hayes, General James Garfield, General William T. Sherman, General Phil H. Sheridan, Hon. Thomas Drummond, U. S. Circuit Judge; Hon. Henry W. Blodgett, U. S. District Judge, and Governor Shelby M. Cullom as honorary members. This met with instant approval. All were duly elected.

Almost as controversial as the political issues this year was the question of whether the Club should set up its own restaurant. The politically minded members considered a restaurant an unnecessary luxury, while the more social minded saw it as an essential feature of an up-to-date club. Finally, at a board meeting on December 7, a communication was read from R. S. Critchell wherein Critchell and eleven other members offered to advance $100 each on dues for the next four years "towards defraying the costs of fitting up the restaurant." This proposition, giving the Club $1,200, was accepted. An appropriation of $2,800 was authorized, and a committee composed of Ira Buell, Phil Hoyne, and William Penn Nixon was appointed to act with the Room Committee to make the necessary plans. Critchell later wrote:

"At this time, the growth of the city having proceeded with great rapidity, there was a real demand for a gentleman's club in the heart of the city, in addition to one already existing, which would conduct a first-class restaurant, and whose membership would be exclusive. . . . The strictly 'dyed in the wool' Republican politicians like John Wentworth, Phil Hoyne, Judge Bradwell, and others whom old man Salisbury had got in at the start, did not sympathize with the social and restaurant feature at all, and, to get the restaurant started, it became necessary for me, with a few other men, to sign a written guarantee to be responsible for all costs of outfitting the restaurant beyond the amount of cash on hand in the treasury, which was as much as these gentlemen, who were the temporary board of directors, would vote."

The restaurant would have to be good, as Chicago at that time had several notable eating places. There was the famous Kinsley's on Washington between Dearborn and State, which "lacked nothing calculated to please either the eye or the palate." Race Bros.' New England Oyster House, "lighted with countless gas jets," was on Madison Street. There was a Henrici restaurant on Madison and another on Randolph. The Palmer House, Sherman House, Brevoort House, and Grand Pacific Hotel were among the hostelries specializing in good food.

The rapid growth of the Club during this first year is shown by the figures quoted in the first annual report, in January, 1881.

The Honore Building at Dearborn and Adams, where the Union League Club leased clubrooms in 1880.

The Board of Directors pointed with justifiable pride to the fact that "The Club now closes the first year of its existance (*sic*) with 260 members representing all professions and the various avocations of life in talent and character equal if not superior to the members of any similar club in the world." The treasurer's report showed that total receipts for the year were $10,237.50 and expenditures $6,996.79, leaving a total of $3,240.71 in the treasury. All bills paid.

Critchell summed up the Club's status thus: "During the first year of the Club's existence, it fell to my lot to preside at nearly all the meetings, on account of the absence of the president and the other vice-presidents. I had some decided views about the management of the Club, which differed somewhat

49

from those of many others, and I was sufficiently interested in the success of the Club, which I felt depended, to some extent at least, on my views being carried out, to make it a habit to be present at Club meetings. One of the most important things to my mind was the exclusion of Chicago visitors who were not members of the Club. The political element were quite willing to have everybody allowed the privileges of the Club at all times, which would from my standpoint have made the Club so common, and cheap, that there would be no object in joining it.

"On this issue, largely, turned the second election of officers and directors, those who were elected favoring the policy of exclusiveness. At this election I was made secretary of the Club, and the ticket on which I was elected was composed of men who as officers and directors represented the idea of an organization more social than partisan, and the partisan and office-seeking element were ignored, thus giving the Club a distinct feature other than what some of those active and prominent in the first year of the organization desired."

In this second election, John C. Coonley became president, with Charles E. Culver and Silas M. Moore as vice-presidents, and William Penn Nixon as treasurer. As far as Nixon was concerned, the political aspects of the Club were unchanged, despite Critchell's comments.

The Club now began to formulate certain rules. On February 4, 1881, it was decided to keep the doors open from 7:30 A.M. until midnight. There would be no tipping. Smoking was not to be permitted in the dining room, nor would dogs be allowed inside the Club. A "No gambling" rule was proposed. Dues were to be raised from $25 to $40 yearly beginning June 1. Members were sent cards asking whether bottled ales, wines, and liquors should be served at restaurant tables. The vote was 142 Yes and 94 No.

The long-debated restaurant was opened on March 1, 1881,

with an appropriate banquet, and soon became a celebrated and very popular feature of the Club. In the dining room were one long table and many smaller ones. Thomas Kane, who joined the Club in 1881, later said he took lunch each day at the long table "generally for the reason that Emory Storrs, when in the city, usually sat at the head of the table and entertained us with an almost unlimited supply of anecdotes."

Even Long John Wentworth came there. All others would pause in their eating, and conversation would cease as Long John strode into the dining room and took his seat at one of the smaller tables. He never removed his tall, Lincolnesque hat and he ate alone, indicating by his attitude that he did not wish to be disturbed. He apparently felt he had aided in forming a club which had quickly outgrown him and whose members to a certain extent ignored him. In later years he was to say, "I only come here once a year, for a drink."

Similarly, Orrin Salisbury, the man whose idea had started the Club and who had served as assistant secretary and assistant treasurer during the first year, soon dropped out of sight. His name does not appear on the later rosters of members, and when he died in 1887 and was buried in Rosehill Cemetery, no mention of his death was made in the annual report of that year.

Despite the limited quarters of the Club—which consisted of a moderate-sized assembly room, a considerably larger dining room, with cloakroom facilities adjoining and a kitchen in the rear—between eighty and one hundred members gathered there daily for lunch. "The interest of the members in the patriotic objects of the Club was strong," Andrew MacLeish recalled some years later. "At no time in its subsequent history has this been surpassed. We were not far enough away from the experience and perils of the great War of the Rebellion to forget that openly avowed loyalty was the duty of every citizen."

But the Club was now becoming better organized, and new

conveniences and improvements were steadily introduced. On March 28 the action of the Rooms Committee in putting in a Bell telephone was approved. A livery stable service was arranged for the convenience of the members. Andrew J. Wright, the oldest liveryman in Chicago, with stables at 15–17 Quincy Street, later was authorized to put in a private telephone connecting his stables with the Club. A member had merely to lift the receiver, wind the phone up, and order a coupé or a carriage. If he were going for "more than one mile and not more than two miles" he could hire a coupé for one or two persons at $1.00. A carriage for three or four persons the same distance would come to $2.00. Or he could rent the coupé for $1.00 an hour and a carriage for $2.00 an hour, either of which "if kept waiting more than twenty minutes" would cost fifty cents extra.

Ira W. Buell (left) and Orrin H. Salisbury (right) both took an active part in forming the Union League Club.

The matter of the change in the Club name came up on November 14. Ira Buell had already made arrangements to obtain the charter of the old Union League Club of Chicago, long inactive, and now on a motion made by Buell it was "resolved that it is desired that the name of this club be changed to the Union League Club of Chicago." A special meeting of the Club was held on January 10, 1882, to vote on the change, and the motion was unanimously carried.

Two weeks later the annual report of Treasurer Nixon showed that the Club had 561 members (with the membership then limited to 600) and a total balance of $6,484.28 in the Club's coffers.

Writing in 1916, Colonel Bliss, then the only survivor of the original founders, dwelt on the first days of the Club thus:

"In retrospect, it may be said that one early difficulty was due to the fact that the purposes of the Club were defined as purely political, which might mean much or little, depending upon the motives of the leading spirits of the organization. While no one associated with the undertaking, even at that early day, believed that the purposes would be limited to the purely political, yet, under the charter, there was no power to make other representations. The result was the management was inclined to let the organization drift in whatever direction the membership might indicate. That it has drifted considerably from its original moorings is a fact, for today a great majority of the membership never think or speak of the Club as a political body."

Chapter Four

CHICAGO IN 1880

AT THE TIME THE UNION LEAGUE CLUB WAS ORGANIZED, DYNAMIC changes were taking place in Chicago, in the nation, and through-out the world. Club members at their luncheon meetings and gatherings, when not discussing business, engaged in arguments over the promised marvels of airplanes, automobiles, radioteleg-raphy, electric lights, and moving pictures. The 1880's were the springtime of science and invention. Karl Benz in Germany was using a three-wheeled motor car of the combustion-engine type. Alphonse Penaud in France was making successful flying models of airplanes and helicopters, and writing on the theory of flight. He even patented a design for an amphibian monoplane, streamlined and with retractable landing gear.

Thomas Edison already had patented the phonograph—it had reproduced "The Last Rose of Summer" perfectly—and had just completed the first central electric power plant in the world on Pearl Street in New York City. Lighting by electricity was assured, and Jesse Spalding, insurance man and one of the founders of the Union League Club, headed a group of five in-corporators of the Chicago Electric Light Company with a capital stock of $100,000—a "company organized in faith that the Edison light would be an immense thing."

A Californian was taking serial photographs of race horses in motion and exhibiting them by the "zoopraxiscope"; and Edison, himself, was busy on his "peep-show," or "kinetoscope," which

CHICAGO IN 1883.

Chicago in 1883 was a bustling commercial city, sprawling over the wide prairies. Its population was now over half a million.

he would market in 1893. James Maxwell and Heinrich Hertz were studying electromagnetic waves, which were to prove practical for Marconi's successful experiment in communication in 1895.

The telephone! Alexander Graham Bell's instrument was a rather curious and formidable contrivance. Superior Court Judge Jesse Holdom, in reviewing events of Chicago and the Union League Club during the 1880's in a book entitled *The Spirit of the Union League Club*, recalled that the Chicagoan of those days who was enterprising enough to put one of these instruments in his office carried a small card in his vest pocket. This card was his telephone book. It had printed upon it his own name and 251 other names. The telephone user "belonged to a very small and exclusive group of people possessing this novel means for intercommunication. It was several years before telephone numbers were extended to residence districts."

Chicago was entering upon a period of prosperity, too. Behind were the uncertainties of the Reconstruction period, the devastation of the great fire of 1871, the financial debacle of 1873. The Chicago *Tribune*, in its annual review of January 1, 1881, reported that the year past had been the most prosperous in the city's history. Business had increased 17 per cent over 1879.

Population of the city had increased approximately 500 per cent in twenty years. The latest census showed 503,000 people. Commerce had increased, in a like period, about 900 per cent. The Club itself was in good shape at the end of its first year, with a cash balance on hand of $3,240.71.

The Union League Club member, if walking to his club for lunch, would make his way over wooden sidewalks of various levels, his footsteps resounding on the planks. If he drove, his carriage would roll over wooden blocks in which the wheels of traffic had often made deep ruts.

The clubman might occasionally ride the jogging horsecars, or the cable cars on main thoroughfares like State Street. The horsecar or cable car accommodated "all ranks and colors and was a great leveler." Straw on the floor kept the passengers' feet warm in winter. Whether walking or driving, the clubman would find on either side buildings of five or six stories—no higher, for the skyscraper was not to appear until a few years later.

He would stroll past a gaily painted wooden Indian standing in front of a tobacconist's shop, holding a bunch of cheroots in one hand and a tomahawk in the other. He would see here and there the barber's pole, striped in red and white, "guiding the unshorn citizen to a place where he could be relieved of the surplus growth on head or face."

The well-dressed clubman would tip his high silk hat to a lady who was gingerly making her way from her landau to

Marshall Field's great shopping emporium or some other State Street store. Her dress hem dragged through dirt and dust and caught on splinters in the sidewalk. The clubman would reason that it was well to assume that women had ankles. "Some may have daringly indulged the hypothesis that women had calves and knees; but of this there was no visible proof." Only the fact that the block-paved streets, often deep in mud and abounding in treacherous holes, gave occasion for a discreet lifting of the skirt at times, "advised the male observer that women were in truth bipeds."

In crossing the street the clubman would be wary of the butcher's boy in his light cart, which "he drove, like Jehu, with irresponsible fury." He would be careful, too, of the large drays

Horse-drawn cabs and carriages were familiar sights on Dearborn Street in the 1880's.

Typical of the many fine residences in Chicago's fashionable residential neighborhoods was this home on Prairie Avenue at 20th Street.

hauled by magnificent horses with furry fetlocks. The high-wheeled bicycle might offer a peril, as daring riders "trundled perilously over none too friendly pavements."

In summer, dust and unpleasant smells from the Chicago River and, if the wind were right, from the stockyards, caused the clubman to hurry along. In winter, snow and slush made the going hard and dangerous.

Chicago was already known as a sprawling city of the prairies. But it sprawled in a much smaller way than today. Lincoln Park, to the north, was outside of the city limits, as were Garfield and Douglas parks on the west side. Hyde Park, to the south, was a village and had not yet become a part of the metropolis, and Jackson and Washington parks were far out in the country.

The clubman, being successful and prosperous, would live in a fine residence of brick or brownstone, possibly with a marble front, set in spacious grounds. In front of the mansion, on the curb or road or driveway, quaint little Negro boys of painted cast iron served as hitching posts. On the lawn lay bronze dogs, considered as essential for outdoor decoration. In such houses lived Clubmen William Penn Nixon, at 743 Clark Street; John R. Walsh, 2133 Calumet Avenue; H. N. Higinbotham, 2838 Michigan Avenue; O. W. Potter, 130 Lake Shore Drive; Edson Keith, 1906 Prairie Avenue (right across the street from Marshall Field); and Hempstead Washburne, 534 Jackson Boulevard. Thus the Union League Club was represented in the sections of distinction.

On the West Side, Washington and Ashland boulevards were the residential thoroughfares of wealth and fashion, comparable with Michigan Boulevard, which in those times began to be a street of mansions a few blocks south of the Chicago River and so continued into the exclusive region of Prairie, Indiana, and Calumet avenues. The North Side had its fashionable quarters on Dearborn, Cass (now Wabash), and Pine (now Michigan) streets, with east and west streets running from Dearborn to the lake shore. The North Side was considered fashionable and select, but not too crowded, with Cyrus H. McCormick's recently built three-story mansion of Lake Superior sandstone, decorated by Marcotte of New York, dominating the scene at Rush and Huron streets. With twelve residences of the McCormick family in this section, it became known as "McCormickville."

Members of the Union League Club would be, of course, in and out of the Exposition Building—where the Art Institute now stands—Chicago's greatest structure in those days, where in this year of 1880 thundering oratory could not nominate Grant for a third term. They were there for the May Festival, when the Theodore Thomas Orchestra was proving to the world that Chicago was a city of people who thought of other things besides butchering hogs and building harvester machines. The concert hall was patterned after a German Tivoli garden, and foaming steins of beer helped make the music even more enjoyable. In the winter the hall became an ice-skating rink for young people.

Opposite the Exposition Building, with its three ornate domed towers and vast expanse of clean-span roof, was another impressive building. This was the Pullman Building on the other side of Michigan Avenue. On pleasant mornings Marshall Field and George W. Pullman could be seen separating here after a walk downtown from their Prairie Avenue homes.

Possibly an incentive to the art collection later acquired by the Union League Club, and most certainly the nucleus of the magnificent aggregation of pictures, statuary, and *objets d'art* now in the Art Institute of Chicago, was the art gallery in a building at the corner of Michigan Avenue and Van Buren Street. "The Beheading of John the Baptist," by Charles Sprague Pearce, and "Les Amateurs," by T. Alexander Harrison, were the first two paintings acquired and were to pass on later to their present home in the Art Institute.

When the first of the month rolled around, the Club member would be forcefully reminded of the splendid shops and stores on State Street where the latest fashions from Paris and New York were on display to tempt the feminine members of his family. Nor did he have to go to Bond Street in London for the best in men's attire. It could be found in the Chicago tailoring and haberdashery shops.

The Club member would also know the more seamy side of the city. Picking up a *Tribune* from the Club reading room table, he would read a scorching letter by Mayor Carter H. Harrison to Police Captain Fred Ebersold. "State Street from Van Buren to Jerry Moore's place is a disgrace to the city. It seems to be given over by landlords to prostitutes. These women live upstairs and at night make unseemly calls from the windows.

Situated on Michigan Avenue where the Art Institute now stands, the Exposition Building had been built originally for the Fair of 1875.

They run down to the street and turn the sidewalks into open bagnios. They go into the saloons and drink with the men and even fight. I have been loath to believe all I have heard on the subject, but last night I made a personal observation and found that the picture had not been overdrawn. In a city like Chicago we cannot prevent prostitution, but we can, and must, prevent its being made an open calling."

A man and woman were arrested on a disorderly conduct charge for boldly smoking cubeb cigarettes on the street. It had just been learned that over at 126 Washington Street the Ladies Grain Exchange had been opened in Room 60. There was a telephone and a blackboard and comfortable chairs. The "mustached sex" was barred. The telephone was connected with a bucket shop at La Salle Street and Board of Trade Alley, and the latest quotations (obtained by some devious method) were sent to the Exchange. Ladies were gambling on corn and wheat. The only objection offered, apparently, was by the men in the Pit at the Board of Trade, who now missed the ladies from the gallery, where flirtations were carried on with the same fervor as buying and selling grain.

Judge Holdom believed that Chicago society maintained something of more primitive democracy in this era, as seen in the fact that "when certain husbands of prominent social leaders urged upon their wives the importance and desirability of completing their education by teaching them to dance, these kindly ladies organized what was known as the South Side Dancing Class. It was delightfully informal. The ladies came in high-necked dresses; the gentlemen in their ordinary day apparel, despite the evening hour at which the classes were held. Social historians trace to this dancing class the origin of the big society balls, which were, however, in every sense *de rigueur*, and which belong to a later period."

Colonel Bournique and his wife had established a dancing academy in 1865 in Twenty-fourth Street between Michigan and Indiana avenues. For decades his dancing classes were uniquely the place where the children of Chicago's better families learned their social graces. His son, Augustus E. Bournique, who became a member of the Union League Club in 1916, was occasionally put in charge of balls at the Club.

Gay attire would be in order for the races on Derby Day, held at Washington Park. Society blossomed in all its splendor. The ladies and their escorts came in smart carriages, "as much to watch each other as to watch the horses in their contests for speed. The grandstand presented a brilliant and colorful scene, and on the greensward many a group gathered for an *al fresco* lunch."

This year a mild sensation was caused at the park when

Fashionable Chicago gathered at Washington Park Race Track on Derby Day.

Susan B. Anthony, a demure little woman with solemnly contemplative countenance, occupied a seat among the spectators. Hers already was an ominous name—"it stood in the mind of all male creatures for an incipient revolt of the fair sex." She was the bold leader of the newly born movement for women's rights, and mere man trembled in her presence. She was in Chicago this summer for a convention of suffrage workers.

Derby Day, the dancing classes, the visitings and dinners, and the new thrill of roller skating, then at its height, were not all the diversions for the clubman and his family. There was the theater. Everyone went to the theater, and there was entertainment to suit a variety of tastes, from the distinguished performances at McVicker's Theater and Hooley's Opera House to the crude variety shows and the dime museum with its freaks

63

and waxworks. Joseph Jefferson, Mary Anderson, Salvini, Rhea, Modjeska, and Henry Irving were popular stage celebrities in those days. Gilbert and Sullivan's lilting operas—especially "H.M.S. Pinafore"—Hoyt's comedies, and "Evangeline" and "Ermine" were among the popular offerings.

The *Tribune* was in the midst of a controversy as to whether it was proper for an audience to hiss actors. The *Tribune* defended this right, but received many letters for and against the practice.

To those partial to contemplation of silent but thrilling spectacles there were the panoramas, later to be called cycloramas, of the "Siege of Paris," "The Crucifixion," and the "Battle of Gettysburg." The panoramas were in buildings especially erected for them on opposite corners at Wabash Avenue and Hubbard Court.

Barnum's Circus was in Chicago during the summer. The Chicago Spelling Reform Association met at the Sherman House and was advocating such substitutions as "tho" for "though" and "thru" for "through." The Baltimore and Ohio Railroad was advertising "palace sleeping cars" to Washington. There was no end of good reading matter coming off the presses, and the public was engrossed in Henry George's *Progress and Poverty*, Tennyson's *De Profundis*, Sir Edwin Arnold's *Light of Asia*, and Ernest Renan's *Lectures*.

And there was baseball! J. Frank Aldrich, one of the first members of the Union League Club, was to recall with other later members—Victor F. Lawson, William Dickinson, William Whitehead, George M. Moulton, Henry A. Blair, and Chauncey Keep—how as young men back in 1865 they had played baseball on a vacant lot. Unable to buy either a baseball, mitt, or bat in Chicago, they had sent east for their balls and mitts and persuaded a local planing mill to fashion some bats for them.

But in 1880 Chicago now had its famed White Stockings,

The Palmer House, its barbershop paved with silver dollars, was one of the celebrated show places of Chicago.

who that very year were in the lead for the baseball championship, though they were not to capture it until two years later. William A. Hulbert in 1875 had brought Albert G. Spalding from Boston to be the manager of the White Stockings. Spalding, as a Rockford boy, had been the hero of the diamond, and his skill as a pitcher had enabled his home team to become champion of the region. On his return to his native state from Boston he brought with him three notable players, Barnes, McVey, and White. Spalding, later to be a familiar sight around the Union League Club, became owner of a chain of sporting goods stores.

The clubman would not spend all his leisure hours at his club. He might be found, on occasion, at the Palmer House, the Grand Pacific Hotel, or perhaps the Sherman House, the latter the birthplace of the Union League Club. But in 1880 the Palmer House was Chicago's show hotel. Nothing could compare with it this side of New York. Built at a cost of $2,000,000, it stood six stories high, and among other unique features had a barbershop the floor of which was inlaid with silver dollars. Later these silver dollars were found to have been split in half before being inlaid in the floor, but many visitors returned to their homes to boast of how they trampled silver dollars beneath their feet in the great city of Chicago. One could live at the Palmer House for from $3.00 to $6.00 a day, including meals.

The old Grand Pacific Hotel, on Jackson Street, was a hostelry of distinction. John B. Drake, one of the early members of the Union League Club, was the genial host. The hotel was famous for its annual game dinner, and was a great resort for Republicans.

The Sherman House was the favorite stopping place for the commercial traveler. It was named for Francis C. Sherman, three times mayor of Chicago, who built it in 1836. Lincoln had stopped there as early as 1848.

In such a year and amid such surroundings was the Union League Club born. But now it had work to do, and was to begin the first major battle of its long fighting career.

Entrance to Jackson Park, a favorite spot for country outings.

Chapter Five

THE PURITY OF THE BALLOT BOX

In the chicago municipal election of april 3, 1883, george Washington cast his ballot in the second precinct of the Ninth Ward. So did Thomas Jefferson, John Hancock, James Madison, Abraham Lincoln, and many other distinguished Americans. Such a turnout of notable men had never before—nor since— been recorded in any one voting place in the United States. And regardless of former political preferences, they one and all had voted the straight Democratic ticket.

Naturally this attracted some attention. It was especially noted by the investigators for the Union League Club who were making a check into the "fearful conditions of our local elections" and who had selected the second precinct of the Ninth Ward as a typical example for study.

Illegal voting was not new in Chicago. Lawlessness, scenes of violence, interference with bona fide voters, repeaters, ballot-box stuffing, colonization, and all manner of frauds had been practiced since the early days of the city. Candidates printed their own ballots. Judges of election "counted" ballots by tossing those not meeting with their approval into the Chicago River.

John Wentworth, the first Republican mayor of Chicago, in his inaugural address delivered on March 10, 1857, had deplored the scandalous conditions which, it had been charged, were prevalent on the day of election. He said:

"He who deprives one of his fellow-citizens of a free access to the ballot box deprives him of his inalienable rights, and acts the part of a tyrant and an oppressor. And he who votes, not having the right to vote, or is accessory to the voting of others who have no such rights, perpetrates a fraud upon his countrymen, and strikes a blow at the only safeguard of our Republican institutions—the purity of the ballot box."

Again, in 1860, when he had become mayor for a second time, Long John cautioned, "There is a great need of a new registry law, and of efforts to purify the city of fraudulent voters and protect the elective franchise."

Thus when the founding fathers of the Union League Club stated in their Articles of Association that one of the primary objects of the Club was to "preserve the purity of the ballot box," they were not simply voicing an abstract idea. They had in mind a very concrete situation in their own city of Chicago.

In September, 1880, when the Union League Club had been organized but a few months, J. W. Steward, county commissioner, met with the Club's Committee on Political Action "to consider with regard to the policy of largely increasing the number of polling places or districts and other matters that require prompt action by this Board." Chicago was growing at such a rate and precincts were becoming so populous that it was difficult to handle voters properly or to detect fraud. An increase in the number of polling places, it was felt, would be the first step toward insuring honest elections.

A week later the committee, through Chairman George E. Adams, submitted a report recommending that the voting precincts should be as small as possible and that no more than 250 or 300 persons should be received at one polling place. Several months later, on May 10, 1881, the Committee on Political Action further recommended that the registration laws be amended "so as to require the registry books to be closed two weeks prior to election, and no one allowed to vote at an election whose name was not on the registry."

Col. William Hale Thompson, father of Chicago's ebullient future mayor, "Big Bill" Thompson, suggested that a committee be appointed to visit Springfield to present the legislature with these proposed amendments to the election law. This was done at once, with Colonel Thompson heading the committee.

While revision of the election laws was being pressed, the mayoralty election in the spring of 1883 decided the Club on more prompt and decisive action.

The Republicans had become somewhat disheartened over successive reverses of their city tickets. They were turning out the vote, but without result. Newspapers charged that the campaign of Carter H. Harrison, running for a third term on the Democratic ticket, was being conducted by gamblers under the leadership of Democratic Boss Mike McDonald and his secretary, Joseph Chesterfield Mackin, who controlled the party machinery, and certain aldermen "who had the worst elements of the population subject to their commands."

These charges proved odious to good Democrats as well as to Republicans. A committee of citizens representing both parties was organized to consider the accusations, and to take action in reference to placing a "Reform Ticket" in the field. This committee met in Fairbank Hall, Central Music Hall Building, and became derisively known as the "Fairbank Hall Silk Stockings." The Republicans also held a convention, and a compromise was effected with the "Fairbank Hall Silk Stockings" whereby Judge Eugene Cary was nominated for mayor. Judge Cary, a member of the Union League Club, had been on the Political Action Committee during the first year of the Club's existence.

Apparently it was expected there would be considerable illegal voting at this election, for on March 31, three days before the election, the Board of Directors of the Union League Club

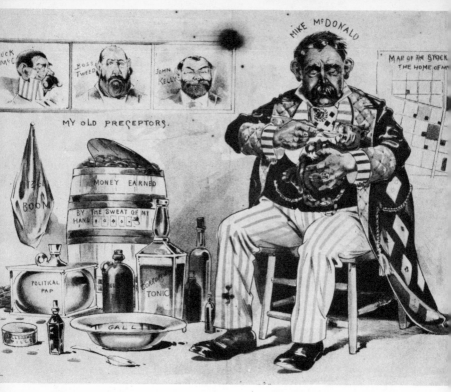

Democratic Boss Mike McDonald, special target of the reform element.

met and resolved that "a reward of $300 be offered by the Union League Club for the apprehension and conviction of any persons who shall be guilty of voting illegally at the election to be held in Chicago, Tuesday, April 3, 1883."

But despite the efforts of the Reform Ticket, Carter Harrison emerged victor. Swept into office, too, were the Democratic candidates for city treasurer, city attorney, and city clerk.

The persistent charges of fraud continued, and the Union League Club employed two investigators to make a spot check in one of the polling places. On June 12 the Committee on Political Action made its report to the Club, stating that it believed "there is great danger that the criminal minority of our city will by fraud permanently control the majority."

"To prevent this," the report read, "it is first necessary that the people should clearly understand the situation, and we have concluded that we could not do a more timely service than to place before you and the public a sample of the fearful conditions of our local elections."

From a number of similar precincts they had chosen the second precinct of the Ninth Ward for the purposes of investigation.

"Selecting carefully competent men personally known to members of our committee, we have had every house visited and, this being about the time when the Directory canvassers were making their rounds, we were enabled without suspicion to make a thorough canvass. Upon application to the City Clerk through another party we were unable to gain access to the poll book but were furnished a certified copy under the Seal of the City Clerk. This, with the lists of the canvassers duly sworn to, is herewith presented."

Careful comparisons of the two lists under personal supervision of the committee revealed "a condition of affairs beyond belief."

"The poll book has only 1,112 blanks for voters," the report pointed out. "They were filled to the last line. Not satisfied with this, however, the judges and clerks swore to receiving seventy-one more. Their affidavits read that 1,193 votes were given, so many for this candidate and so many for that, while the record is but 1,112. When you recall that the returns from the precinct were received among the very earliest (shortly after eight o'clock on the evening of the election) the only conclusion is that this poll book was written up mostly, if not entirely, at some time before the day of election."

Out of the total number of 1,112 recorded votes, 907 were fraudulent. Thirty-six were recorded as voting from vacant lots. Factories, foundries, stores, vacant buildings, houses of evil repute, and especially saloons were all represented as having a large number of voters.

"Occasionally the writers seem to have attempted to be funny," the investigators' report read. "Names of ex-presidents and other distinguished Americans were written together with names of men formerly living in the neighborhood but long since dead, while F. Jourdain is recorded as voting from Jordan."

On hearing this report, members of the Union League Club were roused to action. In the growing lawlessness of election campaigns, they realized Chicago was facing a situation which was potentially as great a threat to its liberties as the threat of military insurrection in Civil War days. To deal with this danger —to restore honest elections and to reform voting procedure— was a project worthy of a club which had as its watchword loyalty to the Union. Thus the Club embarked on its first great crusade in the cause of better government.

The facts were placed in the hands of Luther Laflin Mills, state's attorney and one of the charter members of the Club. Three judges and two clerks of election in the second precinct of the Ninth Ward were arrested, and indictments quickly followed. The Club employed one of its members, General J. B. Hawley, to aid in the prosecution, and the case came before Judge Joseph E. Gary in the Criminal Court on November 20. The five defendants were tried on an indictment which charged conspiracy.

"Mike McDonald and his faithful lieutenant, Joseph Chesterfield Mackin, were there as observers," the Chicago *Tribune* reported. A jury was waived by the defendants. There was such an array of prosecution witnesses that Judge Gary had to let them remain in the courtroom "because I haven't a big enough place elsewhere to put them."

Typical of the witnesses was one Andrew Cant, who said he had voted but was given no credit on the poll book.

"State what you voted for?" asked one of the defense counsel.

"Mayor, city clerk, city attorney, treasurer."

"Voted for everything the Republicans nominated," said Judge Gary facetiously.

"Yes, certainly," was the reply.

"Showed his good sense," added General Hawley. Judge Gary had to rap for order.

The next day Samuel Ditty, a Negro janitor, testified he had "voted under difficulties." In fact, he had been struck on the head while handing his ballot to the clerk. He complained to a policeman outside, who "called him a damned liar and ordered him away." Edward C. Rockwell, a furniture dealer, said his ticket was torn up before his eyes and a Democratic ballot shoved into his hand. He also protested to the policeman on duty and was told "to get out quick" or the policeman "would assist him."

The defense denied all allegations and the trial closed at the end of the second day.

The following day, Judge Gary ruled that under the Criminal Code of Illinois the judges and clerks of election must be acquitted. He could not find them guilty.

The *Tribune* in a scathing editorial said: "Judge Gary's verdict of acquittal in this case may be taken as an authoritative declaration that the safest crime a man can commit in Chicago is ballot-box stuffing." Also, "All that remains to law-abiding citizens of all parties is to content themselves with the dutiful payment of their taxes, and submit to the rule of criminals, saloonists, and loafers of the city." Yet the *Tribune* hastened to say that Judge Gary himself was "a man of unquestioned integrity and great legal ability."

The Committee on Political Action at a special meeting of the Club on December 10 made a lengthy report of the whole case and concluded thus:

"The committee suggests the passage of a law providing for the appointment of officers under the state laws, exercising their duties similar to those exercised by the election supervisors under the law of Congress, would go far toward securing fair and honest elections in this city. Such a law would secure the attendance at each poll of an approved citizen of each party, who would supervise the registry and election and see that from the opening of the polls until the returns were made out the election was fairly and honestly conducted, and would in addition furnish the means for securing the punishment of all persons participating in any frauds at such election."

Now came the presidential elections of the year 1884. The excitement attending the Democratic national victory, which brought Grover Cleveland to office, had not died away in Chicago when the discovery was made that a "bold and treasonable fraud" had been perpetrated in the second precinct of the Eighteenth Ward. Ballots had been tampered with so as to reverse the result in the precinct, giving a fraudulent majority for State Senator Rudolph Brand, Democrat, as against Henry W. Leman, Republican. Brand promptly announced that he would not accept an election which was in doubt, and demanded a recount.

Indignation and excitement were evident on all sides. A Citizens' Committee of Safety was formed in the Eighteenth Ward for the purpose of "hunting down and bringing to justice the miscreants who had perpetrated the frauds." Many Union League Club members co-operated in this movement. W. Nelson Blake, A. A. Carpenter, Melville E. Stone, General I. N. Stiles, Edwin Lee Brown, A. M. Day, E. F. Cragin, Erskine M. Phelps, Melville W. Fuller—later Chief Justice of the United States Supreme Court—and many other prominent representatives of both political parties formed the committee, with A. M. Day as chairman.

Luther Laflin Mills, crusading state's attorney, and Carter H. Harrison, Democratic mayor of Chicago during the Club's fight for electoral reform.

Examination of the ballot box of the second precinct of the Eighteenth Ward showed that after it had been placed in the custody of the county clerk and was in the vault of his office, the original ballots had been abstracted and a number of bogus or forged ballots, printed as facsimilies of the genuine ones—with the exception that they contained Brand's name instead of Leman's—had been substituted.

The apparent motive for the crime lay in the fact that the General Assembly election was to ballot for a United States senator, and a careful canvass of the state had shown that the senate and house were apt to be in a tie between the two parties. More completely to carry out the fraud, the entire tally sheet accompanying the ballots had been forged so as to correspond, and clever counterfeits of the signatures of the judges and clerks of election were affixed. The Eighteenth Ward's Citizens' Committee, with the Federal authorities co-operating, brought about the arrest of judges and clerks, except one who decamped to Canada.

An enterprising reporter for the *Daily News* discovered that the bogus tickets had been printed at P. L. Hanscom's printing office on Madison Street, and obtained a proof slip of the spurious ticket containing Brand's name. The Wright brothers, junior members of the Hanscom firm, stated that Joseph C. Mackin, secretary of the Cook County Central Democratic Committee, assistant secretary of the State Central Committee, and secretary of the Cook County Democratic Club, had ordered the tickets printed, and that they had been delivered to his room in the Palmer House. Mackin later was found guilty of perjury in connection with the spurious ballots and sentenced to five years in Joliet Penitentiary. Governor Joseph W. Fifer ordered his release in 1889, but for many years "jomackinism" was a term applied to fraudulent voting, as coined by the *Tribune*.

This scandal gave impetus to the efforts of the Union League Club to get its new election law on the books. The Club did not have to go outside of its membership for experts to draft such a law, and soon mass meetings were being held to acquaint the public with the provisions of the proposed measure. On January 4, 1885, the Chicago *Tribune* carried a story with the headline: UNION LEAGUE CLUB URGES REVISION OF STATUTE LAW DEALING WITH ELECTIONS. In the same issue was an editorial on "Simple Electoral Reform."

"There is not the slightest doubt that the Illinois Election Law, as far as it applies to Chicago, is a wretched failure," the editorial said. "Under its operation it is possible for a gang of unscrupulous men to disenfranchise the majority of the voters. This is not a matter of speculation. The thing has been done at two city elections, and would have been done again at the late November election if the preparation of ballot-box stuffers had not been exposed by the public press and defeated by the unexampled energy of the honest citizens, aided by the United States election officers."

The exposure of the prevalence of election frauds and the

boldness with which they were executed led to unusual pre-cautions for a fair municipal election in 1885. The citizens who had been active in the prosecution of the Mackin case organized a Committee of Seventy to guard against illegal voting. Articles printed in the leading newspapers from day to day showed where illegal registration had been carried on to a large extent, and the full registry lists were published as well in the hope of preventing frauds by the persons registered illegally.

This had the result of deterring frauds to some extent, but at the election, repeaters, by collusion with venal judges and clerks, resorted to affidavits to swear in their votes, and these affidavits were subsequently stolen from the polling booths before the returns were made to the city clerk. In the Second Ward the poll-book record showed 821 of these affidavits used, and none was returned; and a similar condition of affairs was shown in the First, Ninth, and other wards. The result of the city ticket, canvassed by the council, showed Carter H. Harrison (Dem.), 43,352, and Sidney Smith (Rep.), 42,977. However, the Republicans won the offices of city clerk and city attorney.

Rampant violence and intimidation were prevalent at this election in the Second and Ninth wards and at the rougher precincts throughout the city. The closeness of the vote between Smith and Harrison made a contest inevitable, which was speedily inaugurated in the courts by the Committee of Safety. But by a ruling of the judge in the County Court, which made it obligatory for the contestants to prove up each fraudulent vote *seriatim*, they were compelled to abandon the contest, and the suit was dismissed.

The better element of Chicago's citizenry was now thoroughly aroused by the result of this election and the con-stant repetition of frauds at the polls. The Union League Club pressed the matter of the new election law. The Citizens' Asso-ciation and the Iroquois and Commercial clubs now lined up with the Union League in favor of a law which would have the effect of repressing and preventing these frauds.

Among the leaders of this movement were Marshall Field, A. A. Carpenter, Melville E. Stone, General I. N. Stiles, S. Corning Judd, A. F. Seeberger, and John A. King. A bill, to become known as the Citizens' Election Bill, was drafted by A. M. Pence, S. S. Gregory, and Alderman Thomas C. Clark. It was submitted to the legislature and passed.

There was some doubt as to the constitutionality of the measure, but pending a decision of the Supreme Court, the law was submitted to the voters in the fall election of 1885. It received a majority in every ward in the city and was also adopted by voters of the Town of Lake. Following its adoption, County Judge Richard Prendergast appointed Francis Hoffman, Jr., Daniel Corkery, and Samuel B. Raymond, the latter a member of the Union League Club, as election commissioners. In compliance with the provisions of the law, these commissioners engaged a clerical force, re-districted the city into precincts containing not more than three hundred voters each, located new polling places, and selected lists of judges, preparatory to the town and aldermanic elections of 1886.

Under the new law, one each of the election commissioners must be a member of the two leading political parties. Of the three judges and two clerks in each election precinct, "at least one judge and one clerk shall be selected from each of the leading political parties." Each political party could have a challenger at the polls, as well as at the place of registry. Judges of election were constituted the Board of Registry for each precinct, and no person could vote unless he was a qualified registered voter. Election day became a legal holiday.

The question of constitutionality was argued before the State Supreme Court in November, 1885, with A. M. Pence, an active member of the Union League Club, representing the Club before the tribunal. The court affirmed the constitutionality of the law on January 19, 1886.

The Union League Club had won its first big fight. It had spared neither money nor effort in putting through the new election law. "The Club is justified," is the comment entered in regard to the new statute. There would be further modifications and improvements in later years, but the foundations for honest elections were now firmly laid.

This new election law led also to the adoption of the Australian secret ballot several years later. For seventy-three years of the state's history there had been no such thing as entering a booth alone, behind a curtain, to mark one's ballot. In the former order of elections, ballots were bandied about the streets by interested politicians, who pounced upon voters as they came in sight and either pressed into their hands a ballot already marked, or "insisted intrusively" on helping them mark the names of the candidates. The Union League Club agitated for the Australian system of secret balloting, and in 1891 the bill became a law.

In numerous ways since the enactment of the Cities Election Act, the Club has sought to realize this one primary object—"to aid in the enforcement of all laws enacted to preserve the purity of the ballot box."

The Political Action Committee and its successor, the Public Affairs Committee, joined forces with other civic agencies in the detection and prosecution of vote frauds. In 1934-35, for example, ninety-nine persons were prosecuted for ballot frauds and thirty-seven jail sentences resulted. The attendant publicity undoubtedly helped to obtain the enactment of the Permanent Registration Act by the 1935 session of the General Assembly. The Club also co-operated to place that measure on the statute books as an effective deterrent to fraudulent voting.

Improvement in the election procedure became a frequent objective to enable the county judge and the Board of Election Commissioners to administer Chicago's election machinery with greater efficiency and economy.

The Club took a leading part in the adoption of the voting machine as a means of reducing election errors and expediting the voting process. This activity became associated with every step of the process of enactment of the enabling statute in 1941, the successful voting machine referendum in 1946, the bond issue to purchase voting machines in 1947, and the program for purchase and installation of voting machines. In the latter phases, the Club's representatives functioned under the aegis of the Joint Civic Committee on Elections.

Mindful that voting, like charity, begins at home, the Club regularly has urged its members to register and to vote. Twice the registrations of its members residing in Chicago were checked on the official records and polite reminders sent to those for whom no precinct listings were found.

For many years prior to 1940 the Club recruited hundreds of citizen volunteers from among its members to serve as poll watchers in selected Chicago precincts with long records of fraudulent voting practices. In 1940 the Club joined with twelve other civic agencies as sponsors of the Joint Civic Committee on Elections to systematize and expand this poll-watching program.

In each major election since that time, the Joint Civic Committee has recruited, trained, assigned, and supervised citizen volunteers for service as observers to watch the casting and counting of the votes. Armed with credentials issued by County Judge Edmund K. Jarecki and the Board of Election Commissioners, the mere physical presence of these observers at precinct polling places undoubtedly discouraged fraudulent election practices.

Chapter Six

WELCOME TO LOYAL HEARTS

THE UNION LEAGUE CLUB HAD BEEN IN ITS CRAMPED QUARTERS in the Honore Building scarcely a year when its members began to agitate for a clubhouse of their own. As the Club grew in membership and also in prestige, a larger and more permanent home seemed a necessity. The first move in this direction came on December 13, 1881, when a proposal was made to erect a building on the 100 x 131 foot lot on the southeast corner of Dearborn and Monroe streets. A six-story building, it was estimated, would cost $500,000, and to finance it the Club would sell perpetual memberships at $1,000 each. At that time there were 531 members in the Club.

When this plan later was discarded, the Club was offered the opportunity to purchase the north half of the Honore Building, as Timothy B. Blackstone, president of the Chicago and Alton Railroad, said his company desired to purchase the south half. This offer was declined, and though agitation increased among members for permanent quarters, the annual report of January 23, 1883, called attention to the fact that "the Club can just as well promote the public good from the old rooms" as in a new building.

It was on November 15, 1883, that the proposal was offered which later was to be accepted. General John L. Thompson, a prominent attorney, suggested that the Club lease a 50 x 99 foot lot on the southwest corner of Jackson Street and Fourth Avenue (later Federal Street), and purchase the adjoining lot of 25 x 99 feet at $1,200 per foot. This property was owned by Charles W. Bonynge, then a resident of Paris.

The project was beginning to take shape. In January of 1884 the most important move was made when George F. Bissell, Albert L. Coe, and Rollin A. Keyes obtained corporation papers for the Union League Auxiliary Association. This association, with a capital stock at first of $50,000, was to play the major role in obtaining the property and building the Clubhouse.

By February 20 it was announced that the capital stock had been fully subscribed. John V. Farwell, L. L. Coburn, George F. Harding, John R. Walsh, Levi Z. Leiter, R. S. Critchell, and J. McGregor Adams had each taken five shares at $100 a share. J. B. Leiter, Andrew J. McNally, and Murry Nelson had each taken two shares. W. H. Rand, D. H. Burnham, Lyman J. Gage, George M. Pullman, Ferdinand W. Peck, and others had subscribed for the remainder. William V. Jacobs, treasurer of the Club that year, as trustee had taken twenty shares—the largest block. These stocks were "to be full paid and nonassessable."

Nine directors for the Auxiliary Association were elected, with General Thompson serving as president of the board. J. McGregor Adams, who had been elected president of the Club that year, was named vice-president of the board of the Auxiliary; Albert L. Coe, real estate dealer, was treasurer, and Rollin A. Keyes, secretary. The Union League Auxiliary Association was legally organized as a corporation on February 22, Washington's Birthday.

Now the problem was to obtain a suitable property on which to build. At a meeting on Monday, March 3, it was resolved to enter into a ninety-nine year lease with Bonynge for his property at Jackson and Fourth streets.

It took great faith in the future of this district for the Club even to consider—and later to decide upon—this location for its permanent quarters. It was an isolated section. The only structure of any size nearby was the Customs House and Postoffice, just across Jackson Street. Ten years before, in July of 1874, a fire had swept away one thousand houses in the fifteen blocks below Van Buren between Clark and Wabash streets, and the area had been only partially rebuilt. Nelson Thomasson later said that the man who had sponsored him for membership, Josiah Lombard, had lamented the fact that the location "was too far out," although it was only a block south of the Honore Building. "I heard many other members predict that a club that far from the center of business could not help but fail."

The Auxiliary Association, through General Thompson, offered to lease the property for $4,200 a year for ninety-nine years. General Thompson wrote Bonynge on March 7, stating, however, that the proposition was subject to revocation by telegram to Bonynge "any time before receipt of a telegram from you accepting it."

On March 17 the proposition was revoked by cable to Bonynge, evidently because his representatives here wanted more money, and negotiations were started at once with C. C. Heisen for a lease on the property on the northeast corner of Dearborn and Quincy streets at $8,000 a year for ninety-nine years. The Union League Auxiliary Association also agreed to pay the cost of paving Quincy Street with granite cobblestones.

Papers were ordered drawn up, but before the deal went through, Bonynge indicated that he would consider another offer, and Albert Coe was authorized on July 7 to negotiate with the Frenchman "up to $7,300 per annum for 99 years." Eight days later these negotiations culminated when Vice-President Adams and Eugene E. Prussing, acting secretary, were authorized to draw up a lease for the 75 x 99 foot lot at $6,800 annually.

The dream of a clubhouse was now becoming a reality, and

on July 21 a Building Committee was named. The Union League Club could easily find within its own membership men to perform any sort of duty, so on July 28 William E. Hale moved that an architect who was a member of the Club be selected to draw up plans for the new building. On August 1, Wetherell, chairman of the Building Committee, reported that only two of the five architects in the Club were willing to submit competitive plans. It was then decided to waive competition and select Major William LeBaron Jenney, a brilliant architect and builder, who had joined the Club two years before. As the results were to prove, the committee could not have made a better choice.

Jenney, who has been credited with being the "inventor" of the modern skyscraper, had come to Chicago in 1868 after an impressive war record as chief engineer of the Fifteenth Army Corps. A man of daring, he had first startled Chicago by putting a brick façade on an office building. This "radical departure" from conventional building in those days consisted of pressed brick with elaborate stone trimmings. The Portland Block, erected right after the fire of 1871, had another innovation. The first passenger elevator was used in this building.

In 1884 he gave the world skeleton construction, making possible modern city building and revolutionizing the architecture of the world. Jenney always insisted that the skyscraper was not an invention but an evolution; "but it was Mr. Jenney who made general over a whole building what in a small detail way had been done before."

This method, in which the frame holds up the walls, became known as the "Chicago construction." Jenney's Home Insurance Building, at La Salle and Adams streets, actually of ten stories but of the height of a twelve-story building, was the first skeleton construction building in the world. It was while he was engaged on this building that Jenney was approached by his fellow-

The ten-story Home Insurance Building, designed by Major William Le Baron Jenney, was the world's first skyscraper.

members of the Union League Club with the proposition that he design and build the new clubhouse. He accepted the invitation at once.

The cost of the building was not to exceed $150,000. On October 9, 1884, at a joint meeting of the Club and the Auxiliary Association, Jenney brought in plans drawn by his young helper, William Bryce Mundie. These plans were finally approved on October 21.

A few weeks before Jenney formally submitted his plans to the Club, the *Inland Architect and Builder*, whose editor was watching this new project with interest, ran a story which undoubtedly had the Club members scratching their heads. It appeared, from the editor's view, that "the ladies" were having quite a lot to say about the new building. "Though the interior plans have been practically finished," the journal said, "the ladies—who seem to have a voice in the matter—suggested many changes, and this, if considered, will interfere largely with making the building comfortable alike to gentlemen members unless better counsel prevails and the plans that suit the convenience of the gentlemen are acceptable to the ladies as well."

For instance, the editor continued, "it seems out of place to destroy a beautiful entrance on Jackson Street because the ladies wish a special entrance and suite of apartments to themselves on Fourth Avenue. This, architecturally considered, is almost impossible considering the size of the lot and requirements of a properly planned clubhouse."

But the ladies were to have their way. They had their private entrance, which possibly spoiled the "beautiful entrance" on Jackson Street. And while it may be true that some members harbored feelings of resentment, the *Graphic News* nevertheless reported: "While ladies have hitherto been excluded from the pleasures of club life, the Union League desires their presence, and has accordingly fitted up apartments for their comfort and convenience. Hereafter the rights of the ladies will be recognized."

It was now decided to increase the capital stock of the Auxiliary to $100,000, and this was done on December 5. Three days later authorization was given the Auxiliary to make a lease of the building to the Union League Club. This lease, dated January 31, 1885, leased the "clubhouse, art gallery, and library," to be completed on January 1, 1886, or as "soon thereafter as practicable," to run from that date to September 1, 1983. The lease was signed by John L. Thompson and Rollin A. Keyes, president and secretary of the Auxiliary, and J. McGregor Adams and Sidney Corning Eastman, president and secretary of the Club.

Financing this project became the major problem. On June 22 it was decided to negotiate a loan of $50,000 on ten to twenty year bonds at 5 per cent per annum. These bonds were authorized on July 1. They were of $1,000 each to total $50,000, payable to the Merchants Loan and Trust Company in twenty years after date. This matter was arranged through Byron L. Smith, vice-president of the bank, and one of the first members of the Union League Club.

Then came another important matter. This was the selection of a suitable inscription for the mantel over the fireplace in the lounge. Jenney, on his drawing of the fireplace, had left the space vacant except for the words, "Ye Inscription." Now Jenney, General Thompson, and J. McGregor Adams were named as a committee to decide on what the inscription should be.

Members of the Club were invited to submit suggestions for an appropriate motto, and several hundred ideas were received. Of these the committee discarded all but five, which were displayed on a large chart in the lounge of the old Club, and comments were invited from members. However, the committee in the end had to make the decision.

General Thompson and Major Jenney favored the simple sentence, "Welcome to Loyal Hearts." A few of the Club members, however, had indicated their preference for a quotation from a letter which Rufus Choate on October 1, 1855, had addressed to the Whig convention at Worcester, Massachusetts: "We join ourselves to no party that does not carry the flag and keep step to the music of the Union." So, as a compromise, both sentences were used as the Club motto.

As in the case of any new building, many troublesome problems arose to plague the Auxiliary Association. Unforeseen expenses developed; estimates were exceeded; members wanted changes and additional improvements—all of which cost money. In the middle of January a resolution was offered that "immediate steps be taken to provide a bowling alley in the new Clubhouse." H. M. Bacon remembered well the concern this caused Jenney.

"The seriousness of the burden of settling this, and other difficulties, was apparent in his voice and manner when called upon at this critical stage," Bacon recalled. "He (Jenney) arose with great deliberation and with some hesitation, remarking that as to the alley 'if the young men wanted bowls (pronounced by him broadly "bowels") he supposed we would have to put it in, although there were some difficulties and troublesome expense.' Major Jenney hardly openly dared turn down the request of the younger members, but just let the matter go on and on and we never got our 'bowels.' "

The Auxiliary Association also decided that the new Clubhouse should be lighted by electric lights. Mr. Coe was told to use his own judgment about "procuring a lightning rod for the tower" of the new structure.

On February 1, 1886, President Thompson of the Association reported that in order to complete the Clubhouse the Union League Club had advanced a sum "in excess of $30,000 over and about the $150,000 expended by the Association, and a plan should be devised to repay this sum." This proved simple, for on February 24 the capital stock was increased to $130,000.

On May 10, 1886, the Clubhouse was first occupied. There still were many things to be done. Uniforms for waiters . . . mantels by Pullman . . . stained glass for the tower . . . a laundry room . . . prices of sleeping rooms which were to be auctioned off to the highest bidders . . . fire escapes . . . house rules—no smoking permitted in the dining room . . . rules for ladies . . . insurance . . . furnishings.

At last everything was ready for the grand opening on June 10.

This was a gala evening for Chicago. Society turned out en masse, for the Club carried on its roster of membership the wealthiest and most influential men in the city. Invitations had been sent to some five hundred friends, and the greater part of

The Union League Clubhouse as it appeared at the opening celebration in 1886.

these attended, with their wives and families. Two thousand five hundred persons were entertained at the new Clubhouse that evening.

As night fell the building, regarded as the last word in club structures, presented a handsome and brilliant appearance. Its architectural style was modeled after the fourteenth-century Florentine and Romanesque renaissance. Bright lights streamed from every window. At many of the windows groups of ladies and gentlemen in full evening dress could be seen. Carriages moved up in a continual stream.

Canvas-covered arches, lighted by electricity, extended along the sidewalk on the Fourth Avenue and Jackson Street front, and a larger arch covered the sidewalk just at the main entrance on Jackson Street. A crowd of persons collected on the opposite side of Jackson Street and watched as the carriages drove up and the guests stepped out. A police sergeant and a detail of ten officers were stationed on the sidewalk to keep the crowd back and preserve order.

Alighting from their carriages, the guests ascended the stone steps over tile floors, through the heavy doors of hardwood and plate glass, into the magnificent reception room. Here they were greeted by the official reception committee of General Joseph B. Leake, former United States district attorney and Civil War hero; Israel Parsons Rumsey, commission merchant and first president of the Chicago Citizens' Law and Order League, and Major Jenney. Near the tower window of the library stood President J. McGregor Adams and ex-presidents L. L. Coburn and E. G. Keith.

While Major Jenney proudly explained to some guest that unpressed brick had been made especially for the building and was chosen to heighten the picturesqueness of the structure, and that the trimmings of red sandstone and terra cotta could better be admired in daylight, William A. Angell, purchasing agent of the Pullman Palace Car Company, who had furnished the house, might be telling another:

"We did not aim to lumber the rooms with useless truck, however ornamental it might be. The house itself is rich enough to withstand the effect of interior treatment, and as nothing was to be gained by elaborate furnishings we thought it best not to sacrifice taste to common custom. You will notice as you go through the house the lack of decorative jim-cracks."

The first guests had come at eight o'clock. The rush started an hour later. A *Tribune* reporter, making his way through the press, found that "the ladies were gorgeous in silks and laces, and vied with each other in the fragrance of their flowers and the brilliancy of their jewels."

Chicago's women were enjoying their triumphant entry into club life. The *Tribune* reporter further found that "they were grateful for the hospitality with which they were received into the club, and expressed their gratitude openly. The Union League Club is the only club in the country which extends to the ladies of the members the same privileges which it does to the members themselves. For the present there is virtually no difference. If a lady is accompanied by one of the members, the house is hers to do as she pleases in." Possibly as a note of warning, or perhaps one of feminine pride (the reporter may have been a woman) the writer said, "The time may come when she will not even be required to burden herself with a male escort." (The prophecy was correct, as the rules were changed in 1933 to permit women without escorts to enter those parts of the Club house available for their use.)

Taking note of the ladies' entrance, their own reception room ("a model of modest elegance"), private dining room, and a private elevator for their convenience, the reporter felt that "Mr. W. L. B. Jenney must have had the idea of feminine occupation in his mind when he designed some of the rooms—so

An artist's view of the Main Lounge of the first Union League Clubhouse.

Architect's drawing of the fireplace in the Main
Lounge, before the Club's motto was added.

dainty is the arrangement, so homelike and cheerful and bright."

The *Tribune* devoted more than half a column to describing the costumes of the ladies. Mrs. Henry W. Blodgett, wife of the Federal judge, wore a "toilet of jet, with close-fitting turban trimmed with pomegranate silk." Mrs. J. B. Mayo, "pale-blue silk with brocade and rose silk trimmings." Miss Minnie Kelley had a "black lace dress, with heart-cut bodice of black velvet." Mrs. J. L. Day had on a "white tennis cloth trimmed with swan's down." Mrs. N. M. Chittenden, "black satin de lyon, with white carnations and onyx jewels." Miss Crilly, "pale, pink-tinted romchudda silk under olive tulle, with a bouquet of *bon silene* roses and maidenhair ferns."

The guests wandered from one brilliantly lighted room to the other. Flowers were everywhere, peonies chiefly, but roses here and there and potted plants. The fireplace was festooned with growing ivy. The main hall was described as "a stately room, with a quantity of delicately-tinted wall space, and with pillars and arches of Corinthian design. Here and in the parlors and café the gentlemen most do congregate and discuss the club and its workings, its birth and its history," observed the *Tribune* reporter.

The chief attraction was the Main Dining Room, extending through two stories and during the day commanding a fine view of Lake Michigan. This was said to have been "probably one of the richest rooms in the United States," having, among other features, a circular skylight window of stained glass which covered the whole northeast corner of the ceiling. From its window one could gaze in every direction. When lighted up with electric lights, the decorations and brilliancy of this apartment made it "something indescribable."

In one corner of the dining room, seated behind a carved screen in a little gallery, were the musicians—members of the Chicago Mandolin Orchestra. The *plimpy-plamp* of their instruments was agreeably softened by the screen, but this did not "mar their music." The private supper rooms of the Club were used for the banquet. Here the table appointments made many guests gasp in admiration. "The silverware, made expressly for the club, the elegant crystal of many designs, the exquisite china service were so attractive that they almost overshadowed the charms of the perishable material upon them." The punch bowls "were of very graceful pattern and are said to be unique, and were purchased with the understanding that they were to remain so and that no duplicates were to be made of these or of the other dishes."

The dancing did not begin until late, and was necessarily restricted then owing to the great press of people. Four quadrilles and ten round dances made up the program. The rests between numbers were long, "and the conversation seemed to be enjoyed more than struggling about the room and lurching at every moment against another revolving couple," the *Tribune* decided. The Chicago *Inter Ocean* concluded its own account in these words:

"In the entire surroundings there was a quiet elegance, good taste and simplicity, and not a person departed rightfully thinking otherwise. Every provision directed the progress of the festival. More remains not to be said. The Union League has now had its social baptism, brilliant even for monarchial offspring; its political immersion it has already experienced even to the heel. Now equipped as it is this club may sally forth to do great deeds for Chicago, for not even in the heel should this young hero be considered vulnerable."

The cost of the building had been $170,000, while that of the furnishings aggregated $45,000.

After eighteen months in their new home, the Club members received the sad news that there was a deficit of $24,210.03. The total running expenses were shown to be $83,193.60 a year.

The Club dining room was serving "only one meal a day on which there is the least profit." "Free lunches" were being given for Saturday evening entertainments. These were to be abandoned in favor of a "$1 table d'hôte."

There were now 850 regular members and 150 nonresident members. By increasing the dues from $60 to $80 a year for resident members and from $30 to $40 for nonresident members, an additional sum of $70,800 could be provided. The increase was accordingly authorized.

The new Clubhouse had been opened during trying times in Chicago. There was great social unrest which threatened the city's welfare—and the Union League Club had another fight on its hands.

Chapter Seven

ALLEGIANCE TO AMERICAN
INSTITUTIONS

THE THOUSANDS OF LABORERS AND ADVENTURERS WHO WERE attracted to Chicago during the rebuilding era following the fire of 1871 were for the most part uneducated newcomers, ignorant of the underlying spirit of American institutions. Chicago was the western distributing point for a vast European immigration. With the good came the bad, and borne along by this stream were the scum and dregs of countries where despotism had made paupers and tyranny had bred conspirators. From Russia came the Nihilists, described by one newspaper as "the gift of centuries of Slavic slavery and cruelty." From the German states came the Socialists, the offspring of military exactions and autocratic government. And from Europe generally, including Great Britain and Ireland, Chicago "drained the feverish spirit of human resentment against laws and life; of property and of conduct which it had no hand in making or enforcing."

During the extraordinary activity of rebuilding the city after the conflagration, there was plenty of work and little trouble. But when work became slack, thousands were laid off and a financial depression gripped the city. The workingmen were discontented and ripe for trouble.

This became more evident in 1877 during a nationwide railroad strike. While the majority of Chicago's idle had no direct interest in this strike, they joined in the demonstrations at the behest of agitators. There was much violence and bloodshed.

The settlement of this strike did not bring peace. Foreign agitators came to Chicago and preached their disturbing theories. Anarchy was advocated. The term "revolutionary socialism" became more popular than the milder form of "political socialism." This in turn resulted in avowed anarchism. Violence was urged. Dynamite bombs were manufactured.

There were armed groups of anarchists in the city, similar to the communists of Paris. Among the most desperate of these were several companies of the *Lehr und Wehr Verein*, the Bohemian Sharpshooters, and several independent groups. They boldly paraded the streets with arms and carried red flags. Their agitators made incendiary speeches in the Lake Park, Market Square, Greif's Hall, and other places of similar resort.

An infernal machine was found on the premises of Judge Lambert Tree. Another was discovered in the building occupied by the Chicago, Burlington & Quincy Railroad. Finally, in January of 1886, the leaders of the anarchist movement grew so bold as to solicit from Melville Stone, editor of the *Daily News*, the publication of an interview. He sent a reporter to see August Spies, a recognized leader of the anarchists and editor of their organ, the *Arbeiter Zeitung*, and George Schilling, one of the leading labor agitators.

The story appeared in the morning edition of the *Daily News* on January 14 and occupied three columns on the front page. It carried the ominous headline: DYNAMITE IN CHICAGO. Spies and Schilling, unidentified in the story, gave the reporter a lengthy statement in which they announced that they intended to join in the demands of the trades-unions on May 1 of that year for an eight-hour law, and that if strikes resulted and the police interfered, they intended to give battle. They would place dynamite bombs in the manholes of sewers and explode them. They allowed the reporter to take a sample bomb to Stone, one "which happily had not been charged with explosives."

Melville Stone used the bomb as a paperweight. As he studied it from time to time he became occupied with grave fears. He sensed that all this agitation might lead to mischief. He had sought to awaken the public mind to danger by publishing the story, but to no avail.

May Day was approaching. Agitation for the eight-hour day became more marked. The *Daily News* in March pointed out that 225,000 persons of a hundred or so trades would be affected by such a measure. This would be revolution on a vast scale. The first of May came and with it the threatened strikes. The next day the *Tribune* said it did not expect industrial war, "but compromise and yielding in part," and predicted that "The real crisis will come when the eight-hour system has worked out its inevitable effect of inflating prices and reducing demand and has taken 20 per cent of their present comforts and necessaries away from the laborers."

But on the very next afternoon industrial warfare did come. It was on Blue Island Avenue, known to the labor leaders as the "Black Road," leading to the McCormick Harvesting Machinery Works. Here a battle resulted between the strikers and police who were protecting the "scabs." Shots were fired. One striker was killed and others may have died from their wounds.

On the night of May 4, the anarchists called a meeting in Haymarket Square on Randolph Street between Desplaines and Halsted streets. Mayor Carter Harrison had ordered police to watch the meeting, which had been heralded by a violent circular headed REVENGE! The Mayor himself rode up on his blooded Kentucky mare at one point in the meeting, listened for a time to the speeches, and then departed. Police came shortly after Harrison had left. A bomb was thrown by an unknown hand—the first dynamite bomb hurled in the United States. One policeman was killed outright and sixty-seven were injured. Seven of these died later. A tremor of horror swept the city.

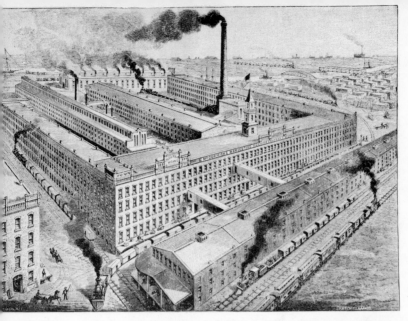

The McCormick Harvesting Machinery Works on Blue Island and Western avenues, which saw an early outbreak of labor violence.

The explosion reverberated within the walls of the Union League Club, as it did in other clubs and homes of the wealthy in the city. In the Union League Club gathered such men as Cyrus McCormick, Jr., whose Harvester works had been the scene of tragedy; Joseph Medill, editor of the *Tribune;* Melville Stone, who had sounded the warning; Philip D. Armour, who was having labor trouble in the stockyards; Marshall Field; John V. Farwell; Lyman J. Gage, the banker; and Julius Grinnell, state's attorney, who was to be the prosecutor of the Haymarket Riot defendants.

One member of the Club, walking along the lake front, had heard a speaker inveighing against the government and advocating the throwing of bombs. This member, Sidney Corning Eastman, a prominent attorney, now drafted an "Open Letter to the Union League Club," had it published in a twenty-one page pamphlet and distributed among the members. He placed the issue squarely up to Club members and urged a "revival of American patriotism," as a cure for a social illness.

Eastman stressed the fact that in the "school census" of 1884, of the total population of 630,000 there were to be found 150,000 Americans, 209,000 Germans, 48,000 Scandinavians, 28,000 British, 28,000 Bohemians, and 23,000 Poles. These foreign groups were highly nationalistic, he claimed, and in many cases their laudable societies had been taken over by more radical elements. The socialistic societies of the Bohemians, for instance, were so organized as to embrace entire families "even down to thirteen-year-old girls." The Turner societies of the Germans, founded upon noble principles, had deteriorated into anti-American groups. Eastman found that "national life is degenerating," and was "threatened by dangers from within."

"No system of legislation will cure it," he wrote, "although many abuses might be cured by wise laws, but the trouble must be met from within. We need, WE MUST HAVE A REVIVAL OF AMERICAN PATRIOTISM."

It should not be the patriotism of "Knownothingism, the Chinese wall of insular prejudice, but the patriotism which comes spontaneously from a broad, intelligent appreciation of the *merits* of American civilization." The responsibility, he said, "lies at the conscience of every one of you. Have you done your whole duty as an American citizen? Do you do your best to uphold the laws? Do you do all you can to purify elections? Do you take an active, vital interest in all public questions, and use your best thought and activity for the prevalence of sound views through the community, or do you not rather let things slide along with an occasional sigh at the degeneracy of the times?"

After these soul-searching questions, he stated that "We, as members of this patriotic organization, owe it to ourselves to try to henceforth do our full duty as citizens and TO SAVE OUR COUNTRY FROM THE DANGERS WHICH BESET ITS PATH."

All Chicago was horrified by the violence of the Haymarket Riot. The handbill shown below, printed in both English and German, helped stir up the passions of the malcontents.

REVENGE!

Workingmen, to Arms!!!

Your masters sent out their bloodhounds — the police —; they killed six of your brothers at McCormicks this afternoon. They killed the poor wretches, because they, like you, had the courage to disobey the supreme will of your bosses. They killed them, because they dared ask for the shortenin of the hours of toil. They killed them to show you, "Free American Citizens!", that you must be satisfied and contended with whatever your bosses condescend to allow you, or you will get killed!

You have for years endured the most abject humiliations; you have for years suffered unmeasurable iniquities; you have worked yourself to death; you have endured the pangs of want and hunger; your Children you have sacrificed to the factory-lords — in short: You have been miserable and obedient slave all these years: Why? To satisfy the insatiable greed, to fill the coffers of your lazy thieving master? When you ask them now to lessen your burden, he sends his bloodhounds out to shoot you, kill you!

If you are men, if you are the sons of your grand sires, who have shed their blood to free you, then you will rise in your might, Hercules, and destroy the hideous monster that seeks to destroy you. To arms we call you, to arms!

Your Brothers,

John V. Farwell, Marshall Field, and others sought a more direct way. Farwell and his brother, who had been on a hunting trip out west, had come back to Chicago in 1877 with a trainload of soldiers from Fort Laramie. The merchant was impressed by the fact that when "they [the soldiers] arrived there was not much trouble in quieting the strike and riots, because the strikers and rioters knew the regulars meant business."

Later Marshall Field arose before the Commercial Club and made one of his rare speeches, in which he said he thought there should be a regiment of soldiers nearer Chicago "instead of a thousand miles away, like Fort Laramie or Fort Riley." With both Field and Farwell back of such a measure, the Commercial Club raised money to buy 632 acres of ground thirty miles north of Chicago and presented it to the government. This was to become Fort Sheridan.

"The theory was that if they had some troops nearby, it would act as a preventive and prevent a lot of riots occurring in Chicago because the soldiers could get there so quickly," Farwell later explained.

But there were those in the Union League Club who did not feel this solved the problem. Efforts would have to be made to strike deeper at the roots—to educate the newcomers in the principles upon which America was founded and bring before them the ideals of the men who had held the nation together.

Chicago had been caught up short on May 4, 1886, they believed. A vital thing had been neglected in the mushroom growth of the city. There were disloyal citizens in their midst through their own negligence. The Club itself, but six years old, felt the weight of responsibility and was made conscious of its own Articles of Association, which in part read: ". . . to encourage and promote by moral, social, and political influence, unconditional loyalty to the Federal Government, and to defend and protect the integrity and perpetuity of the nation."

The members of the Union League Club were not long in making up their minds. The Committee on Political Action, headed by Abram M. Pence, a prominent attorney, laid aside all other matters temporarily and sought some means to revive patriotic ideals as a means of counteracting subversive radicalism.

The unanimous decision was that this could best be done by sponsoring annual celebrations on Washington's Birthday. The committee was of the opinion that the "history of the nation in its formative period centered about the revered figure of George Washington." No other name, in the belief of the committee, "was so well fitted to evoke the memories and associations which would give significance to a patriotic celebration." To perpetuate "the ideals of loyalty which were personified in Washington by an annual tribute to his character as a man and his service as a military leader and president" would exercise an elevating influence upon the life of the community.

With this in mind, the committee determined to bring to Chicago some speaker of distinction, identified with the public life of the country, and to invite the public to hear him.

Just four days after the jury to try the Haymarket Riot anarchists had been sworn in the Criminal Court of Judge Joseph E. Gary on July 15, this committee decided to invite James Russell Lowell to be the speaker for the first Washington's Birthday celebration. Lowell, both as an admired literary figure and as an American of the old New England mold, would, they believed, add a special luster to the occasion.

Mr. Pence addressed an invitation to Mr. Lowell, who was then in London. Pence pointed out in his letter that "The Club contains a membership of about one thousand gentlemen, drawn from our leading professional men and merchants. One of its chief objects is to inculcate a higher appreciation of the value and sacred obligation of American citizenship."

Lowell was asked to indicate his attitude by cabling "Yes"

or "No." In August Pence received a four-word cablegram which read, "Pence, Chicago. Yes. Lowell."

Meantime, the trial of the Haymarket anarchists, which had dragged on for three months, came to an end. A jury found the eight defendants guilty. Seven, including the anarchist agitator, August Spies, were condemned to die as accessories to the crime; one was sentenced to prison. Two of the condemned men, however, had their sentences commuted, and were later pardoned.

Judge Gary, known as one of the "most affable men on the bench," had a serious responsibility in this case. It was without precedent in law. Defense counsel had argued that there could be no accessories to murder without a principal. The State must prove that "somebody was a principal in committing murder before it can convict others as accessories." This the State had failed to do. It was believed that the bomb had been thrown by a certain Rudolph Schaunbelt at the command of Spies and another of the defendants, George Engel. But Schaunbelt had disappeared. There was no direct proof, the defense contended, that he had been the "principal."

Judge Gary had an answer for this. He said that "if the bomb was thrown in pursuance of the prisoners' advice, the instructions as to the law of accessories before the fact applied to the case, and the instruction to the jury was proper." He pointed out that "the law is common sense" and "holds each man responsible for the natural and probable consequences of his own acts."

"It holds that whoever advises murder is himself guilty of the murder that is committed pursuant to his advice, and if men band together for a forcible resistance to the execution of the law and advise murder as a means of making such resistance effectual, whether such advice be to one man to murder another, or to a numerous class to murder men of another class, all who are so banded together are guilty of any murder that is committed in pursuance to such advice."

The outcome of this case started a social war which lasted for many years. The Haymarket Riot Case, as it became known, was termed by some a "miscarriage of justice." Many prominent citizens became involved in the controversy. As late as 1893, Judge Gary felt called upon to defend his decision in the trial in a thirty-page article in *Century Magazine*.

But whatever its legal merits or faults, the Haymarket Case convinced many Chicagoans of the need for a more positive program of education in the fundamentals of American democracy. The Union League Club's Washington's Birthday celebrations were a notable step in this direction.

Shortly after sentence had been passed on the anarchists, Pence once more wrote to Lowell, requesting him to name a subject for his lecture. A month later he received this reply:

> DEERFOOT FARM
> SOUTHBOROUGH, MASS.
> Nov. 13th, 1886

DEAR SIR,

  I was writing to you when I came accidentally upon your letter of 16th October which had been mislaid.

  What I mean to speak about is Politics—*our* politics—with no reference to party.

  You will not be responsible for my opinions. Will that be what you want? I have no doubt you will make Chicago pleasant to me.

> Faithfully yours,
> (*Signed*) J. R. LOWELL

A. M. Pence, Esq.

The committee responded immediately, saying that the subject was entirely satisfactory and that it wished Lowell to treat it in his own way and speak his own opinions.

All was quiet again until the middle of January, 1887, when another letter was dispatched to Lowell calling his attention to the fact that the Harvard Club had arranged to give him a reception in Chicago on Monday, February 21, but "on con-sultation with us, that club saw the impropriety of anticipating our reception to our invited guest and consented to a later day."

At the same time the Club sent the invitation of its president, J. McGregor Adams, for Lowell to be his house guest during his stay in Chicago. To this letter Lowell on January 26, 1887, made the following reply:

DEAR SIR,

I accepted the invitation of the Harvard Club, not because I like even semi-private dinners where one is expected to speak, but because I thought it would seem churlish to refuse. I did not expect any public compliment of the sort. I hoped to come quietly to Chicago, deliver my lecture, and come back quietly.

This is what I should prefer. This does not mean that I am in any way insensible to the honor implied in your invitation, and rather than disappoint your very kindly intentions I put myself entirely at your disposition, after stating what my own preference would be. I shall write to the Secretary of the Harvard Club, who has informed me of their willingness to change their day, accordingly.

He ended this letter by saying he was sorry "that I shall be unable to accept the generous hospitality of your president, having already promised to be the guest of Mr. Wirt Dexter during my stay in Chicago."

Thus Lowell, even before he reached the city, laid the foundation for a series of controversial and disappointing in-cidents in connection with the Club's first Washington's Birthday celebration. Lowell was a "mugwump," or independent Re-publican. His host, Wirt Dexter, general solicitor of the Chicago, Burlington & Quincy Railroad, was also a "mugwump." But the majority of the Union League Club's membership were regulars or "stalwarts" in the Republican party.

Chapter Eight

JAMES RUSSELL LOWELL
CHANGES HIS MIND

JAMES RUSSELL LOWELL GOT OFF ON THE WRONG FOOT THE minute he arrived in Chicago and absent-mindedly inquired of someone the way to the Southern Hotel. This hotel was in St. Louis. Chicago was quick to react to the implied slight. The *Daily News* scolded, "Mr. Lowell's visit to this city has been marked by several unfortunate occurrences. . . . In the first place he shocked patriotic Chicagoans by professing to have confused Chicago with St. Louis."

This was but the beginning of a series of "unfortunate occurrences" by the author of the *Biglow Papers*, lately ambassador to England and eminent man of letters, which were to make his eagerly expected visit a comedy of errors.

Meantime, Union League Club members, still not forgetting the primary reasons for inaugurating the Washington's Birthday celebrations in behalf of inspirational patriotism, were anticipating with interest but somewhat mixed emotions the prospect of a redhot mugwump speech from their distinguished guest. "Mugwumps were anathema in the Union League Club of Chicago," Melville Stone later noted in his memoirs, though he did admit that while a mugwump himself, he had been elected vice-president of the Club in 1896.

Public curiosity, too, was whetted by the expectation of hearing something out of the ordinary, and as early as four o'clock on Tuesday afternoon the entrance of Central Music

Hall at State and Randolph streets was packed with men and women in response to the Club's invitation to hear Lowell's lecture. Carriages lined State Street from Washington to Randolph, and a long procession jammed the sidewalk. "Expressions indicative of the strong interest in the speaker were heard on all sides, and everyone elbowed his neighbor in impatient haste to be within," one reporter observed.

At four-fifteen o'clock the organ "pealed forth in a medley, of which 'Yankee Doodle' was a prominent part, as though the organist had feared Mr. Lowell might have forgotten the air during his long sojourn abroad." Every seat in the galleries and parquet was filled. In the foyer men and women stood four or five deep, "craning their necks to catch a glimpse of the distinguished orator." Every box was filled, and "it would have been well-nigh impossible to have gathered together an audience that could have better represented the brains, fashion, or wealth of Chicago society."

Central Music Hall, where James Russell Lowell switched speeches at the Club's first Washington's Birthday celebration.

On the stage were seated members of the Union League Club and many of the clergy of the city. The Club members wore long faces and none smiled or looked happy. The reason for this was soon evident. At four forty-five o'clock the thunderous tones of the organ ceased and General George W. Smith, president of the Club, solemnly rose to present the distinguished speaker.

Then the bombshell exploded. Mr. Lowell "in his gracefully easy manner" announced that he, like other entertainers, must change the program at the last moment. He had agreed to talk on "American Politics," but "had concluded upon reflection that the present occasion and the club auspices" would not permit him "to speak as frankly on that subject as was his custom," and therefore he would speak on "Literature," with a few words at the beginning on criticism, and a short discussion about *Richard III* and Shakespeare.

"When it became known that the lecturer had changed the subject of his lecture . . . many expressions of regret and disappointment were rife among those who stood in the foyer," commented the *Daily News*. "It may have been this regret that caused so many to leave their seats before the lecturer had completed his discourse, although the action hardly bore the stamp of courtesy towards the club whose guests they were."

Lowell, in making known the text for his remarks on criticism, recited Wordsworth's lines:

"A primrose by the river's brim
A yellow primrose was to him,
And nothing more."

Those of the audience who remained sighed and fidgeted in their seats. Lowell went on to say that it was a relief to meet people who saw things as they were, especially in criticism, and particularly when each critic "seemed determined to dive deeper than his fellows and to bring up something which nobody had ever before heard of." The ruffling of fans and whisperings might have indicated to Mr. Lowell that he had dived pretty deep and come up with something surprising.

He talked about Goethe and his "catholicism of spirit," quoted Shakespeare's Mercutio, and finally "addressed himself to the consideration of *Richard III* and the question of its authorship."

To those gathered to hear a political speech, Mr. Lowell cited *Richard III* as the finest dramatic work of the great master, but he held to the belief that "the play as it has been handed down to us has suffered from the hurried work of careless copyists, or incorrect hearing of shorthand writers."

After developing this theme at some length, Lowell concluded by saying that "I have always wished that in our great universities and colleges there could be established professorships for Shakespeare, as the Italians did in their temples of learning for Dante. I value Shakespeare for this particularly: That for those who know but one language there is as much learning in his works as in any of the ancients—I had almost said in all of them combined."

There was polite applause when Lowell finished. But the guests filed out and formed into groups in the foyer where a lively discussion ensued. Why had Lowell changed his subject at the very last moment? Many a spicy bit of anecdote was developed, most of them at the expense of mugwumpism.

"Mr. or Mrs. Wirt Dexter is to blame for it," explained an ardent admirer of Lowell, "and possibly both of them. Wirt Dexter is a mugwump. The members of the Club are stalwarts. They don't like Mr. Dexter's political views, and have no hesitation in saying so. They felt sore when they learned that Mr. Lowell, a man of learning and national reputation, who was

James Russell Lowell, eminent poet and statesman, whose visit to the Union League Club caused a furor remembered for decades.

coming to Chicago to speak under the auspices of the Club, should be the guest of so conspicuous a mugwump. The directors held a secret meeting, and there was a long and hot debate whether to extend Mr. Dexter the courtesy of an invitation to the banquet or not, and there was a mighty strong opposition to sending the invitation, too. Some fiery speeches were made, and Mr. Dexter heard of them. That made him as hot as any of the clubmen, and he and his wife quietly set to work to take their revenge by persuading their guest not to speak on the subject that might prove offensive to his hosts. From the buzz the change of lectures made in the Club, their revenge must have been very sweet."

But Dexter "unequivocally and most emphatically" denied this charge. He said he had no previous knowledge of what address Lowell had prepared, and therefore had no influence in the change nor even conversation about it.

The *Daily News* took a direct means of finding out. A reporter was sent to ask Lowell, "Why did you change your lecture?"

"My reason for not delivering a political lecture," he answered, "was lest I should either not do justice to the one faction or too little justice to the other. I had determined, therefore, before I left Boston not to deliver a political lecture, but had I then known the condition of mind here as I do now, I should have delivered the political lecture."

President Smith of the Club said he had had no knowledge of the switch in plans "until shortly before the hour set for the address," but he believed it to have "emanated from a desire on Mr. Lowell's part to avoid any possible offense to either party."

The controversy over Lowell's switch in subjects was just beginning to warm up by evening, when the Union League Club gave him an elaborate banquet in its new Clubhouse.

At the speakers' table were Joseph Medill, J. McGregor Adams, George Hunt, E. G. Keith, E. W. Blatchford, Lyman J. Gage, Marshall Field, George F. Bissell, L. L. Coburn, Gwynn Garnett, Thomas M. Cooley, Thomas Drummond, Francis Fairchild, the Rev. Frank M. Bristol, the Rev. S. J. McPherson, and the Club president, General Smith. Sitting directly across from Lowell was Wirt Dexter. Three hundred members of the Club occupied some dozen long tables.

At ten o'clock, when cigars and brandy came and the clubmen pushed back their chairs, General Smith arose and introduced the honored guest. But General Smith took occasion to say that "as American citizens, we need have no fear here or at any time of expressing honest opinions. (Applause.) This Club is not organized for the purpose of keeping silent." (Applause.) He went on to say that the Club represented no one political party, and that the members, whether Republicans or Democrats, were first of all citizens. He welcomed Lowell as a student of letters and a student of democracy, invited him to say something on the subject of politics, and asked the company to join him in a toast to their guest.

All arose and drank.

Standing in front of a portrait of George Washington, Lowell began his speech. He was, he said, "particularly struck with what your excellent president said just now—that the business of your club was not to keep silent; and I am exceedingly glad to hear it."

Lowell was now at his best. He spoke of the politics and governments of cities, states, and nations. He warned that the rapid growth and prosperity of Chicago did not indicate success. He mourned the degeneracy of the parties of that day as compared with those of a century before. As to government, he thought: "If a government be a necessary thing—and perhaps it is—there are two forms of government, and but two. The one form of the government governs you, and the other leads you. Now what is the result? It is a question of immense importance who the men are that lead and in what direction the leading is.

"We ought to be choice in our leaders for this reason: that here, more than anywhere else, especially in the chief place in this nation, it is the man who makes the place and not the place that makes the man. . . . The President's chair can alternately be a pillory or a throne, as the character of the man who sits in it."

He concluded on a moral note: "Now, gentlemen, is there a great city in this country that—I won't say is well governed—but that is decently governed? (Cries of No! No!) Now whose fault is it? I tell you that the loss of money is very considerable. I mean by that it is a thing to be considered. The loss of money is great, but it is the smallest loss. It is an infinitesimal loss. The loss of morals is the greatest loss. (Applause.) You can recover your pecuniary loss—that is easy enough; we are energetic people, and we do not mind that kind of thing; we can recover that fast enough; but I tell you that your moral loss is every day going on at compound interest, and that the sternest accountants that are known to human history are keeping accounts." (Applause.)

The *Tribune* reported Lowell's speech in full, devoting in all five and one-half full columns to the Union League Club affair. The circulation of the paper at that time was around sixty thousand daily, and thus Lowell's political speech was made available to many thousands more than the audience who might have heard him talk on this subject at Central Music Hall.

But the mere fact that he had changed the subject of his speech was of far more interest than anything he might have said. Lowell was sniped at from all sides. The *Daily News* said: "Mr. Lowell may have talked about Shakespeare on Washington's Birthday because that lamented bard bears a strong resemblance to the father of his country in one particular. They are both dead."

Writing Lowell's biography at a later date—1901—Horace Elisha Scudder decided, "The Union League Club was a Republican organization under the control of the Blaine wing of the party. It had succeeded in getting rid of those Republicans who had been hostile to Blaine, among whom was then the gentleman who was Lowell's host." The fact is, however, that Lowell's host, Wirt Dexter, had never been a member of the Club. Subsequent historians of Chicago have repeated this error, without taking the trouble, as Scudder also failed to do, of checking with the Club to be sure.

Something, however, had changed Lowell's mind—but what it was will probably never be known.

While the first observance of Washington's Birthday by the Club had resulted in a fiasco, the celebration was continued with but one interruption through succeeding years. It soon attracted favorable attention, and other cities followed the example of the Club, so that February 22 throughout the land became an occasion for cherishing the memory of the nation's first president and renewing allegiance to the ideals for which he had given himself so unreservedly.

On its fourth observance of Washington's Birthday, in 1890, the Club devoted the morning to school children. Eight thousand filled the new Auditorium Theater, and four thousand were seated at the Central Music Hall. Patriotic addresses were given and patriotic songs sung. In the annual report for that year the Club records read: "This service has elicited commendation from thinking people in other states, and alone has given the Club a wider reputation than that of any other in the United States."

From that time on, the school children were included in the celebration, and the Washington's Birthday programs became an annual public civic observance. The largest halls available—Central Music Hall, the Auditorium, Orchestra Hall, and the First Regiment Armory—were selected as meeting centers, and the most distinguished public figures were invited as speakers.

Among the celebrated statesmen and men of literary renown who have been the orators of the Club on these occasions are the following: 1888, Chauncey Depew; 1893, Edward Everett Hale; 1894, William McKinley; 1895, John Ireland; 1896, Theodore Roosevelt; 1898, Benjamin Harrison; 1902, Albert J. Beveridge; 1904, Elihu Root; 1906, William Howard Taft; 1907, Grover Cleveland; 1908, Charles Evans Hughes; 1912, Jean Jules Jusserand; 1923, Charles G. Dawes.

In 1923 a new plan was introduced in the Auditorium program under the influence of John Benham, chairman of the committee. This program provided for different types of school activities: massed glee clubs, massed bands, a flag raising by a high school R.O.T.C. unit, and a musical tableau by costumed

The Washington's Birthday Banquet held at the Club in 1902. Such banquets, featuring noted guests, were annual events for more than four decades.

Patriotic tableaus by high school students were featured in the annual celebrations held at the Auditorium Theater.

The Union League Club awarded special medals to winners in annual high school oratorical contests as part of its Washington's Birthday celebrations.

players. The program also included the finals in a city-wide oratorical contest, with each high school competing in district elimination contests. The Public Affairs Committee also sponsored an annual poster competition for high school pupils, with an entry from each high school. Art scholarship awards were given as prizes.

The new plan was continued with variations for eight years and was expanded to include all senior high schools in Cook County. During the superintendency of William J. Bogan, the public schools inaugurated the "Annual Civic Assembly" with specimen activities from the various high schools and the presentation of high school awards.

In 1930 the Club appropriated $5,000 for a study of civic education in the schools by a special citizens' commission. Four years later the Club inaugurated the annual vocational conference for Chicago high schools, which in spirit is a continuation of the educational and inspirational purpose for better citizenship of the Washington's Birthday programs, discontinued some years before.

Chapter Nine

GRAND OPERA FINDS A HOME

ON THE MEMORABLE NIGHT IN 1889 WHEN THE AUDITORIUM Theater was dedicated, Adelina Patti ignored the hundreds of other persons in the audience and sang to one man. That man was Ferdinand W. Peck. In Mr. Peck's box was the President of the United States; nearby were the Vice-President, the governor of the state, and the mayor of Chicago, while on either side were the George M. Pullmans, the Marshall Fields, the Robert T. Cranes, and others of Chicago's Four Hundred. But while she sang "Home, Sweet Home," the divine Patti never took her eyes from Peck.

It was an accolade well deserved by this one man who, more than any other, had at last given Chicago a permanent home for grand opera. Ferdinand Wythe Peck, tall, distinguished looking, was a native Chicagoan and a founding member of the Union League Club. Born to wealth, he was still a man of the people. Louis Sullivan, the great architect, described him as "a dreamer for the populace, one who declared himself a citizen with a firm belief in democracy."

The dreamer and the practical man were ideally blended in Peck. He had the time to dream and the money and business acumen to make those dreams realities. Peck's father, one of the very first settlers who came to Chicago, had made a fortune in real estate speculation. Ferdinand Peck, the youngest of seven sons, was born in the family home at Jackson and Clark streets,

Ferdinand Peck, later president of the Union League Club, who brought grand opera to Chicago.

and as he grew up entered the legal profession, principally as a means to equip himself to manage the affairs of the vast Peck estate.

With leisure to travel abroad, his interests led him to visit the music capitals of the world, and after each journey his dream of a permanent home for opera in Chicago became more vivid. Chicago had had opera before, of course, but in a score or more of locations and often under unsatisfactory conditions. Peck was determined to provide opera for Chicago on a grand scale, and not for just an exclusive set but for the enjoyment of all the people.

The initial attempt at opera in Chicago had been "inaugurated under far from flattering auspices," to use the words of an early historian. In more apt language, it had been disastrous.

The opera was *La Sonnambula*, given at Rice's Theater on Monday evening of July 29, 1850. The opera troupe, consisting of three or four singers, had come by boat from Milwaukee. Great was the excitement among the thirty thousand inhabitants of the raw prairie town when it was announced that a real grand opera would be given there for the first time.

The opening performance went off well, and the next day everyone was talking of "the opry." But on the next evening, as the curtain rose for the second act, the tenor's aria was interrupted by offstage screams of "Fire! Fire!" The theater was emptied without loss of life, but the building burned to the ground. And so ended Chicago's first "season" of opera.

Rice, a resourceful and enterprising man, rebuilt his theater on Dearborn Street, and on October 27, 1853, began a "second season" of opera. From that time forward opera came and went. It was presented variously at the Globe Theater, Shelby's Academy of Music, McVicker's Theater, Hooley's Theater, Wood's Museum, Central Music Hall, and the Rink Opera House, but nowhere found a permanent home. Once, on the opening of Crosby's Opera House on Washington Street between State and Dearborn, on April 20, 1865 (the date had been postponed because of the assassination of Lincoln), Chicagoans thought opera had found a home at last. But the fire of 1871 left little of Crosby's but the memory.

For several years after that there was talk of Chicago's need for a grand opera house. Schemes were suggested and discussed, but all were discarded because they were of too aristocratic or too exclusive a scale to meet general approval. What was needed was opera for everyone.

Peck had an idea at last, and its success was to be the forerunner of a greater idea. His first thought was to install in the Exposition Building on the lake front, where the Art Institute stands today, a vast auditorium with a huge scenic stage, and give there opera for two weeks, engaging artists of world fame.

The plan looked good. Peck conferred with several fellow-members of the Union League Club, including George Schneider, Edson Keith, George F. Harding, Eugene Cary, William Penn Nixon, R. T. Crane, and George M. Bogue. The question arose as to the matter of acoustics in so vast an amphitheater.

There were those in the Club who could solve this problem: Dankmar Adler, the architect, and his young partner, Louis H. Sullivan. Adler, later wrote Sullivan, was the "only man living, at that time, who had the intelligence to discern that the matter of acoustics is not a science but an art—as in fact all science is sterile until it rises to the level of art." Adler and Sullivan were consulted. They said the thing could be done.

The Exposition Building had been opened in September, 1873. It operated at first with a deficit, but in later years Potter Palmer, Joseph Medill, and other backers realized sizeable profits. Athletic and sporting exhibitions were held there, as well as the Republican convention of 1880, the Summer Garden Concerts, the Thomas Orchestra seasons, the May Music Festivals, the Republican and Democratic national conventions of 1884, mass meetings, "and many other entertainments of high order, and meetings of public importance for which the building had an unfailing accomodation and advantage."

Now there was to be an opera festival organized by the Chicago Opera Festival Association of which Peck was president. Eight of the ten members of the board of directors were members of the Union League Club. The most stupendous feature of this enterprise was the erection of a vast opera house within the north end of the building, seating more than six thousand hearers in comfortable chairs. The stage was of vast dimensions, 80 x 100 feet. The hall was handsomely decorated, and the stage well appointed with new scenery. The expense of fitting out the house was said to have reached $60,000.

Sullivan thought the effect thrilling. He said the audience "saw and heard; heard even the faintest pianissimo. No reverberation, no echo—the clear untarnished tone of voice and instrument reached all. The inference was obvious; a great permanent hall housed within a monumental structure must follow. This feeling marked the spirit of Chicago in those days."

Adelina Patti, operatic idol of Europe and America, whose appearance in Chicago was hailed with tremendous public enthusiasm.

This first opera festival was given during the two weeks of April 13-25, 1885, and consisted of fourteen performances. Artistically, almost everyone except Sullivan thought it not too remarkable. The space was too great for the smaller voices; too large for the dramatic parts of the performances. It was conceded that in several of the operas the stage settings were fine, and in all the Patti performances "the Festival achieved its intention of giving opera at lower prices than had ever before been known with Patti the star. The enthusiasm of the public upon her nights was something long to be remembered, the vast hall being a sea of heads and a flower-garden of brilliant costumes."

The financial success of the venture was beyond any criticism. At the annual meeting and banquet of the Chicago Opera Festival Association in the Union League Club on May 2, President Peck announced the gratifying news that gross receipts had amounted to $132,000, the largest sum, it was believed, ever taken for fourteen consecutive performances of opera anywhere in the world. After defraying expenses, a handsome balance was left. It was a gala dinner, and opera was the magic word.

Between the arms of the table, which was arranged in the

form of a horseshoe, was a large floral lyre with "Music for the People" in carnations in the center. In front of this President Peck stood as he said that "it is a fair statement that no such audience had ever gathered anywhere upon the Eastern Continent to witness such presentations as were seen at the Chicago Festival. But," he went on, "the people now ask, 'Cui bono beyond this?'" He wound up by saying that it had been shown "beyond peradventure that Chicago's great need was a large temple of music or hall where entertainment could be given for the people at large on a scale commensurate with their means, the demand for such a structure having been abundantly proved by the wonderful attendance at the festival." Mayor Carter Harrison advocated the erection of a permanent hall which would seat six thousand.

By the following year this idea had taken definite shape in Peck's mind. In a speech before the Commercial Club in June, 1886, he approached the subject in a businesslike manner and assured his listeners that an investment in a proposed Auditorium Building, which would house a hotel and an office building as well as provide a home for opera, would be no donation, "but one that will bring direct returns."

By January, 1887, the work of excavation began on the site which fronted Congress Street, Michigan Avenue, and Wabash Avenue, and building started in June. Before the structure was half finished it was turned over to the executive committee of the National Republican Convention, which fitted it with seats. Hardly had Benjamin Harrison walked out as the Republican nominee for President than workmen rushed in to complete the structure.

When the Auditorium reared its magnificent form above the Chicago skyline, civic pride soared into hyperbole. "The useless pyramids shrink into insignificance and the Eiffel Tower is but a toy," rhapsodized one writer. Citizens were proud of the fact that this was purely a Chicago enterprise, costing $2,700,000 on property worth $1,000,000. It was built by Chicago men on designs by Chicago architects—the same Adler and Sullivan combination—and had the finest organ in the world.

President Harrison and his entourage arrived in Chicago on the morning of December 9, 1889, to attend the dedication cere- monies, and were escorted to the Union League Club where a luncheon and reception were held. Hundreds crowded the Club- house to meet the President. By evening a huge crowd had gathered in Congress Street in front of the Auditorium Theater entrance, overflowing into Michigan and Wabash avenues. "This is a well-dressed mob. It therefore has wit enough to become exasperating," sighed Wirt Dexter, straightening his clothes after running the gantlet.

Nearly three hundred policemen struggled with the mob, which got entirely out of hand by eight o'clock when the car- riage crowd began to arrive and the superb costumes of the society women could be seen.

An enterprising reporter heard such as this:

"Scrumptious!" cried the mob when an importation from Worth got daintly from her carriage.

"Ain't she fine," cried the mob as the importation penetrated its ranks.

"Golly!" yelled the mob as the importation became engulfed in its midst.

"Oo-oo-oo-o-o-o-ooh!" sighed the mob in a vast, heaving, bottom- less sigh, as the importation vanished through the portals in a blaze of electric light.

That evening some five hundred carriages, estimated at one- third of the total number in Chicago, drew up and departed. Many other music lovers came in cable cars, hansom cabs, and street hacks. Chicago had never witnessed anything like it. When the women of the *haut monde* settled in their boxes, their gowns and jewels became even more dazzling against the background of gold and ivory walls, glowing with scintillating electric lights from magnificent cut-glass chandeliers.

There was Mrs. Marshall Field in a breath-taking Josephine creation of pale brown brocade with diamond ornaments. Mrs. Ferdinand Peck wore a gown of shell-pink brocade with roses and violets mingled in her bouquet. Mrs. Potter Palmer, radiant in scarlet crepe, wore a diamond aigrette in her hair and a necklace of diamonds. Mrs. Levi P. Morton wore a décolleté costume of black Brussels net with diamond ornaments in her hair. She carried a bouquet of white roses and orchids. Fans waved in recognition and diamond-studded lorgnettes were raised in haughty scrutiny. President Harrison, in Peck's box, leaned over and whispered to Vice-President Morton in the next box: "New York surrenders, eh?" The *Tribune*, which was

Elegantly gowned women delighted the eyes of the crowds gathered about the entrance to the Auditorium on its opening night.

Boxes in the "golden horseshoe" were filled with notables of Chicago society.

to devote three solid pages to the affair next day, said the Auditorium had "opened with ceremonies of unprecedented impressiveness."

Mayor Dewitt Cregier spoke. Everyone roared for Ferd Peck. Peck spoke and invited the audience to call on the President for a speech. The President spoke and said everyone wanted to hear Patti; Patti, "the petted darling of two continents." Then came the ode by Harriet Monroe, art critic of the *Tribune*. "Hail to thee, fair Chicago! On thy brow America, thy mother, lays a crown." Miss Monroe, later to edit *Poetry*, a magazine of modern verse, wrote then in the classic style.

Finally Patti stood before them. Women caught their breaths as they looked upon her gown of black-and-white striped satin, the front and bodice exquisitely trimmed with silver drops and jet passementerie. Black mousquetaire gloves reached above her elbows, and on her neck and breast gleamed diamond ornaments. Men sighed at her charm—"so essentially feminine." A hush fell over the hall. Patti's clear, fluid notes came forth in the song "Home, Sweet Home." She sang without ornament, and her rendering was simplicity itself. She seemed to be testing the new theater with her voice. She sang this song "not as your mother sang it," one critic said. "She sang it better."

When the last note died away everyone was on his feet. Patti nodded to the conductor. Her encore was the bravura favorite, Eckert's "Swiss Song," with its echo effects and pretty embellishments. The crystal drops on the chandeliers trembled. When Patti finished, she would sing no more.

"Two little songs can hardly be called a triumph, and yet the event of last evening will be likely to be cherished as one of the

Climax of the opening ceremonies at the Auditorium was the appearance of Adelina Patti singing "Home, Sweet Home."

most memorable in her long and successful career," wrote a critic.

It was to be a memorable event for many others. It was a memorable night for Chicago, and Chicago would not forget it for many a year.

The dedication was followed by a season of four weeks of Italian opera which was considered "one of the most successful, musically and financially, ever given in this country." Franklin H. Head, manufacturer and banker, had auctioned off the boxes in the Auditorium. George M. Pullman was the highest bidder, his box costing him $1,600. Robert T. Crane, Marshall Field, and Samuel Allerton paid $1,000 each for theirs. This led a contemporary to say of these four Union League clubmen: "It was a testimonial to the municipal patriotism of the four highest bidders that not one of them was particularly interested in music." But all were stockholders in a highly successful venture —the Chicago Auditorium Association.

Many of the Union League Club members who had been responsible for permanent opera later used their influence and money for the establishment of a permanent symphony orchestra for Chicago. Club member C. Norman Fay, who had known Theodore Thomas for ten years, met the famous orchestra conductor in New York in 1889.

"Would you come to Chicago if we could give you a permanent orchestra?" Fay asked Thomas.

"I would go to hell if they could give me an orchestra!" exclaimed Thomas.

Fay and four other incorporators of the Chicago Orchestra Association—Alvin C. Bartlett, Nathaniel K. Fairbank, Charles D. Hammill, and Ezra B. McCagg—met on December 17, 1890, to organize the orchestra. All incorporators but McCagg were Union League Club members, and thirty-two of the fifty-one

Michigan Avenue in 1889 was a boulevard lined with stately buildings.

guarantors who contributed to a $50,000 guarantee fund were members of the Club. First named the Chicago Orchestra, it later became the Theodore Thomas Orchestra, and finally the Chicago Symphony Orchestra.

In 1904, Club member Daniel H. Burnham and ten friends raised $750,000 to endow the orchestra and the building of Orchestra Hall on Michigan Avenue. Many other Club members have been active supporters of the orchestra. George E. Adams, president of the Club in 1892, was president of the Orchestral Association from 1894 to 1899. Club member Edward L. Ryerson was president from 1938 to 1952, and a board member from 1930. Scores of others were active at various times, including J. McGregor Adams, Marshall Field, H. N. Higinbotham, Victor Lawson, Martin A. Ryerson, Charles H. Wacker, T. B. Blackstone, Ferdinand Peck, Frank O. Lowden, Julius Rosenwald, Ralph H. Norton, Paul H. Davis, Percy B. Eckhart, Stanley G. Harris, Charles Ward Seabury, and Jeffrey R. Short.

Chapter Ten

THE WORLD'S FAIR LIVES ON

SCARCELY HAD THE EXCITEMENT OVER THE ESTABLISHMENT OF the Auditorium as the home of grand opera in Chicago died down than the Union League Club was caught up in the initiation of another great civic and cultural project.

In 1889 there was already under way a national movement for a great World's Fair or Exposition to commemorate the 400th anniversary of the landing of Columbus, and loyal Chicagoans were determined that this Fair should be held in their city. As a matter of record, the first man to suggest publicly that Chicago be the site of a Columbian Exposition was Edwin Lee Brown, an iron-works manufacturer, first president of the Illinois Society for the Prevention of Cruelty to Animals, and one of the first members of the Union League Club.

The germ of the idea for the World's Columbian Exposition, Brown always maintained, sprang from an annual meeting of the stockholders of the Chicago Inter-State Industrial Exposition Company, owners of the Exposition Building on the lake front. At this meeting, held on November 14, 1885, Brown offered a resolution "that it is the sense of this meeting that a great World's Fair be held in Chicago in the year 1892, the 400th anniversary of the landing of Columbus in America." Brown said this idea had been suggested to him by George Mason, vice-president of the Excelsior Iron Works. Mason, in looking up his family history, had found that when Illinois was finally and definitely ceded to England by France, the first white settlers came to the place where Chicago now stands and took up their homes there in 1792. This was the 300th anniversary of the landing of Columbus on the island of Guanahani, and Mason thus conceived the 1892 celebration as honoring both the city and the explorer.

The matter was referred to the executive committee for consideration and report, but the resolution created a great deal of public comment and served to advertise Chicago throughout the country. The newspapers of the city and many public men who were interviewed heartily commended the proposed World's Exposition, and it was deemed particularly appropriate for Chicago, the youngest great city, to celebrate the landing of the great navigator upon the new continent.

Fresh impetus to the movement for a World's Fair was given in 1889 by the Chicago celebration of the centennial of the inauguration of George Washington as first President of the United States. One hundred thousand people gathered in eight mass meetings to take part in the celebration, while two hundred thousand children in two hundred meetings added to the general enthusiasm. These meetings had been sponsored by the Union League Club, which climaxed the celebration with a banquet honoring two hundred distinguished guests.

A month later the City Council asked Mayor DeWitt C. Cregier to appoint a citizens' committee of one hundred to obtain the Fair for Chicago. On his own initiative the Mayor appointed two hundred and fifty. There were eleven standing committees, all with one secretary, Edward F. Cragin, a successful real estate promoter, who at once established his headquarters at the Union League Club. Shortly thereafter he requested and obtained permission to entertain guests there in connection with World's Fair business without the formality of first writing for permission.

A Congressional movement to promote Chicago as the scene of the great event was initiated by an honorary member of the

Union League Club, Senator Shelby M. Cullom. On August 13, 1889, he organized a committee for this purpose and in December of the same year introduced a bill in Congress providing for the holding of the exposition. New York, Washington, and St. Louis were also eager contenders for the honor of being host to the Fair. Minneapolis and St. Paul made strong bids.

Brown watched his idea grow, but he was too ill now to participate in the work. By the time of his death, on July 22, 1891, Chicago had been assured the Fair. Congress already had set the date for opening in 1893, and two fellow Club members had been presidents of the World's Fair Association—Lyman J. Gage, vice-president of First National Bank, and William T. Baker, president of the Board of Trade. Had Brown lived, he would have seen a third member of the Club take over the presidency— Harlow N. Higinbotham.

The Club would have liked to see one of its members as World's Fair mayor, as well. At that time it was fighting to free Chicago from the spoils system, and had endorsed a bill before the state legislature for the adoption of the merit system in cities over 100,000 population. This fight took shape in the nomination of the millionaire packer, Samuel W. Allerton, as a non-partisan candidate on a genuine civil service platform. The Political Action Committee's report tells the story: "But for the phenomenal popularity of the opposing candidate (Carter Harrison) due to his possession of dazzling personal qualities which peculiarly adapted him to discharge with grace the delicate duties of the world's host during the World's Fair, the committee believe that the merit system would have been endorsed by a majority of our citizens and an honored member of this Club would have long since put it into successful operation in all departments of municipal service." Harrison won over Allerton with a plurality of 19,695 votes.

From the beginning, the Union League Club, both as an

The Fine Arts Palace, architectural gem of the Columbian Exposition. Now rebuilt, it houses the Museum of Science and Industry.

A trip on the Ferris Wheel
was a thrilling experience
no visitor to the Exposition
wished to miss.

organization and through the activities of individual members, had wholeheartedly supported the World's Fair, and it could now take honest pride in the nation-wide recognition resulting from its efforts. "During no period in its history has your organization enjoyed greater prosperity or filled a more important place in its relations to the community than in 1893— the year of the Columbian Exposition," read the annual report of the Board of Directors of the Club on January 23, 1894.

The Union League Club shared in the general pride in the great "White City," as it was popularly called, with its 150 buildings of Romanesque, Greek, and Renaissance architecture. Its members had fought for the Fair, invested heavily in it, and been foremost in planning it. Club member Daniel H. Burnham had supervised the designing and construction. Most of the architects and builders were Club members, and Dankmar Adler and Louis H. Sullivan were particularly noteworthy in initiating functional architecture with their Transportation Building.

The facilities of the Club were hospitably extended to the many distinguished guests who came to Chicago from all quarters of the world. An assessment of $20 had been made on each member to refurnish the Clubhouse throughout for the year of the Fair, and a total of $22,220 had been spent, with only nine members failing to pay their share. Some of this money was spent in purchasing adjoining property occupied by a saloon and constructing a new main entrance on the site. The lounge was enlarged and other improvements completed to make the Clubhouse attractive "and to promote hospitality on the part of the Club and individual members in connection with the great influx of strangers in our midst; and your organization has in many ways during the year exerted an important influence in the advancement of our city."

More champagne flowed in the Club that year than at any time in history. Steve Kelley, who was then wine clerk, was

The Court of Honor, surrounded by buildings in the classic architectural styles, was the heart of the Exposition's great White City.

kept busy thinking up new types of drinks. This veteran employee, who retired in 1954 after completing sixty-five years with the Club, later recalled: "I remember how one member suggested that I plug a watermelon, pour in an entire bottle of champagne, and then replug it and let it stand for a time in the icebox. This proved a popular refreshment during the Fair. We also installed a machine to freeze champagne and were able to serve champagne ice. Mint juleps were in demand, and to keep everyone satisfied I merely crushed a little of the end of the mint stems. There were those who argued that mint should not be crushed and others who said it should be crushed. Even Kentuckians could not agree."

Kelley became noted for his *pousse cafés*, a tricky drink made with layer upon layer of different-colored liqueurs. Taking advantage of the specific gravity of the various cordials and brandies, Kelley first poured into the glass some red apricot cordial. On top of this he poured a layer of brown crème de coca, then white crème de menthe, followed by yellow chartreuse, then green chartreuse, and finally topped off with cognac brandy. Carefully made, the liquors did not mix, and as Kelley said, "pleased the eye as well as the taste."

Privileges of the Club had been extended during the year to resident consuls and to the foreign commissioners and chiefs of departments of the Exposition. There were 1,272 guest cards issued during the year. The register showed 5,279 names of visiting men and 1,500 visiting women, besides the great number of persons entertained in the private dining rooms.

During the World's Fair year the Club had 1,184 resident members, including most of the wealthiest and most influential men in the city. At that time it was estimated that there were more than two hundred millionaires in Chicago, most of them men who had built their fortunes by their own efforts and from small beginnings in this city of opportunity.

With such a representative membership, it is not surprising that the government requested the Club to be official host to the Duke of Veragua and his brother, the Marquis of Barboles, lineal descendants of Christopher Columbus, at a Spanish breakfast. These distinguished visitors, who came for the opening of the Fair on May 1, had been much sought after by Chicago's society leaders, but since they were unable to accept so many invitations, it was decided to provide the breakfast and reception at the Club on May 6.

The ten-course breakfast proved a brilliant affair. The Duke of Veragua, an imposing figure with clean chin and upper lip and a profusion of side whiskers, a pleasing face and broad forehead and narrowed eyes, sat directly on the right of the Club president, Ferdinand W. Peck. On Peck's left was the Duke's brother, also a handsome man. The several hundred Club members and notables, including many foreign representatives to the Fair, no doubt pondered on what a wealthy man the Duke would be if he could but make good his claim to that portion of all the riches of the New World that was originally guaranteed to Columbus and his successors through all time.

After eating his way through a Spanish menu—which included *ostras frescas* (fresh oysters), *aceitunas* (olives), *pimiento frito* (fried peppers), *tomatoes con cebollas* (tomatoes with onions), *huevos con arroz* (eggs with rice), *filete de ternera con salsa castellaña* (veal chops with Castilian sauce), *supremes de pollo, à la Alfonso XII* (chicken), *sorbete Infante* (sherbet), *chochas asados* (roasted woodcocks), *ensalada de lechuga* (lettuce salad), *fresas con kirsh y bizcochos* (strawberry shortcake with kirsch), and washed down with sherry, Château Leoville, Pommery sec, Malaga, coffee, and cognac—the Duke got up and responded to the address of welcome in perfect English.

There were many more magnificent entertainments, of an official and private nature, but more important to the Club was its part in making many of the Fair's prized exhibits permanently available through the founding of the Field Columbian Museum—now known as the Chicago Natural History Museum.

The Columbian Museum was one of the outstanding attractions of the World's Fair. The great collection of birds and beasts, of ores and precious stones, and of exhibits depicting the habits and customs of peoples from all over the world had been gathered together over years of effort and the spending of a large amount of money. One of the most interesting collections was that of American Indians, owned by Chicago's wealthy lumberman, Edward E. Ayer.

Many visitors to the Fair expressed the hope that in some way this collection might be preserved as a permanent contribution to Chicago's educational and artistic development.

Among these was Judge Sidney Corning Eastman. Judge Eastman thought about the matter and talked about it at the Club.
He wrote a letter to the Chicago *Tribune*, which was published
in the Voice of the People column, but apparently attracted
little attention.

However, a few days later Judge Eastman, while making
the steamboat trip from Lincoln Park to the World's Fair
grounds, met a fellow Club member, James W. Scott, publisher
of the Chicago *Herald*. Eastman showed him the *Tribune* clip-
ping, which Scott had apparently overlooked.

"An excellent suggestion!" exclaimed Scott. "I am going to
send one of my staff to interview you on the subject."

The reporter called and several stories, as well as editorials
on the subject, were published by the *Herald*. Still nothing
happened of a constructive nature. However, at the next meeting
of the board of directors of the Fair, Scott brought up the
subject. It met with enthusiasm, and a committee with George
E. Adams as chairman and Eastman as secretary was appointed
to see what could be done.

"After the Fair is over Chicago will have one of the finest
museums in the world," the *Herald* enthusiastically announced
on August 12. It pointed out that the museum would be one of
the numerous relics of the great exposition, and added that all
that remained to be done was that citizens, independent of the
directors of the Fair, form an organization and take possession
of the material then contributed to the museum. A number of
foreign commissioners already were willing to donate their
entire displays if the proper arrangements could be made.

Such arrangements were made. A group of men, including
Andrew McNally, the publisher; Levi Z. Leiter, the merchant;
Ferdinand Peck, capitalist; E. E. Ayers, Judge Eastman, George
M. Pullman, Melville E. Stone, and Philip D. Armour applied
for a charter for "The Columbian Museum of Chicago." This

was granted September 16, and a few days later the trustees of the museum met at the Union League Club. Edwin Walker was made temporary chairman, with Eastman secretary. A finance committee was appointed, composed of Ayer, John C. Black, and James W. Ellsworth.

These members of the finance committee pledged themselves to provide a fund to endow the museum. Ayer and Ellsworth went to see Marshall Field.

"Mr. Field," said Ayer, "how many young men today even know the name of that great merchant of only a few years ago, A. T. Stewart? Yours, likewise, may be lost unless you do something outside of a business way to perpetuate it. In the second place, how will the teachers, students, and others who want to know about natural history have an opportunity to study representative collections unless you or somebody else provide them, and what other opportunity will ever be presented as favorable as the present one?"

"Let me think of it a few days, and then come to see me," said Field.

In a few days Ayer and Ellsworth were back.

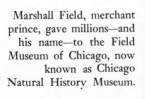

Marshall Field, merchant prince, gave millions—and his name—to the Field Museum of Chicago, now known as Chicago Natural History Museum.

"Well, Mr. Field, what do you think you can do?" Ellsworth asked.

"Well, I'll give you a million," was the offhand response. But he insisted that $500,000 must be pledged by other business men, and $2,000,000 in World's Fair stock assigned to the trustees.

Pullman, on hearing of Field's pledge, gave $100,000. Leiter gave another $100,000, but he did it on condition that the museum not bear Field's name. He and Field, former partners, were then at outs. When Cyrus H. McCormick learned this condition he raised $85,000 in less than an hour, and a few of Field's friends made up the balance. Leiter's subscription was cancelled.

Ayer gave his Indian collection worth $75,000, and the museum was housed in the Fine Arts Palace in Jackson Park, one of the most celebrated of the Exposition buildings. It first bore the name of the Field Columbian Museum, but in 1905 this was changed to the Field Museum of Natural History. In his will Field remembered the Museum with $8,000,000, bringing the total of his gifts to $9,430,000.

In the course of the years many more exhibits were added. Explorers and collectors sent rare specimens from all over the world. When eventually the old World's Fair building began to show the ravages of time, the museum was moved to a splendid new building erected on the lake front at Twelfth Street, endowed by the Field family. In 1943 the more civic title of Chicago Natural History Museum was adopted, but the name of Field Museum still lingers on affectionately in the memories of many Chicagoans.

Chapter Eleven

THE PUBLIC CONSCIENCE
OF CHICAGO

IN THE BACKWASH OF THE WORLD'S COLUMBIAN EXPOSITION came industrial strife and economic troubles. Union League Club members felt the pinch with others as the country was gripped by the panic of '93. Business and bank failures were reported throughout the nation, and with the closing of the Fair, there was widespread unemployment in Chicago, variously estimated at from 36,000 to 200,000. Mayor Carter H. Harrison, shortly before his assassination at the close of the Fair, predicted there would be riots by the destitute within the city unless Congress appropriated money for some sort of relief work.

The rapidly growing city of some 1,500,000 inhabitants was wide open, with vice, gambling, and corruption flourishing brazenly. The City Council was selling public utilities franchises for cash on the line, and even the legislators were not above accepting a bribe here and there. Michael ("Hinky Dink") Kenna and John J. ("Bathhouse") Coughlin were in political ascendancy. Coughlin had been elected an alderman in 1892. Kenna would gain this office in 1897, and the pair would become two of Chicago's most notorious aldermen. Describing the Democratic primary in the First Ward on October 2, 1893, the *Tribune* said that three hundred men had lined up before the polling place. "Bathhouse John," wearing a skullcap and gumshoes, was "ably assisted by Thomas Jefferson McNally, the Leidendecker boys, and the man Carter H. does not know

"Hinky-Dink" Kenna, who with "Bathhouse John" Coughlin dominated Chicago's First Ward politics.

[Kenna] in the formation of the 'voters.' Of the whole batch not more than twenty were legal voters, and it is extremely doubtful if one-tenth of the number could read the names on the tickets thrust into their hands by 'Bathhouse John.' "

Need of some reform organization which could combat the growing evils, as well as alleviate the suffering of the starving and jobless, was apparent to all good citizens. But the one to take the initiative was a complete outsider—William T. Stead, a visiting English journalist who had come to write about the World's Fair and remained to publish his highly controversial book, *If Christ Came to Chicago.*

Under labor auspices, Stead called a mass meeting in Central Music Hall on Sunday, November 12, 1893, as a protest against the deplorable conditions existing in Chicago. At this meeting a committee was formed to organize a federation of all good citizens to unite in a vigorous crusade for relief of the poor, for industrial conciliation, to battle against the vicious elements of society and slum conditions, and to improve the municipal government. The Civic Federation of Chicago, with its great central committee and active councils in each ward, resulted.

Turlington W. Harvey, millionaire lumberman and active member of the Union League Club, was chairman of the committee of nomination. In notifying those who were to serve on the executive committee, he sent out notices which read: "The object of this organization, briefly and in general terms, is the concentration into one potential, non-political, non-sectarian center all the forces now laboring to advance our municipal, philanthropic, industrial, and religious interests, and to accomplish all that is possible towards energizing and giving effect to *the public conscience of Chicago.*"

The response was immediate. Lyman J. Gage, also a Club member and president of the First National Bank, was named president of the Federation. Mrs. Potter Palmer became first vice-president; J. J. McGrath, second vice-president; R. M. Easley, secretary; and E. S. Dreyer, treasurer. Jane Addams was a trustee. The Club was represented also by such men as L. C. Collins, Victor F. Lawson, William Penn Nixon, A. C. Hesing, George E. Adams, Marshall Field, Cyrus H. McCormick, and H. N. Higinbotham.

Reform was the watchword, reform in all phases of municipal government the most important goal. "If we are to shoulder our share in the governing of the city, we must begin where the process of government begins," said William A. Giles, retired jewelry manufacturer, at a meeting of the Federation in the Union League Clubhouse on April 10, 1894. He said the Federation must go into politics, "practical politics." In the fall of that year, at another meeting in the Clubhouse, 344 members of the Club raised $4,000 within ten minutes "to help catch election law violators and send same to Joliet." Lyman Gage announced that $50,000 would have to be raised, and he had hardly spoken before a telegram was handed to him from Victor F. Lawson, owner of the *Daily News,* which read: "Yes: Gladly subscribe $1,000 to the Civic Federation's guarantee fund."

Yet with all the money and the backing of prominent citizens, satisfactory results still were not obtained. The Federation took upon itself the duty of showing how the streets could be cleaned for less than the city was paying; how it could suppress gambling by organizing its own raids. The vice lords and the professional politicians merely "laid low" until things quieted down, and then went back to operating as usual.

In the midst of all this, Stead's jeremiad of 460 red-hot pages came off the press. If Christ came to Chicago, the London editor wrote, He would be horrified at the sordid and irreligious state of affairs. Stead spared no one in his book. He inveighed against the way churches were run; he excoriated the "boodlers" or public plunderers; he classified Marshall Field, Philip Armour, and George Pullman as the "Chicago Trinity," admired and respected more by young men than the Saviour. He dwelt on "Whiskey and Politics," the "Scarlet Woman," the "Boodlers and the Boodled." He incurred the wrath of Chicago's women society leaders in his chapter on "Who Are the Disreputables?" by saying, "Those women who have great opportunities only to neglect them, and who have great means only to squander them upon themselves, are more disreputable in the eyes of God and man than the worst harlot on Fourth Avenue." Stead's book left Chicago's moral reputation in shreds.

In his book Stead was endeavoring to spur on the Civic Federation, of which he had been the inspiration. The Federation struggled along, promised a lot and tried hard. Great things were to be done at the primaries and even greater things on election day.

But President Gage finally admitted that "for some reason, they had failed." He made this admission before a group of 250 citizens representing the Union League, Marquette, Commercial, Iroquois, and Hamilton clubs. He had called them together in January, 1896, to ask their aid in carrying on the work. At this meeting a committe of fifteen was appointed, later to report a plan for organization of a ward committee of one hundred, the original committee of fifteen to be continued in an executive capacity. Thus came into being the Municipal Voters League.

The League was to accomplish the work vainly attempted by the Political Action Committee of the Federation. This job was "to rescue the city from the band of conspirators, known as the Council 'gang,' " as the benign, white-haired Judge Murray F. Tuley told a crowd of fifteen hundred people at Central Music Hall on the night of March 16. Judge Tuley explained that the newly formed League's task was "to clean out the City Council, which is degrading Chicago before the world," and also added that "the League has no machinery." Then he turned and looked at the stocky form and pugnacious face of a man on the platform. "I have said the League has no machine. I will take that back—we have this little sawed-off giant of reform, George E. Cole. He is our machine, tireless and fearless. He has X-ray eyes and can look right through a candidate and see whether he is a boodler at heart or not."

This was George Cole's first introduction to the public. Cole, stationer and printer, and veteran member of the Union League Club, had tackled a formidable job at which others had failed, and one which prominent men had refused as impossible to accomplish. "Citizen" or "Old King" Cole, as he became known, *was* the League. He had been president of the Fourth Ward Council of the Federation when he was called one night in February by William T. Baker, who had succeeded Lyman Gage as president of the Federation, to appear at the Federation's headquarters. Baker told the surprised Cole he wanted him to head the Municipal Voters League. Others had refused the job.

A short, stocky man, Cole by Lincoln's concept had legs of adequate length, "as they reached to the ground." He stood now on those legs and said: "Gentlemen, you have not named me as

"Citizen" George E. Cole pitted his energy and determination against Chicago's politicians— and won.

first, second, or third choice; it is merely 'Hobson's choice.' But I made up my mind a year ago that I would act the coward's part no longer, and would assume whatever civic duty came to me unsought. I will accept the appointment as a leader of a forlorn hope, *on condition* that I am to name the secretary and executive committee, and am given full authority to run things to suit myself. You are to furnish $10,000 and I am not to know who contributes."

Cole's first move was to select the men to work with him. He named Hoyt King, formerly assistant secretary to Police Chief Major Robert McLaughry, as his secretary, and an executive committee consisting of fellow Club members William H. Colvin, Edward Burritt Smith, R. R. Donnelley, James L. Houghteling, Francis Lackner, and Allen B. Pond. Two others were M. J. Carroll, printer and one-time president of the Chicago Typographical Union, and Frank Wells.

For these men Cole had a simple, forceful formula: "Now let's get down to brass tacks. God helps those who fight like the devil, and to hell with the libel suits. We'll make this fight with facts alone. Take nothing for granted. 'I think' and 'I guess' are taboo here."

An investigation by Secretary King showed that fifty-seven of the sixty-eight members of the City Council at that time were "crooks." Cole's job was to defeat the undesirables for re-election. Mass meetings of citizens were held in Central Music Hall and elsewhere. At one of these meetings, Frank O. Lowden, later governor of Illinois, said: "Corporate interests too must learn that every immunity or benefit secured unfairly from the public becomes a menace, not a gain. . . . It finds at the same time that if those interests bribed a council or a legislature, it sowed a crop of dragon's teeth which has sprung up into an army of mailed highwaymen."

Hoyt King later recalled that the investigation of the League disclosed that the City Council "was a market for the sale to corporations of rights in the streets, over them and under them, with no adequate compensation to the city." The name connected with such sales was usually that of Charles Tyson Yerkes. Yerkes had come to Chicago in 1881 from Philadelphia and opened a brokerage office. A year later he became a member of the Union League Club. He was an art collector, contributed to charity, had a fine home on Michigan Avenue, was a respected but soon-to-be feared citizen. He had bought a majority of the stock in the North Chicago Street Railroad Company, and a year later in the West Side lines. In 1895 he had changed to electric power and turned his attention to elevated railways. Chicago's famous Loop was his idea.

"And then this little stationer turns up, with no experience and no money, to oppose him," said Hoyt King. "Yerkes had brains, long experience, money, and no conscience. He had built up complete control of the Council, fixing a market value for votes. Other corporations fell in line."

The Chicago *Record* had been more specific about the

"market value of votes" in the City Council. On February 19, 1894, it had asked, "How much does it cost to pass a franchise ordinance through the Council?" and answered the question by saying the highest price paid was when four members received $25,000 each for their votes on a measure giving valuable privileges to a railway corporation, passed in the face of public opposition. Others who voted for the ordinance received $8,000 each. For the past four years, the paper said, "$5,000 per vote" was the high-water mark. When it became necessary to pass an ordinance over the mayor's veto, 25 per cent was added.

The sinister hand of Yerkes now was seen in an ordinance giving the "McGann Road" rights in Jackson Street (now Boulevard), which had passed the City Council prior to the city election of 1896. This measure provided that the Chicago General Railway Company should be granted a fifty-year franchise to occupy Jackson Street and other thoroughfares with streetcar lines.

The Club, one of the chief opponents to this plan which would bring the car lines in front of the Clubhouse door, was fortunate in having as a member Mayor George B. Swift. Mayor Swift had vetoed the proposed ordinance.

Cole now found that merely electing "aggressively honest" aldermen was not sufficient. In the first test of strength, the Municipal Voters League had secured sufficient aldermen to prevent passage of the ordinance over the mayor's veto. Promptly the "gang" in the Council, in anticipation of the seating of these "good" aldermen, conspired to call a special meeting of the old Council to push through the ordinance before the newly elected members could be sworn in.

Cole did not have much time. He immediately "subsidized the local messenger service," got in touch with reliable aldermen, both holdovers and prospectives, and brought together twenty-nine at the Union League Club on Sunday afternoon, April 12.

Cole explained the situation to them, and they all agreed that the new aldermen should present their credentials to the city clerk and be sworn in before the meeting of the Council Monday evening.

At nine o'clock Monday morning Charles M. Walker, later to become a Federal judge, came to Cole's office in great distress. He had applied to City Clerk "Alphabet" Van Cleave to be sworn in. Van Cleave told him he did not have the proper forms and would meet him at the Council chambers in the evening. Cole asked Walker to draw up the form and had it printed at once. He arranged for someone with legal authority to administer the oath to the aldermen at the afternoon meeting at the Club. But Van Cleave found out about this and was able to "find" his own forms. So the aldermen were sworn in that afternoon, and that night took possession of their seats. Their votes were sufficient to support the mayor's veto. These and subsequent acts broke the rule of the boodlers in the City Council. It was after this that a newspaperman gave the boodlers the name of "gray wolves," indicating a hungry pack on the outside trying to get in.

"Boodler" politics was a favorite cartoon theme of the period.

In 1896, after the first campaign in which the League took part, there were twenty-two aldermen believed to be honest; in 1897 there were twenty-three, and by 1898 there were forty-two aldermen believed to be honest against twenty-eight believed to be dishonest.

This last aldermanic election was to be the showdown between Cole and Yerkes—between David and Goliath. Yerkes had pushed the Allen law through the legislature, and unless enough aldermen were elected to defeat a fifty-year city franchise as provided by that law, it would be clear that the people of Chicago endorsed the law and wished it to stand. But the result of the election was decisive for the League. Out of twenty-nine candidates it endorsed, nineteen were elected.

Cole predicted in the *Tribune* after the election that "This election marks the downfall of Charles T. Yerkes as a dominant force in the City Council. Its results mean his elimination as a factor in our municipal affairs. They mean he will never be the factor he has been in Chicago life. . . . The people have won the first fight on the Allen law. . . . The fight can now be carried into the legislature, and the election of legislators pledged to repeal the Allen law will be of some value to the people of Chicago."

On the evening of December 19 of that year, when the Council convened to adopt a fifty-year streetcar franchise under the Allen law, angry citizens crowded the council chambers, wearing on their coat lapels tiny coils of lynching rope. As the Council took their seats, there was an ominous roar from the milling crowd without. But the "aggressively honest" aldermen had things under control. Forty to twenty-nine was the vote against the franchise.

Yerkes, who had bought the Chicago *Inter Ocean*, with Charles Wheeler Hinman as editor-in-chief, through its columns denounced Chicago as "anarchistic" and said capital would fly

Page 151—

George E. Cole and J. Frank Aldrich, veterans of Chicago reform, casting their votes in a First Ward precinct.

from the city. Next year the legislature repealed the Allen law. Yerkes was through, as Cole had predicted. In 1900 he disposed of his interests in Chicago and went to London.

Another fight for good government had been won, and Citizen Cole, asked about his experience in politics, could say, "I would rather go fishing. If you can find anyone in Chicago who knows or cares less about politics than I do, I would like to see him." But there was more work for him. Although he resigned from the Municipal Voters League in 1899, in 1901 he became president of the Citizens' Association, and in 1902 founded the Legislative Voters League "to clean up the legislature," as he had cleaned up the City Council.

Chapter Twelve

McKINLEY SEEMS TO BE
THE COMING MAN

"FOUR HUNDRED MEN SPRANG TO THEIR FEET, AND WAVING napkins and handkerchiefs, burst into cheers as a medium-sized, smooth-faced man walked into the banquet hall of the Union League Club last night. The cheering grew in volume until the fine-looking man walked across the banquet hall around the end of the speakers' table and then up to the seat reserved for him. As he paused here, Judge Leroy D. Thomas lifted his glass high and said:

" 'Gentlemen, I propose the health of the Governor of Ohio.'

"The toast was drunk standing, the company sat down, and the banquet went on."

Thus did the Chicago *Tribune* on Friday, February 23, 1894, describe the enthusiasm with which Governor William McKinley was received by members of the Union League Club of Chicago. McKinley had been invited to Chicago by the Club as the guest of honor for the eighth annual Washington's Birthday celebration, and had been the main speaker at the ceremony in the Auditorium Theater. More than seven thousand persons had crowded the Auditorium to hear him. Already McKinley was viewed by many as the Republican standard-bearer in the 1896 presidential campaign, although he had given no indication that he would run.

McKinley did not touch on political topics in his short address at the Union League Club banquet, where oddly enough

William McKinley, governor of Ohio, was the "orator of the day" at the Union League Club's Washington's Birthday celebration in 1894.

he found seated near him Congressman William Jennings Bryan of Nebraska, who would be his opponent in the presidential campaign two years later. Bryan—who was there, Club President John P. Wilson jestingly remarked, "because he was able to evade the guards at the door"—also refrained from political talk. When called upon to offer a toast he lifted his glass—containing grape juice, no doubt—and said, "The name of America must always exalt the just pride of patriotism."

Chicago's Democratic mayor, John P. Hopkins, had avoided giving any political endorsement of McKinley by his presence. His chair next to the Governor remained vacant. The Mayor later said he had not understood he had been invited to the banquet, but "would not have come anyway," as he wished to attend a travel lecture at Central Music Hall.

McKinley had arrived an hour late at the banquet. He pleaded fatigue, brought on by his speaking tour of several weeks, and had been resting at the home of his brother-in-law, Lafayette McWilliams, Club member and a partner of Marshall Field & Company. But at each mention of his name the guests applauded and shouted, "What's wrong with McKinley? He's all right!" Justice David J. Brewer of the United States Supreme Court evoked the greatest demonstration when, in boasting about the possessions of the nation, he said, "We have not the English Bill of Rights, but is there not another *Bill* for America to be proud of?" All eyes turned to McKinley, "a shout went up, and glasses tinkled."

The next day, before leaving the city, Governor McKinley told reporters: "I don't care to talk politics—I'm not a politician anyhow and so cannot discuss political questions."

Less than two months later the Union League Club made him an honorary member.

It was in such an atmosphere, friendly to McKinley, that Charles Gates Dawes came to the Union League Club a year later with the determination of doing everything in his power to place the Governor of Ohio in the presidential chair. Dawes, a slender, eager-eyed young man, wearing a mustache on his upper lip, arrived in Chicago from Lincoln, Nebraska, on January 8, 1895. He took quarters at the Union League Club, to which he had been elected on the recommendation of his friend, John R. Walsh, founder and president of the Chicago National Bank.

Dawes, then twenty-nine years old, was on the lookout for a "natural monopoly," and had recently purchased the entire capital stock of the La Crosse Gas, Light and Coke Company of La Crosse, Wisconsin. He was seeking further possibilities in the Midwest. At this early age financial success already was assured for Dawes. He had found his work and fortune in banking and public utilities, and as an outlet for his great energy he had turned to politics. More to the point, he had turned to McKinley politics.

A native of Marietta, Ohio, Dawes had met Major William McKinley in Columbus the year before and had done considerable work in his interests among politicians of Nebraska, Wyoming, and North Dakota. McKinley had been a friend of Dawes's father, General Rufus R. Dawes, in the Civil War; and later when they were together in Congress, Marcus A. Hanna, capitalist-politician of Cleveland, who was in full charge of the McKinley campaign at that time, had asked Dawes "to look after matters in Illinois." No urging was needed, as Dawes's diary of March 10 reveals. He wrote: "McKinley seems to be the coming man."

Although he had offices in the Auditorium Building, Dawes conducted his McKinley campaign mainly from the Union League Club. Here he drew around him several old-time politicians, notably General John McNulta, a fellow Club member, who had seen service in the Republican party since its birth. He enlisted, too, several young men as assistants—men who were to be identified with him during his colorful career, which reached its height when he became Vice-President under Calvin Coolidge.

One of these young men was William Grant Edens, later vice-president of Dawes's Central Trust Company, and who as a good-roads advocate will be remembered as the man who gave his name to the Edens Expressway northwest of Chicago. In 1954, when Colonel Edens had reached his ninetieth birthday, his mind was still vigorous and his recollection clear about those stirring days of the McKinley campaign.

"Back in 1895 I was making myself obnoxious to fellow railroad trainmen by talking of Major McKinley as 'our next president,'" recalled Colonel Edens. "At that time I was chief clerk and cashier of the International Brotherhood of Railroad Trainmen, with headquarters at Galesburg, Illinois. Trainmen for the most part were all Democrats and they tried to silence me. They even argued that, as a trainman, it was treason to be anything but a Democrat."

Edens became a delegate to the Young Men's National Republican League at Cleveland in 1895, and there he met Charles Dawes. Soon after he had returned to Galesburg, Dawes wrote him to come to Chicago and have lunch at the Union League.

"I had never been in a rich man's club before," confided Edens. "My eyes almost popped out at the magnificent way in which the Clubhouse was furnished, and I was speechless when I met such men as Victor F. Lawson, owner of the Chicago *Daily News;* H. H. Kohlsaat, publisher of the *Times Herald;* William Penn Nixon, editor of the *Inter Ocean;* and many other wealthy and influential members of the Club. The only fellow, and I might say the first I saw when I went to the Club, to whom I could talk without stammering, was the check boy, Francis J. Kilkenny."

Dawes was to know and talk, too, with young Kilkenny, and Edens vouches for the story so aptly told by Paul R. Leach, head of the Washington Bureau of the Chicago *Daily News,* in his book *That Man Dawes.*

Dawes had given his hat one evening to the check boy. Kilkenny handed Dawes a large envelope in return.

"What the dickens is this?" Dawes asked, as he turned the neat package in his hands.

"Clippings about Major McKinley, sir," replied the red-cheeked, bright-eyed check boy in a heavy Irish brogue.

"H'm. Where did you get them?"

"I picked them out of the newspapers that had been thrown away, and saved them for you, sir."

Dawes hesitated, smiled, and then said: "What is your name?"

"Francis J. Kilkenny, sir."

"Come upstairs and have dinner with me."

"I am in uniform, sir, and employees are not permitted to eat in the dining room with members."

Dawes waved his hand. "See the manager. Get out of uniform." Kilkenny did, and at dinner Dawes hired him as his confidential assistant. Later, when William McKinley went to the White House and appointed Dawes Comptroller of Currency, Francis Kilkenny went to Washington with him.

Mark Hanna appointed Edens state organizer of the Illinois Republican League and instructed him to report to Dawes. His reports were of great value, as much of the state organization work was based upon Edens' reports, which came from every congressional district in the state.

Dawes, working efficiently and without fanfare, found himself confronted with two other Republican groups, one composed for the most part of members of the Union League Club, headed by Mayor George B. Swift. Though McKinley supporters, they were carrying on their campaign for his nomination independently of the regular Republican organization. Mayor Swift's group, as it was known, consisted among others of Alexander Revell, the furniture man; Charles Ulysses Gordon, real estate man; John C. Spry, lumberman; General Charles FitzSimmons, and William P. Williams, who then was the Club secretary and had delivered the first McKinley speech in Chicago in December, 1895.

The second and more formidable group was that headed by William E. Lorimer, already known as the "Blond Boss" of Chicago and Cook County politics. Lorimer had taken over the local Republican machine in a rough-and-tumble fight, and now in an attempt to play for national recognition was backing an honorary Club member, Senator Shelby M. Cullom, Illinois "favorite son" and a man of high character with the added asset.

that he "looked like Lincoln." Lorimer's group was anti-Swift, and at the state Republican convention a knockdown, drag-out fight was anticipated between the Swift and Lorimer forces.

The three-cornered scrap appeared to concentrate within the very walls of the Union League Club itself. However, Dawes, for his part, scorned local politics. He had a broader vision, and would not become mixed up in the petty squabbles of machine and reform politics. He and McNulta wanted to keep out of local entanglements, and Dawes especially felt that Lorimer and his downstate friends would defeat Swift if the latter attempted to control the state convention.

Dawes's strategy was simple. He wanted the moral effect that a McKinley instruction of the four delegates would have on the nation as a whole. Hanna wanted this, too. Illinois was a pivotal state. It chose its national convention delegates in March and April, ahead of other large states. Thus the publicity accruing from a state victory in April, 1896, would be of great value in influencing other states.

Dawes's brilliant work in behalf of McKinley at the state convention which was held in Springfield on April 29-30, 1896, in which he decisively out-maneuvered Mayor Swift, made political history. He was ably assisted by William F. Calhoun of Vermilion County, a boyhood friend of McKinley's in Ohio, who presented McKinley's name to the convention. On the "critical day," as Dawes termed it in his diary of April 30, after one of the bitterest fights ever waged on the Republican convention floor, the four delegates-at-large were instructed for the Ohio candidate. The resolution was carried 832 to 503 on the first roll call.

At this turbulent session, William P. Williams, secretary of the Union League Club, gave an exhibition of unselfish devotion to McKinley's interests which the Tribune thought worthy of mention. His name had been on the slate along with

Charles Gates Dawes won his political spurs by working to nominate William McKinley for President in the Republican convention of 1896.

those of Calhoun and Attorney General George Hunt in support of the motion to insert McKinley's name in place of that of Cullom at the afternoon session. "Mr. Williams had prepared carefully his speech and had submitted it to Major McKinley, who heartily endorsed it and expressed his ardent desire that the opportunity be afforded him to deliver it before the convention. In the parliamentary tangle, however, and feverish anxiety manifested on all sides for a quick vote on the question at issue, Mr. Williams feared that any further delay would jeopardize the chances of Major McKinley in the convention. The speech was intended as the effort of his life. However, he unselfishly placed personal ambition in the background and instead of going to the world with a warm eulogy of his friend, Major McKinley, he was one of the fiercest advocates of an immediate vote."

Though he received little public recognition for McKinley's victory, Dawes returned to Chicago happy. "The papers as a unit ascribe all credit for winning the battle to Calhoun, although after the army had been collected and drilled through three days he simply appeared as the man on horseback," Dawes confided in his diary on May 1. McKinley was jubilant. But Dawes's work was now just beginning. There was the national convention at St. Louis, and on June 18 came "the day of days in my political career thus far—the nomination of William McKinley for President occurred in the afternoon."

In the press gallery at the St. Louis convention was an editorial contributor to the Omaha *World Herald*, William Jennings Bryan, a boyhood friend of Dawes. Two weeks later in Chicago, shortly before the opening there of the Democratic convention, a newspaper man wrote: "Just three people believe the boy orator of the Platte, who speaks in platte-te-tudes, has a chance for the Democratic nomination. They are: Bryan himself; his wife; and Dawes, a Republican."

Dawes had repeatedly said that if Bryan could speak before the Democratic convention his nomination would be assured. Bryan did speak. He electrified the nation with his "Cross of Gold" speech and became the opponent of McKinley for the Presidency—Bryan as an advocate of "free silver" and McKinley the champion of the gold standard. "I could not but have a feeling of pride for the brilliant young man whose life for so many years lay parallel to mine," Dawes wrote in his diary of July 9.

Busy days were ahead for Dawes. The greatest pilgrimage in American political history had started to Canton, Ohio, where visitors from all over the nation came to meet McKinley on the front porch of his home. They "trampled his lawn and obliterated his carnation beds."

In Chicago, Dawes was keeping account of every cent collected and spent in the campaign—running things "on a business basis." He set up national campaign headquarters for McKinley in the Auditorium Building, but still maintained his unofficial headquarters at the Union League Club, where his contacts with the civic and business leaders of the city proved invaluable. He obtained a contribution of $10,000 from Marshall Field, a fellow Club member. There were entries in his journal such as: "July 20. M. A. Hanna met me at Club and we went to the Auditorium Hotel where we had a meeting of sub-committee of Executive Committee." "September 5. I gave a little dinner party at the Union League Club . . . after which we all went to Central Music Hall to hear Carl Schurz speak."

October 9, "Chicago Day," was a notable event for McKinley. There was an immense "sound money" procession; some twenty-five thousand marched in the parade. "Stood with Caro [his wife] on the reviewing stand reserved for Executive Committee in front of the Union League Club," Dawes wrote. In this parade there made its appearance "an instrument called a 'megaphone,' which first came into use on bicycle tracks, and is calculated to make the most inoffensive whisper sound like a foghorn," a newspaper reported.

On November 3, 1896, McKinley defeated Bryan by a 567,692 vote in the nation. A short time later the President-elect and Mrs. McKinley came to Chicago. McKinley went with Dawes to his Evanston home and there further discussed with Dawes a position in the Cabinet. Here, too, Mrs. McKinley had fitters at Marshall Field's store carry out her design for an inaugural gown. The newspapers used pictures on the front pages and readers learned that the new First Lady would wear "a dress of silver-wrought brocade of Parisian texture combined with *point d' Alençon* lace and silver passementerie threaded with tiny pearls, with lace edging and a taffeta skirt and many frillings and French shirrings."

Young Dawes wound up his diary for this year with the sentence: "Thus ends the year 1896—a tumultuous crowded year for me—and yet a year of blessings in many ways."

Chapter Thirteen

THE CLUB HAS BEEN TRUE
TO ITS TRADITIONS

With the outbreak of the short-lived but dramatic Spanish-American War of 1898, the Union League Club had its first real opportunity to show, under wartime conditions, "unconditional loyalty to the Federal Government, and to defend and protect the integrity and perpetuity of the nation." What the Club did in the Spanish-American War was to be a forerunner of its accomplishments in two later wars.

Since 1895 Americans had watched with sympathetic interest the efforts of the Cuban insurgents to win freedom from Spain, and this interest rose to a war fever as accounts of atrocities committed by the Spanish forces were reported in the press. General Valeriano Weyler, Spanish commander-in-chief, was branded "the Butcher" and burned in effigy. Many Americans left their homes to fight beside those seeking freedom in Cuba. The Chicago *Tribune* fanned the martial flames with fighting words: ". . . it is time for the people of every city, town and village in the United States to rise and declare in their might that Cuba must and shall be free. The time to do that is now."

But in the Union League Club, as in the nation, opinion was divided as to what part the United States government should play in this international crisis. At the annual meeting of the Club on January 26, 1897, Abram M. Pence sought to introduce a resolution which he thought expressed the views of the majority of the members. He urged the Club to endorse the principle of arbitration: "that we condemn the spirit of jingoism which is an assumption that our nation possesses a divine mission to superintend the earth." He pointed out that the United States had greater problems within its own borders than it had capacity to determine, and that it "should build up its own waste places and relieve the misfortunes of its own citizens before it becomes a knight-errant seeking to correct the abuses and misfortunes of others." This argument precipitated an immediate debate, which was peremptorily ended when President Thomas B. Bryan declared the resolution out of order.

Pro-Cuban sentiment in the Club flared up in irrepressible fashion the following year after the U. S. Battleship *Maine* was sunk in Havana Harbor on February 15, and after William Randolph Hearst published a letter written by the Spanish minister in Washington expressing contempt for President McKinley. At the Washington's Birthday banquet at the Club "there was such a display of noise and feeling as the oldest members of that decorous body have seldom seen," one paper reported. But sentiment was still for moderation and for confidence in the national executive, and not for war.

Former President Benjamin Harrison, the guest of honor, brought the banqueters to their feet when he said: "We stand now in the awful shadow of one of the most tragic events that has happened in our history, and yet we stand with the poise and with the self-possession of a people who understand their might and can abide the development of time. We are not an hysterical people. We can wait, and we will know our duty when it shall be revealed. We can understand that in a time like this there are grave responsibilities devolving upon the President of the United States—single responsibilities that he may not divide with any man. Let us stand about him and strengthen him in the calm assurance that this great country desires only that which is right, and can wait until the facts are known, before it issues its proclamation." Other speakers pleaded for patience, too, and ex-Governor Richard J. Oglesby said: "We are at peace with all the world. Are we not great enough to keep this peace?"

But it was not to be peace. On April 22, three days before war was declared, the Club at a special meeting endorsed the course of the President and Congress and pledged the Club's full support. "Not a discordant note was heard in the patriotic paean which was chanted at a special meeting of the Union League Club last night," the *Tribune* reported. National airs were applauded, patriotic sentiments cheered to the echo, and not a dissenting voice was raised against the resolutions.

Embodied in these resolutions, made by Frank O. Lowden, chairman of the Committee on Political Action, was one asking that a War Executive Committee of five be named "whose duty it shall be to devise and carry out under the approval of the board of managers and political action committee, ways and means for assisting the government in the impending crisis."

Ferd W. Peck offered a toast that "We invade Cuba with a loaf of bread in one hand and a bayonet in the other." Colonel George Record Peck, general counsel for the Santa Fe Railroad, once more introduced the term "jingoism," and felt that it was appropriate at this time to explain its derivation. This was to be found in the old music-hall ballad, he said, which went:

> "We don't want to fight, but by *jingo*, if we do,
>   We've got the ships, we've got the men, we've got
>   the money, too!"

Jingoism had a more favorable reception on this occasion and was roundly cheered.

The War Executive Committee consisted of Lowden, a rising young lawyer, as chairman; Edward A. Turner, capitalist;

Frederick R. Babcock, lawyer; and John S. Belden and Joseph H. Strong, insurance men. Their first business was the organization and maintenance of three provisional or "home guard" regiments to become known as the "Union League Club Regiments." These regiments were the first provisional regiments called out by Governor Tanner and were commanded by Col. Charles R. E. Koch, one of the best-known dentists in the United States and past adjutant general of the G.A.R.; Colonel Thomas L. Hartigan, a graduate of West Point, who during World War I became a brigadier general in the Philippines; and Colonel J. B. LaGrange.

There were men from all pursuits of life in the ranks of these Home Guards. Many, of course, were ineligible for combat military service because of age or physical disabilities, but they were valuable to such a noncombatant organization. For instance, in Colonel LaGrange's regiment, Superior Judge John Barton Payne held a commission as lieutenant colonel. Frederick Lundin, in later days a sinister figure in politics as the man behind William Hale Thompson, was a first lieutenant and quartermaster in Colonel Hartigan's "Tigers," as the regiment was nicknamed.

The importance of these regiments was stressed by Lowden after the war when in his report to the Club he said the War Committee "has tendered three full regiments, thoroughly trained, to the President of the United States and the Governor of Illinois," and thus "has preserved a body of disciplined men for the maintenance of peace and order within the state in the absence of all other troops; it has helped to relieve in a measure some of the Illinois National Guard organizations from the burden of maintaining their armories while they were in the service of the national government. . . . The Union League Club has been true to its traditions in the discharge of its duty in this crisis."

In the Club is a roster of thirty-eight members who actually saw service during the Spanish-American War, headed by Theodore Roosevelt, who was to become an honorary member at a later date, and listing such men as Milton J. Foreman and Nathan William MacChesney.

For those who know only the dismal and depressing modern type of war, where National Guard organizations are broken up to forestall a concentrated grief among home folks in case of disaster to one unit; where there are no farewell parades with flags flying and bands playing, and news of heroic deeds in action sometimes is delayed for security reasons, it is difficult to picture the excitement of such a war as that fought with Spain. Day by day came such news as the charge of the Rough Riders up San Juan Hill; the sinking of the collier *Merrimac* in the entrance of Santiago de Cuba's harbor to bottle up the Spanish fleet; the destruction of the Spanish Navy at Manila; General Nelson A. Miles's campaign in Puerto Rico. The public thrilled to the accounts of the heroism and sufferings of the boys from home, and in contrast, was shocked by the tainted meat scandal. Even after peace was restored, newspapers flamed with headlines such as INFAMOUS ENDING OF A GLORIOUS WAR, and TO PROBE WAR OFFICE MISTAKES, and published cartoons labeled "Who Is to Blame?" showing "The Soldier We Sent to War and the Soldier the War Department Sends Back to Us," the latter emaciated and worn, racked by the aftermath of yellow fever.

The Armistice was signed August 12, 1898, and the next day the city's Peace Jubilee Committee met at the Union League Club to make plans for a proper celebration.

The war lasted 113 days, with 1,700 killed and wounded, and cost 141 millions. In Illinois 9,901 men were examined for duty by Lieut. Col. Charles Adams, assistant surgeon general of the Illinois National Guard, who found the interesting fact that their average age was twenty-four—the youngest sixteen and the oldest fifty-eight. The first group of these boys, veterans of Santiago and members of the First Regiment, Illinois Volunteers, returned home September 9, 1898. Alexander H. Revell, heading a Club committee, welcomed them at the station while bands played "When Johnnie Comes Marching Home," "See the Conquering Hero Comes," and "A Hot Time in the Old Town Tonight."

Chicago was to see all the great heroes of the war in the next two years. During the third week in October the city was bedecked in carnival attire in celebration of the Peace Jubilee, the local arrangements for which were made by the Union League Club. The last beam of the Union Loop, the elevated structure which completely surrounds the heart of downtown Chicago, had been put into place the year before. The streets in this district were bridged by triumphal arches—sixteen of

WHO IS TO BLAME?

Public sentiment was shocked by stories of mismanagement and graft in the conduct of the Spanish-American War.

The Soldier We Sent to the War and the Soldier the War Department Sends Back to Us them, with colored bunting and electric lights. There was a "Remember the Maine Arch," a "McKinley Arch," a "Dewey Arch," and thirteen others.

President and Mrs. McKinley arrived the first of the week and went to the Hyde Park home of Captain and Mrs. Lafayette McWilliams, 3961 Lake Park Avenue. Captain McWilliams, early Club member, was one of the partners of Marshall Field, and Mrs. McWilliams was the President's sister.

The President found, among other things, that a new postwar custom which had been given the name of "Hobsonizing" had caught on in Chicago. The term came from the reception New York girls had given to Lieutenant Richmond Pearson Hobson and his crew when they arrived in the city. Hobson had performed one of the great heroic feats of the war in sinking the collier *Merrimac* in the harbor of Santiago and thus blocking Admiral Cervera's fleet, and the grateful women showered him and his crew with kisses on their return home.

Unfortunately the weather was vile during the week and one paper lamented that it "was a lasting blemish on the escutcheon of the city." Arches were blown down and rain-drenched. The illuminated bicycle parade at night was called off and the city streets were filled with "1,000,000 shivering mortals." However, nothing could stop the great Military, Naval, and Civic Parade on Thursday.

The arches had been repaired and the reviewing stand set up in front of the Union League Club. Still everything was not going smoothly. When the President was escorted to the stand, after riding in his carriage over the parade route, he looked around for General William R. Shafter, hero of San Juan and El Candy. General Miles, who a few minutes before had been talking to his old scout and friend, William ("Buffalo Bill") Cody and had returned to him the blooded Kentucky mare Cody had loaned him for his campaign, was in his place. So were

President McKinley reviewing the Peace Jubilee Parade in Chicago from the grandstand in front of the Union League Club.

others members of the President's staff. Mark Hanna turned to F. E. Coyne, internal revenue collector for Chicago, and asked him to find General Shafter.

Coyne went inside the Club and there found the General enjoying a hot toddy with some friends. Thinking to deliver his message in military form, Coyne snapped his heels together, stood at attention and said. "General Shafter, the President sends his compliments and wants you on the reviewing stand." General Shafter arose, drew himself to military erectness and replied: "Well, if the President sends his compliments I guess I'll have to go." Coyne explained later he learned to his chagrin that the "Commander-in-Chief does *not* send his compliments," but his method had been effective.

Still the signal for the start of the parade was not given. Just then Governor Tanner, who had found himself afoot as no carriage had been provided for him, arrived at the stand in a belligerent mood. He saw that the mayor's wife, Mrs. Carter H. Harrison, was seated in the rear, and in a loud voice invited her to come down front and take a place near Mrs. Tanner. This was against protocol. There was a flutter among the members of the Club's Executive Committee and protests were heard, but Mrs. Harrison smilingly complied. Tanner then stalked inside the Club and called for a drink. He began to explain his version of why he was not given a carriage in the parade.

In the first place, he said, the committee "should be ashamed of themselves at the shabby treatment of the mayor's wife," and General John C. McNulta, "my enemy, agrees with me." Several prominent men, he said, had sought to keep him entirely out of the jubilee. "I knew what to expect before I came to Chicago, but I'm going to show my respect to the President, whether or no."

This treatment of the Governor caused considerable stir. "Whether it was an oversight or culmination of a series of objections to the participation of the Governor in any of the Jubilee festivities is a matter of opinion," the *Tribune* reasoned.

Tanner was determined not to be left out again. A year later McKinley was in Chicago, again a guest of the Union League Club, for the laying of the cornerstone of the new Federal Building just across from the Club. He was also to review a parade of Grand Army of the Republic veterans. When the parade was about to start, Tanner appeared and crowded into the President's carriage to sit in the back seat with him. Mayor Harrison started to protest, but McKinley stopped him, although anger showed in his eyes.

McKinley, as usual, was immaculately dressed. Tanner wore an old frock coat and a black felt hat of the Civil War army type. Physically a large man, he sprawled over the back seat, waving his hat from side to side, standing when McKinley stood. He gaped and grinned and guffawed. When the parade ended at the Club, McKinley called Harrison aside and said: "I am cold and nervous. Please get me a glass of whiskey." He was obviously shaken by Tanner's conduct. Just then Tanner came up, lifted his own glass and said, "Mr. President, when I was elected, I called in my cabinet and said, 'Boys! Cut out the liquor! If there's any drinking to be done, I'll do it!' " McKinley looked him steadily in the eye and replied, "Well, Governor, you have kept your word, I hear."

On May 1 of the following year, Chicagoans experienced once more the thrill of the great victory at Manila when Admiral George Dewey, resplendent in gold lace, was on the reviewing stand in front of the Union League Club, and they thought once more of his famous command, "You may fire when ready, Gridley."

The Admiral's aspirations to become the next candidate for President had caused a mild flurry in the Republican ranks. Charles Dawes, writing in his diary at Washington on April 5, said he had discussed this matter with President McKinley. "The President exhibited no feeling whatever of resentment toward Dewey," he said. "His candidacy does not seem to be regarded as a serious matter."

Reuben H. Donnelley, who was a member of the Board of Directors of the Club, was assigned as a sort of bodyguard to Dewey on his arrival. "I recall particularly one little incident," he told later. "The Admiral discovered that in some way he had lost his hairbrush. We happened to be passing Siegel and Cooper's when he told me this, and we went into the store to purchase a brush. The young lady who waited on us heard me call him Admiral, and at once recognized him, and expressed her pleasure in having the honor to wait on him. Her eyes showed true hero worship. She was a bright girl and had such a pleasing manner

Admiral Dewey, the "Hero of Manila," was the guest of the Club when he visited Chicago in 1899.

Lieutenant Hobson, whose military exploits were overshadowed by his fame as "the great osculator."

that the Admiral seemed almost as delighted as she did. It took only a few seconds for the news to spread throughout the store. A crowd quickly gathered, and I doubt if the Admiral was in a worse pinch during the entire war than he was then. We had to use football tactics to get out of the store."

Nothing was seriously to mar the reception in Chicago. The Union League Club had planned a luncheon in the hero's honor. But this was delayed so long by the parade that at two-thirty o'clock a Club attendant crossed the street to the reviewing stand with a white pitcher and two glasses on a salver.

"Here's looking at you!" said the Admiral, turning his back on the parade and lifting his glass. When Dewey finally came in for lunch at three o'clock, the parade was still going by.

Other guests entertained by the Club during the year included Captain Joseph B. Coghlan, of the U. S. Cruiser *Raleigh*, who had been called on the carpet for his poem, "Hoch! Der Kaiser," written in commemoration of Dewey's defiance to the German fleet at Manila; and the "great osculator," Lieutenant Hobson, the hero of Santiago de Cuba. If Hobson had left a trail of kissed feminine lips from New York to Chicago, he was to be at his best in the latter city. He set a record here, kissing 163 women in one evening. Next morning the *Tribune* printed the box score:

Duties of a Hero in Chicago

Number of kisses	163
Minutes required	36
Average kisses per minute	4.444
High run (best single minute)	10

President Alexander Revell of the Club and General McNulta, president of the Naval Reserve Association, had finally rescued Hobson from his female admirers and carried him off to the Club.

Chapter Fourteen

THE OLD GUARD MEETS

ON THE NIGHT OF MAY 24, 1904, THERE MIGHT HAVE BEEN SEEN going up the broad marble stairs of the entrance of the Union League Club singly or in small groups a score or more of distinguished men, all well beyond middle age. Some had been driven up in carriages, others had come on foot, swinging their gold-headed canes, while several had attracted the usual attention by alighting from new-fangled "horseless buggies." The evening was mild and pleasant and a few carried topcoats over their arms.

Other members of the Club reverently stood aside to let them pass, offering such greetings as "Good evening, Senator," "Good evening, General," "Good evening, Judge," and "It's a pleasure to see you, sir." Inside the Club they surrendered high silk hats, black slouch hats, and derbies to the check boy, adjusted Prince Albert coats with satin-faced lapels, double-breasted dinner coats of an earlier time, or more up-to-date single-breasted sack suits of gray striped worsted, and made their way to the banquet room.

This was the first meeting of the "Old Guard" of the Club, the "Class of 1880," or those who remained of the original founding members. They had responded to a letter dated May 12, which had been sent to forty-eight men, inviting them to gather at the Clubhouse that evening. "The Union League Club entered upon the first year of its career in 1880," the invitation read. "In that year the Club had a membership of Two Hundred and Fifty, and now, twenty-four years later, it has on its roll but forty-eight of the original members. It has been suggested that it would be pleasant to have a dinner and camp-fire of the 'Old Guard.'" This invitation had been signed by three past presidents: Lewis L. Coburn, Elbridge G. Keith, and Ferdinand W. Peck, as well as Robert S. Critchell, Ira W. Buell, William Penn Nixon, and Frank B. Tobey—all men who had been important in bringing the Club to its present successful state.

With a history of a quarter of a century, less one year, behind it, the Club had achieved national celebrity. Presidents and ex-presidents had enjoyed the Club's hospitality. It had entertained such distinguished guests as Generals Grant, Sherman, and Logan; Justices Fuller and Harlan; political leaders such as Blaine and Conklin; governors and ex-governors; visiting statesmen, foreign diplomats, and tourists. Men of note in literature and art had continuously received its congratulations and encouragement.

The Union League Club numbered a large portion of Chicago's most distinguished citizens in its membership. Bankers, merchants, capitalists, railroad managers, and officers of great corporations—the "solid men" by virtue of their success in business—state and Federal officers, and the great figures of jurisprudence, politics, divinity, and finance found congenial surroundings in the Club. Scores of members dined there, since it was essentially a daytime club, and wined there on special occasions. Between the lighter pastimes of swapping stories and playing billiards and jackstraws, businessmen found opportune occasion for considering commercial as well as social and political topics. "Probably more enterprises have been started and corporations organized in the Union League Club than have emanated from any other source," said a current publication. "The influence of the Club has been equally felt in the affairs of the municipal government and public policy." Club members were given full credit for not only performing "their social part as well as the best of others, but have a public mission which they perform also."

The Old Guard now formed part of a total membership of 1,626, and their Clubhouse was the largest in the United States; a new annex was being added even that year. The rapid growth of the Club reflected the growth of the city, yet the Club still adhered to its original high standards of membership. Nor did it waver in carrying out the dictates of its Articles of Association.

Of the forty-eight invited to the dinner, only twenty-eight responded. But those twenty-eight represented the backbone of the Club. Among them were seven lawyers, five manufacturers, three insurance men, two each of real estate dealers, jurists, and bankers, and a physician, merchant, printer, and capitalist. The oldest was General Joseph B. Leake, seventy-two, and the youngest Sidney Corning Eastman, fifty-four.

It was an informal gathering, and right from the start the old-timers began to reminisce. General Leake, a picturesque figure, recalled his days during the Civil War. This brought to mind stories by other members. Lewis L. Coburn had been stopping at the Willard Hotel in Washington shortly after the close of the war. "A Confederate officer came up to me in the lobby and introduced himself as Fitzhugh Lee, nephew of Robert E. Lee. He told me he was completely down and out. He asked for a quarter to get a drink of whiskey. I felt this was a small offering to a fallen foe, but I gave it to him and he was grateful."

There was a story, of course, about General William Tecumseh Sherman, who had been an honorary member of the Club since 1880. Now retired from the service, he made his home in Washington and took as much interest in old soldiers as ever. Though he was not very good at remembering names of his old comrades, he took pride in recognizing them as best he could on every occasion. One day, when walking down F Street with his secretary and spying a familiar face approaching, he nudged his secretary and asked, "Who is this man coming toward us?" The secretary did not recall the man's name, but said to the General in an undertone, "He makes your shirts." The General smiled affably as the man came nearer, held out his hand and greeted him with: "Major Shurtz, good morning! How is the Major this morning?"

There was many a chuckle as Robert Critchell told the story of Mark Twain and the prairie chickens. Critchell, who felt he was indebted to Samuel L. Clemens for having written a letter of recommendation which secured him the Chicago agency of the Phoenix Fire Insurance Company, had sent some prairie chickens to Clemens in Hartford, Connecticut, just before Christmas. He received this reply:

DEAR MR. CRITCHELL:

Here's fun and more of it. Your prairie chickens came before your letter did, and I at once jumped to the conclusion that they had been sent by our mutual friend, Robert Law, of Chicago, who has frequently sent me chickens for Christmas, so I telegraphed my thank *to Law*. Now I want you to see him and tell him that I don't take back any of those thanks, but I want to add them to the old account. In the meantime I want to say to you that the chickens came in time for our Christmas dinner; they were very good and I am glad you got the agency.

(Signed) S. L. CLEMENS

Critchell met Law a few days later and asked if he knew a man named Clemens in Hartford. Law said he did and he thought that man "had more gall than any man living." As an admirer of Clemens' writings, Law had previously sent him some prairie chickens for Christmas, but had sent none for the last Christmas, yet had received a telegram thanking him. It looked as if Clemens were testily reminding him of his oversight. "Now what do you think of that?" asked Law. Critchell handed him the letter. Law laughed and said, "We will have some fun over that."

There were stories, too, of the celebrities who had been guests of the Club. They recalled Chauncey Depew and his rare quality of humor; W. C. P. Breckinridge, who brought with him the flavor of the South and who spoke as an American citizen "although he had been affiliated with the Confederacy"; Chief Justice Melville Fuller, Stewart L. Woodward, Edward Everett Hale, William McKinley, and Bishop John Ireland of St. Paul.

There were reminiscences of John Wentworth, of course, and how before he died he ordered his monument, which "was the biggest thing of its kind in the West." Solid marble and weighing eighty tons, it was shipped from Maine by water and taken up the north branch of the Chicago River to Rosehill Cemetery. "What are you going to put on it?" Long John was asked. "Nothing," he replied. "Not a word. It is going to be like me, a plain, unsophisticated monument. No fixin's, no gingerbread, nor a nook or corner where a sparrow can come to build his nest and then defile it. It'll be just like me—big and plain."

Standing sixty-five feet high (it cost $35,000), it still dominates Rosehill Cemetery. "If it had a big inscription on it a man'd say, 'Wentworth, humph! Wentworth, eh!' and go and forget all about it before he left the cemetery," Long John had said. Despite his orders there is an inscription, but few go away and forget about it once they have seen it, nor do they forget about Long John.

Judge Thomas Dent remembered how, during the heated election year of 1884 when Blaine was running against Cleveland, mugwumpism had briefly lifted its ugly head within the

"UNCLE JOE" CANNON

CHAUNCEY DEPEW

GENERAL ULYSSES S. GRANT

JOHN WENTWORTH'S MONUMENT

confines of the Union League. Dent was then a member of the Library Committee, "and some members considered the Library Committee over-indulgent in having in the library files some publications, as for example *Harper's Weekly*, which carried some articles unfavorable to Blaine." But Judge Dent "thought the trouble would soon cease" and refused to remove the obnoxious publications.

The Club had been very strict in the early days, and some recalled with a smile, how, insisting on rigid adherence to the Club rule, Dr. Truman W. Brophy, Charles H. Deere, A. B. Meeker, W. M. Burchard, and Daniel H. Burnham, "all exemplary law-abiding citizens," were suspended for one week because of minor violations. On June 15, 1888, the directors passed a resolution stating that it appeared than one Thomas A. Wright had not been a citizen at the date of his election to the Club. The action of the board in electing him to membership was rescinded and his dues and initiation fees returned to him.

One old-timer always rich in reminiscences was J. Frank Aldrich, who unfortunately was then in New York and could not get to the dinner. Yet it was well known around the Club how in the early nineties he had brought into the Union League Club such notable figures as Joseph G. ("Uncle Joe") Cannon, of Danville, Illinois, and Albert J. Hopkins of Aurora.

"Joe Cannon and Hopkins, like McKinley and some other prominent Republicans, were inclined to 'straddle' the money question at that time," Aldrich would recount. "It was then that I urged them to join the Union League Club. 'You are out of touch with the big men of affairs,' said I. 'Come up to Chicago more frequently, get acquainted with bankers and businessmen. Your farmer constituents are all right in some ways but they are laboring under a serious delusion on the money question. Instead of trying to lead them, as you are in a position to do, you find it easier to let them lead you.' It was surprising to note their change of attitude after they had been members of this Club for a short time."

Aldrich and John S. Miller, who was corporation counsel under Mayor Hempstead Washburne, the Union League's "reform mayor" of 1892, had been delegated by Washburne to attend a banquet given at the Union League Club of New York to further the interests of the Columbian Exposition.

The dinner was for the purpose of arousing New Yorkers to help in making the World's Fair a national institution and to contribute amply to its success, which in fact they did. But it was the stopover at Washington on the way to New York that Aldrich liked to recall. "We had stopped in Washington so that John might file his brief in the celebrated 'Lake Front Case' with the United States Supreme Court. Something in glass lying alongside that brief in his suitcase came to grief; the glass was shattered, and when the suitcase was opened the aromatic odor of *spiritus frumenti* permeated the air, and lo and behold! a yellow tinge had come over the brief, and John was panic-stricken. But he need not have been. Whether it was the nostalgic aroma, or the well-known tinge of yellow that decorated his brief when it reached the grave and serious justices of that court that influenced them, I don't know. But one thing we do know. John won his case and the title of the people to the bed of Lake Michigan and the made land two hundred feet east of the Illinois Railroad right-of-way was safe."

Others recalled how the Union League had become a "Clubhouse on Wheels" when 150 members chartered a special train to attend Illinois Day at the Omaha Exposition in 1900. Hiram R. McCullough and Will H. Clark saw that all the usual comforts, conveniences, and club facilities were provided, and in Omaha the train served as a hotel as well as a club. A telegraph office was installed in one of the cars for use of those who wanted immediate contact with their businesses in Chicago.

Similar delegations of Union League Club members attended the Buffalo Exposition in the following year, the Charleston Exposition in 1902, and the St. Louis Exposition in 1903. The Club got around in those days.

In talking over the improvements in the Club during the past twenty-four years, someone of course retold the story of how an artesian well flowed directly beneath the Clubhouse. In 1889 the Board of Directors was disturbed over the cost of water from the city. They were paying $700 a year. So it was decided to sink their own well. In the first attempt, the engineers hit quicksand, but the next time they struck water at 250 feet. It gushed out at twenty gallons a minute. Total cost for two wells, $1,000. However, this only supplied one-half the water for the Club.

It was remembered with pride that one of their more recent ·members, James B. Forgan, the banker, had popularized golf in the midwest. In the fall of 1892 he and seven others organized the Chicago Golf Club. The first links had been rented at Belmont, where the abandoned station of the C.B.& Q. Railroad served as a clubhouse. The rent was five dollars a year. During 1893, due to the World's Fair and the panic that followed, little progress was made either in golf or in increasing the membership of the golf club. But in 1894 things picked up, and the following year Forgan and others purchased a farm at Wheaton and moved their club there. Recalling golf in those times brought to mind the picture of a man attired in Norfolk jacket and knickerbockers, long knitted stockings with cuffs, white linen spats and brown shoes, topped off with a soft hat made of the same m cerial as the jacket.

So the evening passed, with reminiscence, anecdotes, and laughter as the Old Guard relived the events of the past quarter of a century. When the meeting at last broke up, it was planned to make the reunion an annual event.

For various reasons, however, this plan fell through and it was not until November 28, 1913, that the next call for a meeting of the Old Guard went out. By then, the forty-eight of 1904 had been reduced to exactly half. Twenty-four of the Old Guard now remained, and of these only twelve attended the reunion.

Another call went out on December 20, 1920, for "Early Members and ex-Presidents." The guests of honor included twenty living ex-presidents of the Club and twenty-nine early members, not more than ten of whom, however, were the Old Guard. Four years later there were but six charter members living, and in 1930, when the Club celebrated its fiftieth anniversary only two were still alive—J. Frank Aldrich and Sidney Corning Eastman. Judge Eastman could not come to the celebration on March 25 of that year but sent a message: "We have all a right to be proud of the splendid growth of these fifty years, but my friend Aldrich and myself have perhaps a deeper pride than any of you in the knowledge that we helped to form this great Club. . . . Through all these fifty years, my connection with you has been a source of satisfaction and pride to me. I believe we have done much good; our ideals and standards are of the highest; may our future progress be along the same worthy lines."

Aldrich was now left to carry on for the Old Guard. But he, too, passed away on March 8, 1933, interested to the last in his Club, of which he was assembling material for a Club history.

Chapter Fifteen

ROOSEVELT, CLEVELAND,
AND A LADY'S HAT

THEODORE ROOSEVELT WAS A GUEST OF THE UNION LEAGUE CLUB on two occasions, and as time softened the prejudices against the mugwumps, the Club also extended a belated invitation to Grover Cleveland. The Union League Club wanted to keep its record of having entertained every President of the United States since its founding.

Roosevelt was already a national figure when he first came to Chicago under Club auspices. Graduating from Harvard in 1880 and joining the Republican party the same year, he had served in the New York Assembly, and in 1884 had been a delegate to the Republican National Convention. Two years later he was an unsuccessful candidate for the office of mayor of New York. After spending six years as a member of the United States Civil Service Commission, he was now, at thirty-eight, president of the Police Board of New York City. Gentleman rancher, author, practical politician, and the scourge of law breakers, the vigorous young "Teddy" was invited by the Union League Club to be its main speaker for the Washington's Birthday ceremonies on February 22, 1896. It was a popular choice, with the public as well as Club members.

In Chicago, Roosevelt found a strenuous program planned for him. In the forenoon he addressed the faculty and students at the University of Chicago, pausing before starting his talk while the students roared:

"Who is Teddy Roosevelt?
First in war, first in peace,
First to reform the New York police!"

After an informal luncheon at the Union League Club, he stood on the rostrum of the Auditorium Theater in the afternoon to flash his already famous smile at the hundreds who crowded there to see and hear him. Club member W. A. Douglass vividly recalled years later how Roosevelt "opened his mouth wide and showed his big teeth." At that time he spoke on George Washington and said that "The first lesson of Washington is applied morality." He set the crowd wildly applauding when he mentioned Lincoln: "Like that other great American, the mighty son of Illinois, Abraham Lincoln, he (Washington) never refused to do the best possible merely because he did not think it was the ideal best," he said.

The *Tribune* reported that Roosevelt was "in fine vein" at the Union League Club banquet that evening. At the speakers' table were representative Club members, including President Christian C. Kohlsaat, then a probate judge and later to be a United States circuit judge; E. L. Lobdell, prominent banker and broker; John V. Farwell, merchant prince; and Judge Joseph E. Gary, who had sentenced the Haymarket Riot defendants.

Roosevelt chose as his topic "The Enforcement of Law." He said: "The chief evil from which we suffer is the fact that the lax enforcement of laws of all kinds has given the impression to the average legislator that it is a safe thing at any time to put any law on the statute books, then trust the law will not be enforced, so as to please somebody else."

At one point Teddy said he had talked enough, but there were shouts of "No, no—we've got New York time" (referring to Chicago's brief experiment in going on Eastern time). He continued that there could be no government without law enforce-

As a colonel of the dashing Rough Riders in the Spanish-American War, "Teddy" Roosevelt became a national hero.

ment, or "you have got to come in the end to a government by one man or a number of men—in other words, you must go back to anarchy. To preserve government you have got to have laws enforced."

Club members as well as others were thrilled by Teddy's subsequent career: his appointment as Assistant Secretary of the Navy; his dash and courage at the head of the Rough Riders in Cuba; his nomination as vice-presidential candidate for McKinley's second term; and finally, after McKinley fell mortally wounded by an assassin's bullet at Buffalo in September, 1901, his ascendancy to the office of Chief Executive of the nation. To more conventional politicians, Roosevelt's dynamic energy was a constant challenge. McKinley himself had earlier thought, "Roosevelt is always in such a state of mind." Mark Hanna, the suzerain of Republican politics at the time of McKinley's second election, opposed Roosevelt as Vice-President and had re-marked, "Don't any of you realize that there is only one life between that madman and the Presidency?"

But Roosevelt, as President, was popular in the Midwest. The Union League Club promptly made him an honorary member, and he was "de-lighted." (He was already a member of the New York Union League Club.) It was in Chicago that he made his famous speech on the Monroe Doctrine and added a phrase which was so quickly caught up by the press and remem-bered long after his more important words were forgotten. "There is a homely adage which runs, 'Speak softly and carry a big stick; you will go far.'" Roosevelt had added: "If the American nation will speak softly and yet build up and keep at the highest pitch of training a thoroughly efficient Navy, the

Theodore Roosevelt's vigor—both physical and intellectual—worried his opponents but delighted his admirers.

Monroe Doctrine will go far. I ask you to think this over." But the only part of his speech thought over was his remark about the "Big Stick."

In mid-June of 1904 the Republicans moved into Chicago to nominate Roosevelt for a second term. At the November elections he won an overwhelming victory, and Union League Club members helped Chicago go Republican by a large majority. "Returns were so one-sided that they were received quietly," commented Club member Charles G. Dawes in his diary.

The Club never faltered in its allegiance to Roosevelt. The "square deal," his inveighings against "malefactors of great wealth," his advocacy of the "strenuous life," the enforcement to the letter of the Sherman anti-trust law, caused unrest to some individuals, but were approved by the majority. Dawes, for his part, had no taste for the Rooseveltian strenuous life. Dawes once spent the night at Roosevelt's home in Oyster Bay. When he got up in the morning he saw a tin tub "filled with the coldest-looking water I ever saw in my life and a huge bathing sponge." Dawes walked gingerly around the tub, dressed, and hurried to catch the train back to New York.

Among those Club members who went to Washington for the inauguration on March 4, 1905, was F. E. Coyne, at that time postmaster of Chicago. Coyne found the inaugural ball—held in the old Pension Building, which was "trimmed for the occasion"—a "joke as a ball, but a great delight to all who were there." People went, he reasoned, to say, "I danced at the inaugural ball." A few weeks later, in May, Roosevelt was in Chicago for settlement of the teamsters' strike. The Union League Club would follow Teddy's career through this term which, as one writer put it, was the beginning of the "period of revolt of the American conscience."

It was about the middle of Roosevelt's second term that the Union League Club had its own "revolt of conscience" in regard to former President Cleveland—the only President since the time of Arthur who had never been a guest of the Club.

Mugwumpism, which had split the Republican party and the Union League Club in the days when Cleveland was fighting Blaine, was now dead. So the Club decided to invite the Democratic former President to its Washington's Birthday celebration in 1907. This was to prove not so easy. Frederic A. Delano, as president of the Club, extended the invitation but received only a doubtful acceptance. As the time of the event drew near Delano became worried, and thinking that direct action was necessary, he went to New York to see what could be done.

He decided to make his approach to Cleveland through a friend, Dr. John H. Finley, president of the College of the City of New York. Dr. Finley at that time was an intimate of Cleveland. With the proper introductions Delano then journeyed to

Cleveland's last public appearance was as the guest of the Union League Club at its Washington's Birthday banquet in 1907.

Princeton, wh.evela saw Mr. and Mrs. Cleveland. Cleveland assured him as gi vanted to come, but found it "hardly practicable." Dela much relieved, however, to learn that politics had nothing to do with Cleveland's hesitancy, but that it was his health which made such a trip doubtful. He was under a physician's care, "and too delicate to undertake so much of a journey and so heavy a task." "Furthermore, even if he accepted he felt he might very likely fail us at the last minute," Delano recalled later.

Delano went back to New York. Charles Evans Hughes had just been elected governor of the state, and Delano thought he would be a good man to invite to Chicago. He visited Hughes, and Hughes accepted the invitation at once.

On returning to his hotel he found a telephone message from Dr. Finley to get in touch with him at once. It developed that Dr. Finley had learned through his wife, who had seen Mrs. Cleveland, that she thought the former President could be persuaded after all to go to Chicago "if conditions were right." Delano hurried back to Princeton to see Mrs. Cleveland.

"Mr. Delano, I think this thing can be arranged because Mr. Cleveland is really anxious to make this address," Mrs. Cleveland explained. She added that it could only be done if Delano were willing "to take the trouble of making the trip convenient and comfortable as it can be made for Mr. Cleveland."

"If, for example, you can take him in your private car," she continued. Delano, then president of the Wabash Railroad, readily agreed. Mrs. Cleveland also stipulated that besides herself, Cleveland's physician, Dr. Joseph Bryant, should be taken along, and Delano consented.

But after leaving Mrs. Cleveland, it suddenly occurred to him that now he was in a very embarrassing position. He had two speakers for the Washington's Birthday ceremonies. He could see no way out of this except by absolute frankness. "I accordingly returned to New York and v̶ ̶ once to Governor Hughes' home," he said. "I found hin̶ ̶d proceeded to make a clean breast of the whole episode. ̶ ̶ould not have been nicer than he was. He said that he would, of course, release me, but to this I said 'no,' that was not what I asked for, but what I wanted was for him to *postpone* the date until a year later. He laughed and said, 'Well, that is a long way off,' and so forth and so forth. We parted good friends and he came to us the year following, and in the years since he and I have frequently joked about this occurrence."

Cleveland and his party arrived Thursday, February 21, 1907, in Delano's private car, which had been attached to the Pennsylvania Railroad's "Chicago Limited." The "Sage of Princeton" was welcomed by a committee from the Union League Club headed by Judge Charles S. Cutting. The committeemen were astonished at the change in appearance of Cleveland. Instead of the man of full face and portly presence who had visited Chicago three years before, they saw now a "figure which nowhere would be marked as that of a large man." The former President, leaning heavily on the arm of his beautiful wife, came forward with an uncertain step, but with a genial, though weary, smile. Present to greet him also was James H. Eckels, ex-comptroller of currency and a prominent banker. Eckels, a staunch Democrat, was a member of the Union League Club. During their visit Mr. and Mrs. Cleveland were guests at the Eckels home, 18 Ritchie Place.

That evening the Club gave a reception to which 4,400 guests were invited. The Clubhouse was crowded with Chicago's élite. Mrs. Cleveland, retaining "much of the beauty which made her the idol of a nation when she was a White House bride," wore a white satin gown trimmed with oriental lace. About her neck was a dog collar of pearls, as well as a diamond necklace. The Clubhouse was decorated with American Beauty roses, Mrs. C   nd's own flower. As each woman guest entered, she w   ven a rose.

Mrs. Cleveland herself was not a stranger to Union League Club hospitality. In the fall of 1887, when Cleveland was welcomed to Chicago, Mrs. Cleveland, then described as "very pretty, very polite, very anxious to please," had found the reception and parade too much for her. She slipped away from the parade with an escort and rested a while at the Union League Club before resuming the rest of the program.

Judge Cutting remembered some years later how, before Cleveland made his speech in the Auditorium Theater, he turned and whispered: "Can you tell me where my wife is? When I am going to make a speech I always want to know where my wife sits, because I talk to her, more or less." Cutting replied, "Yes, in the fourth box on the left you will find Mrs. Cleveland." Cleveland counted the boxes, caught his wife's eye, brightened up and said, "All right, she is there. You can go ahead with the meeting."

Cleveland's trip to Chicago was described by Delano as a huge success. "He was a most genial old man; . . . without bitterness or hate even for his political enemies. He was much touched by the reception he received in Chicago at the Union League Club (a Republican organization) and at all the public functions for him." One of the most gratifying things, of course, was the fact that the Union League, which years before had harbored some of his bitterest political enemies, now made him an honorary member.

As Roosevelt's term neared its end, he refused to consider running for office again and yielded the Republican nomination to his genial and portly Secretary of War, William Howard Taft. Union League Club members followed Roosevelt's hunting exploits in Africa and his later tour of the United States. Then, on February 21, 1911, he returned to Chicago as the guest of the

Club, to speak for the second time at their Washington's Birthday celebration.

A typical Rooseveltian program had been arranged, stretching over thirty-six hours, and even the vigorous Teddy exclaimed, "It is a terror!" when he learned of it. He said he would "have to get into shape." John E. Wilder, Club president at the time, remembered how he and other Club members sought to get Teddy "into shape." They thought the best way would be to take him right from the train for a good long hike in Lincoln Park. A few volunteers of the hardier type were called for, and the Colonel was driven by automobile to Diversey Parkway in Lincoln Park. It was an impressive parade, with motorcycle policemen preceding and following the cars and, when Roosevelt and the others alighted, accompanying them as a vanguard and rearguard. Wilder recalled that it was a cold day and some of the Club members wore only light overcoats. Roosevelt had on a fur-lined coat with a fur collar, a black slouch hat, and wore pince-nez glasses and his engaging smile.

"To everyone's astonishment," said Wilder, "after we had gone but a half mile the Colonel stated he thought we had better be getting back to the Club. We began to think our Teddy was a little softer than he had been pictured, and we all felt a little cocky at having tired him out so quickly. But upon our arrival back at the Union League Club, it occurred to me that perhaps the Colonel had not lunched, and upon asking him if he would care for a cup of tea and some strawberries—the strawberries having been gotten as a great treat—the Colonel replied: 'I haven't had anything to eat since breakfast, and I think some ham and eggs would go mighty good.' We had picked him up at two o'clock in the afternoon and it was now around four o'clock. He ate with a splendid appetite."

George W. Dixon, another member, also recalled an incident which showed Roosevelt's remarkable memory for names and faces, one of his famous faculties. As Roosevelt was passing through the lobby of the Clubhouse, Dixon's father, Arthur Dixon, greeted him. Teddy grasped his hand and without a moment's hesitation, said: "If it isn't my old friend, Arthur Dixon! Arthur, how many children have you now?" "At the last census, Mr. President, the count was fourteen," Dixon replied. "You have certainly done your full duty," exclaimed Roosevelt.

The next day Roosevelt spoke at the Auditorium on "Nationalism and Democracy." Then he was the guest of honor at the Union League Club luncheon, after which he rushed off to Hull House to review the "Young Greeks" and Boy Scouts, of which latter new organization he was honorary vice-president and Chief Scout Citizen. He admonished the boys to be gentle and kind, and to begin "by being kind and gentle in your own homes." Accompanied by Jane Addams, founder of Hull House, Teddy then went to the First Regiment Armory, where several thousand "Americans of all nationalities" were assembled under the auspices of the Union League Club. Teddy began by telling these new citizens that they "must stand up boldly" in this country of their choice. At that instant a reporter's chair collapsed. Roosevelt turned with a flash of teeth and remarked that this was not the proper emphasis to place on his idea of standing up boldly for national rights.

When the meeting was over, the Greeks, the Slavs, the Germans, the Italians, and others of foreign extraction crowded around him. In the crush Miss Addams lost her hat. When they got out into the open automobile to go back to the Union League Club, Teddy noticed that Miss Addams was bareheaded and gallantly doffed his own hat despite the cold.

This loss of Miss Addams' hat created a flurry of embarrassment and excitement in the Union League Club. Miss Addams evidently had given little thought to the incident. Hats were of secondary importance to her. "But it was different in the Union League Club," commented the *Record Herald*, which had an inside track on the story because its publisher, Herman H. Kohlsaat, was a member of the Club. "The great hat mystery became the topic of the hour, and discussions of it began in the buttery and percolated into the very inner sanctums of the organization."

Meanwhile, the Club realized it had a delicate duty to perform. It had to square itself with Miss Addams. The Club solons cogitated deeply on the subject. It became a matter for the Board of Directors. Should a committee be appointed to purchase Miss Addams another hat? Brave men grew pale at the thought. President Wilder, a tanner and leather merchant, shook his head sadly. It was out of his line. First Vice-President Francis T. Simmons was an importer of kid gloves. But hats! Second Vice-

T.R.'s views on the direct election of U.S. senators were heartily approved in Chicago.

Jane Addams, who lost her hat, shared the spotlight with Roosevelt at an Americanization ceremony sponsored by the Union League Club.

President Allan B. Pond was an architect. Harry Beach Clow, a director of the Club, was president of Rand McNally & Company. There was a brass founder, a grain broker, and a judge of the appellate court among the remaining board members. All meekly begged to be excused.

At last a brilliant expedient was evolved. Treasurer Arthur Heurtley, a banker, was told to stand by with his checkbook. This was more in his line. Secretary Walter D. Herrick, a lawyer, was ordered to draft a letter. The result:

DEAR MISS ADDAMS:

We are sorry you lost your hat. Enclosed find check for $50. Buy a new one.

(Signed)   BOARD OF DIRECTORS, UNION LEAGUE CLUB.

Red faces became a normal pink once more. Quiet and dignity were restored within the Club. Simple matters of politics, tariffs, and finance again found their places in conversation. But this complacency was not to last. The next day Miss Addams sent her reply:

DEAR CLUB:

Inclosed please find your check for $50. I never wear $50 hats. The one I lost cost only $10. You mean well, of course, but men can't be expected to understand women's hats!

This the Club was forced to ruefully admit. But had the members consulted Mrs. Joseph Bowen, a colleague of Miss Addams, they might have taken the hat incident more lightly. Mrs. Bowen later wrote: "We were always down on the hats she [Miss Addams] wore, for they were mighty shoddy affairs."

When Roosevelt spoke that evening at the Union League Club banquet, his "Big Stick" fell on the heads of peace advocates and those opposed to fortification of the Isthmus of Panama and a reciprocity treaty with Canada. He advocated "peace enforced with 16-inch guns." He had other things to say. He was in favor of woman's suffrage, he believed in a direct election of United States senators (then chosen by the state legislatures), he favored the referendum, and the control of corporations by the government. His views caused the *Record Herald* next day to urge, "Not so fast, Colonel Roosevelt," and to term him a "radical democrat."

This banquet was attended, too, by Count Albert G. Apponyi, former minister of education in Hungary, whose invitation to come to Chicago had incited the Chicago Slavs to such an extent that they staged several violent demonstrations. The Union League Club had been forced to cancel the Count's speech at the Washington's Birthday ceremonies. Local Hungarians, it developed, resented the rigid state control which had accompanied Apponyi's program in Hungary, and claimed he was trying to suppress the Hungarian language as well as Hungarian institutions. "A tyrant at home and peace advocate abroad," was the way local Hungarians characterized him. He had talked at the 20th Century Club, where police in full dress guarded him against a howling mob.

At the Union League Club banquet, Count Apponyi had his opportunity to speak on the world peace movement. He predicted that the United States would assume leadership of the world and take a prominent part in abolishing wars. "It is evident that the United States has been selected by Providence," he said. This was a sentiment after Roosevelt's own heart, although he had a more forcible program for ensuring peace. He rushed forward after the Count's speech and "shook his hand until the nobleman winced," a reporter observed.

Roosevelt left town, Miss Addams' hat problem was solved, but the Union League Club still had on the hand the riot-inciting Count Apponyi. On the evening of February 24 a shouting, hissing, and shrieking mob accosted the Count in front of the Fine Arts Building, where he was scheduled to deliver his last speech. In fleeing the maddened throng, the tall nobleman received a blow in the mouth and another in the eye. Charles R. Crane hurried him to his automobile and managed to get him safely back to the Union League Club. From this haven the Count decided to leave for Washington.

Chapter Sixteen

THE UNION LEAGUE CLUB
ALSO SERVES

WORLD WAR I GAVE THE UNION LEAGUE CLUB ONE OF ITS GREAT-est opportunities for service to the city, state, and nation. "Happily it seized that opportunity, and what it did through its War Committee constitutes incomparably the finest chapter in all its history," said Frank H. Scott, Club president, at the close of the war. Scott at that time could not foresee the far-reaching effects of the work of this committee. It is notable that the War Committee of the Union League Club established a civilian war-time pattern which was to be followed by the government itself in the later great conflict of World War II.

From the beginning of hostilities in Europe, the Union League Club was alert to the possibility of American participation in the war. Some months after Archduke Francis Ferdinand of Austria had been killed by the bullet of a Serbian assassin, and three months after Germany had swept through Belgium, Member Charles Gates Dawes, then president of the Central Trust Company, said in an address before the Club: "The old landmarks by which we guide ourselves and formulate our plans have been swept away. A large part of the world has reverted to barbarism. How much this war will affect us as a nation, or whether we will be drawn into it, no one can tell. If it is much prolonged, it is extremely doubtful that it can be kept within the limits of Europe, Asia, and Africa. There must be preparedness in this nation which wants not war. There must be national preparedness and individual preparedness. I do not, for instance, know what the day's work may be for me. The world may be on the threshold of an elemental convulsion of humanity which will last for a century. Certainly the loss of life and the waste of wealth which this war will bring will profoundly shake the world."

Indeed, preparedness became a reality in the fall of 1915. The country still was stirred by the sinking of the *Lusitania* on May 7, and by the warnings sent to Germany by President Woodrow Wilson. Beginning September 20, businessmen and professional men left their desks and offices for the Business Men's Military Encampment at Fort Sheridan. "Put the Union League Club at the head of the list!" was the "war cry" of the Club, as reported on September 4 by the Chicago *Examiner*. The Political Action Committee, headed by John T. Stockton, president of the Joseph Stockton Transfer Company, and composed of such men as Judge Charles S. Cutting and Julius Rosenwald, president of Sears Roebuck & Company, was designated as a recruiting staff to conduct a campaign among Club members for enlistments.

Already sides were being definitely taken in the overseas conflict. On September 11 Horace L. Brand, president of the Illinois Publishing Company, was barred from the Union League Club, the *Tribune* reported, "because of what members consider un-American utterances in the *Illinois Staats-Zeitung*, of which he is editor." Brand, after withdrawing his application for membership in the Club, sent Warren Gorrell, Club secretary, an open letter in which he protested, "Is pro-Germanism a crime?"

On March 29, 1916, the Union League Club went on record for preparedness. It helped initiate the Preparedness Day Parade and held open house at the time. No move in Washington went unnoticed. America was drawing closer to war. On February 4, 1917, the Club made haste to telegraph its endorsement to President Wilson of his act in severing diplomatic relations with Germany.

Shortly thereafter, the Club expressed indignation over the action of Congressman William W. Wilson, one of its own members, in voting against the armed neutrality bill then before Congress. President Frank J. Loesch drafted what the newspapers termed a "sharp letter" to Wilson and went so far as to raise the question whether the congressman "had not forfeited his right to remain a member of the Club, by not showing unqualified loyalty to the government." Congressman Wilson replied that he had always been for preparedness, but did not think the United States should arm American merchant ships to carry contraband of war.

At the annual meeting of the Club on March 27, 1917, after speeches calling on President Wilson to "uphold the dignity of this country, by a declaration of war," a resolution was passed bearing the signature of William B. Hale, a lawyer, urging Congress to pass at once the compulsory military training and service act, which was to become known as the "draft."

In April war was declared. Soon many members of the Club were in the armed forces, and those who remained behind were not idle. President Howard G. Hetzler, railroad executive, acting under authority of the Board of Directors, appointed what was to become one of the most remarkable committees in the Club's history—the War Committee. This committee at first was composed of nine members, but soon was enlarged to fifteen. Harry A. Wheeler, vice-president of the Union Trust Company, was the first chairman. He resigned in the summer of 1917, and A. D. Sheridan, the vice-chairman, became the head of the committee. Frederic B. Johnstone was the first secretary, but when the committee was enlarged, his post went to Allen B. Pond, the architect. Early members of the committee also included William E. Clow, president of the James B. Clow Company; Harry R.

Kurrie, president of the Monon Route; Edwin Sherman, retired boot and shoe manufacturer; and Marvin B. Pool and Frank H. Scott.

The enlarged committee was composed of Johnstone as chairman, Charles P. Whitney as vice-chairman; Edward M. Skinner, vice-chairman; Allen B. Pond, secretary, and Britton I. Budd, R. W. Childs, Mark W. Cresap, Samuel O. Dunn, Bernard Flexner, John F. Gilchrist, Martin M. Gridley, H. H. Hilton, Morton D. Hull, Edwin S. Mills, and A. D. Sheridan.

One of the first acts of Secretary Pond was to write a letter to President Wilson, outlining the proposed purposes of the committee. The response was almost immediate. Pond received a reply from the White House dated July 17, just four days after his own letter had been sent. President Wilson wrote:

May I not acknowledge with much appreciation your letter of July thirteenth about the patriotic plans of the War Committee of the Union League Club of Chicago with regard to undertaking propaganda with a view to making the purposes and circumstances of the war clearer to our fellow citizens?

You will be interested to know that there are instrumentalities already widely at work for this same purpose and that they are very widespread throughout the country. Committees everywhere are co-operating, and I am happy to believe that the impression that the country is not generally aware of the objects of the war is an erroneous one. In some parts of the country there is very subtle and pervasive agitation against the Government and every possible means should be taken to expose and neutralize that. There are certain agencies at work, for example, in the general region with which the Union League Club would naturally be in touch, which are very determined, very hostile, and very sinister, and I believe that a great deal could be accomplished by the Club if it turned its energies towards meeting these influences directly and running them from cover to their utter destruction. Men like Mr. Nieman of the Milwaukee *Journal* have been very active and very successful in unearthing these influences and exposing them, and if the Club were willing to counsel and co-operate with him in any way, I think some very noteworthy results might be achieved, greatly to the benefit of the country.

Cordially and sincerely yours,

(Signed) WOODROW WILSON

In Milwaukee, Nieman was conducting a one-man campaign against pro-Germanism. He had employed Perry F. Olds, just out of Harvard, to translate for him all German-language articles that were pro-German and were opposed to America's international course. Olds translated some five million words, and this first-hand material formed the basis of the Nieman campaign.

Taking its cue from the President's letter, the War Committee felt there was much to be done towards influencing the sentiment of Chicago citizens of German birth or extraction. At that time there were an estimated ninety-five thousand German families in the city. To these German residents there was directed a series of messages written in the German language, making as clear as possible the situation which confronted them, and pointing out their plain duty. A total of 1,475,000 copies of these messages was printed, including six loyalty editorials in the German press and pamphlets entitled "Prussianized Germany," "A Call to Join the Friends of German Democracy," and "The Lichnowsky Memorandum." The cost of publication and distribution was borne by the committee.

"This work, regarded as most urgent at first, gradually become of lesser import as time showed that the great bulk of the German people in this country would give no aid to their Fatherland in a war against their adopted country," the committee reported after a few weeks, and such work came to an end around November 30, 1917.

Meantime, at a quarterly meeting of the Club on October 25, the Board of Directors unanimously recommended President Wilson as an honorary member, and the motion was seconded

During World War I, the Union League Club emblazoned its motto on the Clubhouse in electric lights.

by Frank H. Scott of the War Committee. He "eloquently spoke to the motion," the Club records report, and the motion was unanimously adopted by a rising vote.

At this quarterly meeting it was reported that Club employees had subscribed $7,550 in 3½ per cent Liberty bonds and had pledged $8,700 to a second issue. After hearing Captain R. H. Knyvett tell of his experiences at the front in an address on "The Real Thing," the Club adjourned following the singing of "The Star Spangled Banner."

The Clubhouse was now thrown open to all Army and Navy men. However, the Club adhered strictly to the law and posted notice which said, "Liquor will not be served to men in the Army and Navy whether in uniform or not." Its own members, too, found that they would have to cut down on food and drink and certain luxuries. "The Union League Club was the only club in the city to observe 'porkless day' yesterday," the *Examiner* told the public on December 16, and on January 30, 1918, the same paper made much of the fact that the Club barbershop had barred egg shampoos as a wartime measure.

In summarizing the work of the War Committee for 1917, President Hetzler, in his annual report, commented that "they have had splendid support from the body of the Club, and have been actively engaged in patriotic work during the year." The committee had procured and distributed "to many classes of our citizenship and to the membership of the Club as well, pamphlets and documents bringing home the facts and issues of the great war. It is recognized throughout the civilized world that one of the potent factors in the present struggle is public opinion, and this Club will continue to do all in its power to educate and solidify public opinion in America in support of the government and its prosecution of the war."

At the beginning of its second year, the War Committee had approximately the same personnel, with the exception that Charles M. Moderwell, well-known coalman, was appointed to take the place of Frank H. Scott, who was elected president of the Club. F. B. Johnstone now became chairman of the committee, with Charles P. Whitney, insurance executive, as vice-chairman. Pond remained secretary.

The committee now enlarged its scope of action, attracting universal attention when on April 20 it announced that it sought the co-operation of some four hundred leading clubs throughout the United States "in undertaking a propaganda to create in the United States a sentiment which will demand that all private interests be put aside until this war is fought out to complete success and a peace is dictated to Germany that will make the world safe from her wanton aggression for all time."

To this end, a letter was sent to the list of clubs, carefully selected because they were outstanding organizations, and without regard to their politics or policies. This letter suggested an undivided support in the prosecution of the war and a vigorous campaign "to counteract the insidious German propaganda which, in spite of all precautions, is known to be active in this country, as in all countries opposed to the conquest program of the Central Powers."

The committee, in addition, prepared plate matter which was supplied free to hundreds of newspapers throughout the state and was placed at the disposal of other organizations which desired to do the same type of work in other parts of the country. The committee went even further. In addition to its educational work and money-raising activities, it assisted in obtaining for the government the services of men who were experts in various lines. It invited speakers of national and international importance to address the Club membership, notably Thomas G. Masaryk, president of the new Czecho-Slovak Republic. President Masaryk, as a guest of the Club, spoke in Chicago on October 9, 1918.

Not the least of the committee's activities was the establishment, jointly with two other Chicago organizations, of a fund of $30,000 for the foundation and maintenance during the first year of the war of the Soldiers and Sailors Club of Chicago.

The second year was the most active for the committee. In speeding up its work it prepared signs and slogans bearing upon the vital importance of labor in the war, and warning against peace offensives put forward at various times by the Central Powers. Material was furnished to Four Minute Men, to clergymen, to lawyers, to teachers, to people everywhere "who by the spoken word could send the message to thousands who might never see themselves the pamphlets prepared by the Club." Union League Club pamphlets were officially endorsed in the Chicago public schools, were used by draft boards and in army

cantonments, and were called for and distributed by the State Council of Defense and similar organizations.

Immediately after President Wilson delivered his speech of September 27, 1918, summing up the national program, the War Committee telegraphed the Committee on Public Information at Washington, requesting fifty thousand copies. The committee received a reply that the documents could not be printed because of a shortage of funds. Realizing that the program laid down by President Wilson in his five speeches, beginning with his famous "Fourteen Points" speech on January 8, 1918, would be the basis of world peace, the committee arranged to publish the entire series in pamphlet form at a cost of two cents a copy. The government approved the plan and promptly afforded the Club franking privileges, a most unusual privilege to a private organization. This document, termed "The Bases of Durable Peace," achieved a circulation of 175,000 copies.

The committee during its existence met some 175 times. Its members devoted almost all their time to its work. Business and professional men themselves, when a few short-sighted businessmen began to repeat in this country "the error which had been so costly in England" and raised the cry of "Business as usual," the committee took up the challenge, and in three articles prepared by Harold G. Moulton of the University of Chicago proved to the businessmen of America that "business as usual" was not possible or practicable. Almost one-half million of these pamphlets were circulated.

The austerities of war were already being realized at the Club itself. In the spring of 1918, diners at the Club, always used to the very best in food, found that the bread, rolls, crackers, and pastry contained no wheat flour. "And most of the diners never would have known the difference if they had not been informed of the fact on their menu cards," observed the Chicago *Post* on May 9.

When the Food Administrator sent out requests to hotels and clubs throughout the country to go on a no-wheat basis, there had been a general protest that "it cannot be done." "The house committee of the Union League Club, however, decided at once it could be done," said the *Post*. "The club, which was founded on patriotic purposes, and had endeavored to live up to its patriotic traditions from that day to this, when its War Committee is spending thousands of dollars in patriotic propaganda work throughout the central west, felt that patriotism began at home and decided that the letter and spirit of the order must be lived up to."

At the request of Food Administrator John McE. Bowen, the Club's recipes were drawn up and sent to other clubs, hotels, and restaurants. One example of making bread without wheat flour showed that the chef used "ten pounds of bran flour, thirty pounds of rye flour, ten pounds of barley flour, one-half milk, and one-half water." Bowen stated: "I wish that every club throughout the United States would take as much interest in the conservation of food as the Union League Club."

A few weeks after the introduction of wheatless bread, the watchful *Herald and Examiner* had a headline on June 14 which read: War Has Done Its Worst, Union League Club Engages 35 Waitresses. No wheat flour, no egg shampoos, meatless days, and other stringent measures—and now for the first time in its history the Club had waitresses! Yet there is no recorded word of criticism from the some thousand male members of the Club.

On November 11, 1918, the Armistice was signed. " 'The tumult and the shouting die, the captains and the kings depart'— and we are left facing the sober duties of world citizenship and the difficult questions of readjustment and reconstruction," the committee's report read on Armistice Day. The Club, with "honorable traditions and a new prestige," felt that upon it was laid the obligation to consider seriously the problems that now arose and to help guide public thought along "the line of their proper and wise solution." These sentiments were repeated three days later when the Club held a "Peace Jubilee" dinner. The Union League Club had vigorously protested German control in Russia, and on August 13 had passed a resolution protesting a peace that permitted the Germans—then called "Huns"—to hold on to their conquests. On September 17 it had lauded Wilson's "No" to Austria, which had been so emphatically given when the President rejected Austria's proposal for a separate peace. This was the line the Club was to follow.

Chicago celebrated the Armistice of World War I with a frenzy of enthusiasm that left downtown streets buried in a sea of ticker tape and confetti.

But there still were problems in America. On December 30, the Union League Club demanded the deportation of all interned aliens, including Count James Minotto, son-in-law of one of its own members. Minotto had been associated with the notorious Count Luxburg in the Argentine. Many other Chicagoans interned at Fort Oglethorpe, Georgia, must go, too, the Club said. These included Max Breitung, cousin of the Albert Breitung who had been arrested on a charge of conspiracy to blow up a munitions ship; Emma Campen, Chicago music teacher, charged with aiding German prisoners and talking in favor of Germany; Hans Merz, former organist of Holy Name Cathedral, who had been a close friend of Kurt Reiswitz, German consul who had fled after a revolutionary plot in India was revealed; Albert Montgelas, former art critic of the *Herald and Examiner* and son of a Hungarian nobleman; and Edward Otto, riding instructor for North Shore children, who had insisted on riding his pupils into Fort Sheridan. A petition was sent to the Attorney General and other members of the Department of Justice, asking that all sixty-eight Chicagoans arrested should be deported.

The end of the war found the Union League Club in an even more important position in the community as a result of its activities. Its work had been recognized by the government, the press, and other clubs throughout the nation. "To say that no other organization of its kind had contributed so much to war work is an entirely conservative statement," President Scott ventured in his annual report for 1918.

Scott stressed the fact that during the entire history of the Club not one single word of the Articles of Association had been changed, nor had the Club ever neglected to carry out their provisions. "It is hoped that in time of peace, the primary objects of the Club will not be forgotten," he admonished. "Their pursuit is no less needed than in time of war, and unless they are kept in mind, the Club will inevitably lose its peculiar claim to distinction."

In the summer of 1919, with racial troubles and a serious streetcar strike threatening the public peace, it was found that the terms of enlistment of the emergency National Guard and Reserve Militia were about to expire. Chicago and the state would be in a precarious condition should further trouble develop. The Illinois National Guard had ceased to exist following World War I. Upon their return to the United States, the members of the Thirty-third Division had been discharged directly to civilian life.

Governor Lowden now requested thirteen members of the Union League Club to serve on a commission to reorganize and rehabilitate the National Guard. Among Club members named was young Marshall Field, who had enlisted as a private and had returned as a captain. A National Guard Recruiting Committee, headed by Gardner Morris, was named as a subcommittee of the Public Affairs Committee, and to further show the interest of the Club in the movement, it was decided to form a "Union League Company," composed of Club members and sons.

Company E of the First Infantry was designated as the Union League Club Company. Members of the recruiting committee were given a list of banks and business houses whose executives were members of the Club, with instructions to interview them personally and obtain their active aid in recruiting men from their offices. Within five weeks a total of sixty enlistments was obtained by the committee. Grant E. Williams, a member of the Club since 1913, was the first man to volunteer, and on December 18, 1920, the Union League Company of the First Infantry attained its minimum quota and was sworn in.

Chapter Seventeen

BOYS' CLUBS AND POSTWAR SERVICE

THE WAR'S END DID NOT BRING PEACE TO CHICAGO. IN THE turbulent postwar atmosphere politics flaunted its corruptness; prohibition ushered in a disregard for law and order; increased building on every side brought on serious labor troubles; the advent of an increased Negro population to fill a wartime labor need precipitated grave racial problems; juvenile crime, as after all wars, was on the increase.

The Union League Club, unique in that its 2,356 membership was a microcosm of the greater city—a compact body of representatives of every profession and every business—felt the responsibility of aiding in resolving and disposing of these and many other problems. As a minor factor, this was necessary for the good of its members; as a major factor, for the good of the city.

To take care of such problems, the Club now brought into being a thoroughly capable and efficient committee—the Public Affairs Committee. This remarkable committee had its genesis in both the War Committee and the Committee on Political Action, conserving on the one hand the energy developed under the impulse of an aroused patriotism during war, and perpetuating on the other the years of consistently unselfish labor in the carrying out of the primary objects of the Club.

The Public Affairs Committee was created on March 25, 1919. The by-laws of the Club were amended, combining the two committees for more effective peacetime service. To the Public Affairs Committee was delegated all the powers of its parent committees, and in certain respects these powers were enlarged so that the new committee might become the active agency through which the Club might function in regard to affairs outside of its immediate domestic interests.

As it passed out of existence, the Committee on Political Action could review a history of nearly forty years of notable achievement. From the time of the naming of the first committee upon the founding of the Club, it had, with varying personnel, been foremost in the battle for honest elections; it had fought Yerkes and the boodlers through the Municipal Voters League; it had successfully brought into being civil service for both city and state; it had been responsible for the Washington's Birthday celebrations; it had agitated for smoke abatement ordinances; it had been in the van in the development of the Drainage Canal. There had been no movement for the betterment of the city during its existence in which the Committee on Political Action had not been actively engaged.

The new Public Affairs Committee began energetically enough. As one Club historian, John C. Shaffer, wrote in *The Spirit of the Union League Club*, it "at once developed a virile life, a life which soon outgrew its limited proportions." Under the new setup the Committee was empowered by resolution to create subcommittees and appoint their personnel. This it proceeded to do, with subcommittees and groups assigned to specific fields and phases of public interest. Subsequent committees followed this pattern, enlisting the co-operation of the general membership of the Club to serve as members of these groups. Upwards of eight hundred individual members now share annually in the work of the committee in its various phases.

William H. Winslow was the first chairman of the Public Affairs Committee, but upon his resignation, Britton I. Budd, president of the Chicago Elevated Lines, took over the chair. Others on the original committee included Marshall Field III, who had returned to Chicago from overseas service with the Thirty-third Division; Harry Eugene Kelly, lawyer; and Graham Taylor, founder of Chicago Commons. There were fifteen in all on the committee proper, with the Club's president, Charles W. Folds, an ex-officio member.

For many years the Club had given attention to the subject of underprivileged boys in the city, and of how to direct their efforts into constructive channels. Specialists on different phases of this topic had addressed annual and quarterly meetings of the Club. John Benham recalled how at a meeting of the Association of Commerce in the Union League Club, where he was the guest of William A. Fuller, there had been a discussion of the advisability of establishing a manual training school for boys. "The discussion lasted a couple of hours," Benham said, "and it looked as if it would merely result in talk when Marshall Field, who rarely if ever gave public utterance, rose and told us that instead of talk we should do something. He said at least one hundred thousand dollars should be raised." Benham did not remember what Field contributed, but it was more than $25,000, and before the evening was over $65,000 had been subscribed in all. The manual training school that stood at Michigan Avenue and Twelfth Street was built as a result. This school later became a part of the University of Chicago.

But within the Union League Club it was felt a more direct contribution could be made to the city's underprivileged youth. This resulted in the founding of the first Union League Boys' Club, which grew out of a dinner at the Blackstone Hotel on the evening of June 12, 1919. This gathering had been arranged by Lewis E. Myers, George Higginson, Jr., Burridge D. Butler, and Britton I. Budd, and was attended by twenty-five of

Chicago's leading businessmen. Also present were William E. Hall and C. J. Atkinson, president and executive secretary of the Boys' Club Federation (International), and John H. Witter, general superintendent of the Chicago Boys' Club.

At this dinner the story of the underprivileged boy and the work undertaken in his behalf by the Boys' Club Federation was told in some detail. Businessmen were admonished of the necessity of helping these boys become good citizens. It was explained that 66 per cent of Chicago's boys were without the proper advantages which should be theirs by right of national heritage, and that "from supper to bedtime they played in the streets and ran in gangs." Such boys rarely went beyond the fourth or fifth grade in school, and as juvenile gangsters sooner or later came in contact with the police. After a boy's first arrest he was looked upon as something of a hero by his comrades, and from that time on the policeman was his enemy. Such boys had warped ideas of the social order of affairs, yet later, as voters or as elected officeholders, they helped to enact the laws.

It was decided at this meeting that an Illinois branch of the Boys' Club Federation would be organized to carry on work in the state, and with this in mind the general subject was presented to the Union League Club's Public Affairs Committee.

Those of the Public Affairs Committee who had served on the War Committee fully appreciated the value of educating boys to become good citizens. During the war, when so many youths were called to the service, this need had been brought out into the open when screenings and tests of draftees revealed the handicaps under which many suffered. The Public Affairs Committee now called a meeting at which Hall and Atkinson of the Boys' Club Federation repeated the necessity of aiding underprivileged boys. Judge Victor P. Arnold of the Juvenile Court and Judge Daniel H. Trude of the Municipal Court were present and told how in these two courts sixteen thousand boys had appeared during the past year charged with a wide variety of offenses.

The Public Affairs Committee took action. A subcommittee consisting of John V. Norcross, chairman, W. F. Hypes, and H. G. Badgerow was appointed to look into the subject and to seek a proper location for such a club. When it was realized that a boys' club could not be operated directly by the Union League Club because of a lack of provisions in its charter, it was decided to organize and incorporate the Union League Foundation for Boys' Clubs. Clarence S. Pellet, insurance man, was named president.

On January 15, 1920, Robert D. Klees, superintendent of the largest boys' club in Philadelphia, with a membership of four thousand boys in the textile district, came to Chicago and was engaged as managing director of the Union League Boys' Club. Klees, a college man, had devoted the major portion of his life to work among underprivileged boys.

Subscriptions to the Foundation were limited. Charter memberships were taken out by forty-three Club members at $1,000 each, while others subscribed amounts to bring the total up to $45,000. The Public Affairs Committee gave $10,000 towards opening the first Boys' Club and its operating expenses. The club was well on its way now, and Benjamin W. Lord, as chairman of the Committee on Building and Location, reported a favorable site at Nineteenth and Leavitt streets. This was a three-story brick building long known by the unsavory name of "Bucket of Blood." It had housed a saloon, a dance hall, and "other institutions of a character that contributed nothing to the making of good citizens." The building was in the heart of one of Chicago's most congested areas, with eighty thousand persons representing twenty-two different nationalities crowded into one square mile. Here was a spot where a boys' club could prove its value to the community.

The dedication of the Union League Club Boys' Club No. 1 was marked with impressive ceremonies.

This structure was purchased for $18,000. The entire building had to be made over and renovated. Business firms contributed shower baths, toilets, plumbing, water heaters; window glass, labor and materials for painting and decorating and rewiring, and other necessary things and services. The Polish Turner Association obtained gymnasium apparatus at a special price. Gerhardt Meyne, a building contractor, later put the center pillars of the building on shores, so a swimming pool could be excavated, and then placed the new foundation under the center pillars and deepened the tank foundations.

Newspapers were watching the progress of the Boys' Club with interest. The *Evening Post* on December 20, 1919, praised the work, expressing enthusiasm at the Club's decision "to take up the case of Chicago's underprivileged boy." The editorial said: "The Union League Club—with its hundreds of fathers who are able to see their own boys have every advantage—lives up to its record for invaluable service to the community by coming to the help of the underprivileged youngster. Not Chicago alone, but America, will owe it a debt of gratitude unpayable if it carries out the project before it and takes up the task of converting the raw material of our streets into useful citizenship."

Police Chief John J. Garrity viewed the developments with satisfaction. "Give us enough Boys' Clubs and we will reduce juvenile crime one-half," he said.

The club, known as Boys' Club No. 1, was opened May 29, 1920. A platform, draped with the national colors, was built into the street in front of the clubhouse, and many notables appeared there for the ceremony. Thomas Faxon and the Chicago Newsboys Band supplied the music. Peter Mortenson, superintendent of Chicago Schools, Judge Victor Arnold of the Juvenile Court, and Clarence S. Pellet, president of the Boys' Club Foundation, spoke. Mathew C. Brush, who rose from newsboy to president of the American International Shipbuilding Corporation, was there, too, and told the boys: "Be a real boy. If you are a ten-year-old boy, be a successful boy of ten; if you are a fifteen-year-old boy, be a successful boy of fifteen."

In July, 1920, the Public Affairs Committee issued the *Union League Club Bulletin* as the first official publication of the Club. Its first editor was Albert Boswell, but in December, S. J. Duncan-Clark, editorial writer for the *Evening Post*, assumed the editorial chair. The *Bulletin*, which suspended publication after eleven issues, to be resumed at a later date, was devoted almost entirely to news of the Boys' Club.

"The Boys' Club might be termed a number of clubs within a club," the *Bulletin* reported in its first issue. "The so-called gangs of the streets retain their identity when they enter the club until they become assimilated. The first gang or group to organize took the name of Yale University. Thirty or forty groups of this kind are meeting at the club one evening each week for recreation and study."

The Union League Club wanted two boys in the Boys' Club for every member of its own. During the first year, 995 boys

Jack Dempsey, an admired visitor at the Union League Boys' Club No. 1.

were admitted, less than half the membership of the Union League. The following year, however, showed better results, with the total rising to 1,269, and the third year there were 1,607. By the end of the third year gratifying results were reported, and it was announced through the *Bulletin* that seven hundred boy members had qualified for positions in the business world, most of them employed by Union League Club members. Holder of Card No. 992 was Ed Malecha. Now a successful insurance broker in the Loop, Malecha recollects:

"My first card cost me a nickel a month. I was eight years old when I joined, and we younger boys paid half of what the older boys did. This small payment made us boys appreciate our membership card, for it wasn't so easy in those days to raise a nickel or a dime every month. The club became the center of everything in the neighborhood. We spent all of our spare time

219

there. We used to march in parades downtown, too, and Mr. Budd as head of the elevated lines would see that we had special cars to take us to the Loop. I can speak for a lot of the boys that the club helped us and put us on the right track and encouraged us to make something of ourselves."

Each year the "Old Timers" of the Boys' Club meet. Such former members as Joseph Baryl, owner of a Loop parking lot company; Stanley Lyson, comptroller of a candy manufacturing company; Johnny Babor, tool manufacturer; Edwin Lukes, auditor for the Commonwealth Edison Company; and many others gather to discuss the old club days.

In 1924 the Union League Club purchased an eighty-acre tract of land enclosing a lake west of Kenosha, Wisconsin, as a summer camp for three hundred boys. Club members dug into

Campfire scene at Union League Boys' Club summer camp near Salem, Wisc.

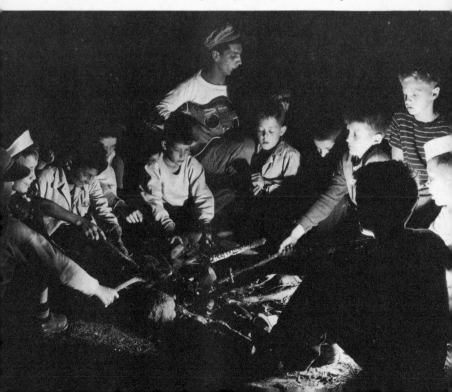

their pockets and paid $64,815.44 for the construction of permanent buildings there. Then in April, 1926, the Foundation established a second Boys' Club at North Walcott and Race streets, and Union League Club members donated $168,543.12 for the property and building. At this dedication Judge Arnold announced that juvenile delinquency in the police district embracing Nineteenth and Leavitt streets, where Boys' Club No. 1 was located, had fallen off 76 per cent after the first year of the club, and even a greater percentage in later years. Time went on, and in January, 1940, Elliott Donnelley, then president of the Union League Club's Foundation for Boys' Clubs, announced that "The Union League Club is spending its second million on boys."

Meantime, Edgar T. Wilkes had succeeded Klees as managing director of the Boys' Clubs. As his secretary, Wilkes later engaged Mrs. Lois Salisbury Sachs. Mrs. Sachs had been working at the Club for some time before she learned that her great-grandfather, O. H. Salisbury, had been so intimately connected with the founding of the Union League Club.

Club members have never lost their enthusiasm for their Boys' Club Foundation. So successful was this service to the community that in later years Pellet, first president of the Foundation, said: "If nothing else of the Club endures, it can be assured that the Boys' Foundation will always remain as one of the finer accomplishments of the Union League Club."

At the end of its thirty-fourth year, the Union League's Foundation for Boys' Clubs has these assets: an alumni roster of more than fifty thousand of Chicago's youth who have been members of its club units, and physical property worth more than $500,000 consisting of two modern clubhouses on Chicago's southwest and northwest sides, and a 200-acre summer camp in southern Wisconsin.

The camp consists of two units—an 80-acre tract acquired

in 1924 and an adjoining tract of 120 acres purchased in 1941, which had served as Camp Nitgedeigt or Camp Abraham Lincoln, a communist-operated summer outing spot. "For removing this blight on Kenosha County," Kenosha Post No. 21 of the American Legion awarded the Union League Club its Certificate of Distinguished Merit.

The Union League Club had anticipated the tragic flare-up between the white and Negro population in 1919. During the war years, because of a labor shortage in the stockyards, mills, and factories, some fifty-six thousand Negroes had flocked to Chicago from the South, more than doubling the Negro population of the city. They were concentrated in a small area on the South Side near the Levee district, and now had overrun Grand Boulevard and Prairie Avenue and pushed south to Sixty-third Street.

In June of 1919 the Public Affairs Committee appointed a subcommittee to study the racial question. This subcommittee, under the chairmanship of Harry Eugene Kelly, was engaged in its study when on July 27 a tragedy occurred at the Twenty-ninth Street beach. White boys hurled rocks at a seventeen-year-old Negro youth as the latter swam across an imaginary line dividing Negro and white waters. The boy was killed. The race riots which followed lasted five days. On the sixth day Governor Frank O. Lowden called out the militia.

Shortly after, the Governor appointed the Chicago Commission on Race Relations "to study and report upon the broad question of relations between the two races." Edgar A. Bancroft, who had been president of the Union League Club in 1903, was named chairman of the governor's commission, and the Club's subcommittee on the racial question was recognized by the appointment of its chairman, Kelly, as a member of the commission. Many of its meetings were held in the Clubhouse.

The commission, after a prolonged study, made its report. It criticized police, prosecutors, and the courts for inequitable and discriminatory handling of cases involving Negroes, and recommended better police protection at beaches and playgrounds. It suggested the condemnation and razing of all houses unfit for human occupancy. It took city officials to task for their neglect in the disposal of garbage and rubbish in Negro communities. The report also wanted authorities "to promptly rid the Negro residence areas of vice resorts, whose present exceptional prevalence in such areas is due to official laxity."

The Public Affairs Committee's subcommittee on the racial question still remained technically in existence, though it yielded all activity in the work to Governor Lowden's commission. Later this subcommittee resumed its independent work, and in later years made valuable contributions to improving racial relations. In 1925 the subcommittee turned its attention to the housing of the Negro and considered this "perhaps the most important aspect of the problem of harmonious relationship between the various racial groups." A foundation, modeled after the Union League Club's Foundation for Boys' Clubs, was established for work among Negro boys on the South Side and two Union League Club members became incorporators and trustees for this new foundation. About 1948 the Club collaborated in getting the Board of Education to establish an adequate trades high school for a preponderately large Negro attendance on the South Side. The old Dunbar High School buildings at St. Lawrence Avenue and Forty-fourth Street had proved inadequate. A program was started by which $5,000,000 was obtained, and by 1954 a site for a new trades school building had been purchased at Thirty-ninth and State streets and plans for the structure were drawn up.

Chapter Eighteen

GRAND JURIES, GRAFT, AND
THE SECRET SIX

UNION LEAGUE CLUB MEMBERS FROM TIME TO TIME HAVE BEEN called upon to donate money for various worthy causes and they always have responded, whether it was for the erection of a monument to the police heroes of the Haymarket Riot, aid for San Francisco earthquake victims, or to found a boys' club. But possibly the most unique call for funds came in the late summer of 1923 when Club members were asked to help pay for the board, lodging, and expenses of a special grand jury.

It was all part of the pattern of the Club's participation in the constant fight against corrupt politics, crime, and graft in which it had been engaged from the days of its founding, and which in the 1920's brought it into conflict with so powerful a political leader as Mayor William Hale Thompson and so phenomenally puissant a gangster kingpin as Al Capone.

The special grand jury had been impaneled in September, 1922, and after its term of a month became so engrossed in Attorney General Edward J. Brundage's investigation into the financial affairs of Mayor Thompson's Board of Education that, under authorization of Chief Justice Michael L. McKinley of the Criminal Court, the inquiry was broadened to include investigation of alleged misappropriations and graft money transactions by public officers under the Thompson regime. In order to accomplish this, it was continued from month to month as a special grand jury. No co-operation was expected from State's

Attorney Robert E. Crowe because of his political squabble with Brundage, so the tribunal was called "Brundage's grand jury."

The Cook County Board, meantime, held the opinion that it could not lawfully appropriate funds to aid in this extended investigation, since its budget for the year had already been made up and did not include an appropriation for such an inquiry. Officers of the Chicago Bar Association were of a contrary opinion, but the County Board did not feel warranted in following their advice. Thus the attorney general's inquiry was on the point of failing entirely for want of funds, and the Criminal Court of Cook County had decided to conclude it on August 3, 1923, unless funds could be provided.

In order to prevent a failure of this investigation, believed by the Union League Club to be "wholesome and necessary," extended conferences were held with Justice McKinley, Brundage, officers of the Bar Association, representatives of various civic organizations, and officers and members of the Union League Club itself. It so happened that Justice McKinley and Harry Eugene Kelly, chairman of the Club's Public Affairs Committee, had been classmates at the University of Iowa, and had remained friends during their subsequent careers. They had several private conferences on the grand jury matter, and later, during the extended term of the grand jury, Kelly and McKinley talked with each other each morning on the telephone to plan the "war strategy" of the day's work.

The result of the conference was that Justice McKinley and Attorney General Brundage were advised that the Union League Club would make available $50,000 for support of the special grand jury. To this end the Club, taking subscriptions from individual members, advanced $46,728.68 out of a special fund thus pledged. For this advance the Club received an assignment of the duly authorized vouchers issued by the attorney general—

Victor Fremont Lawson, Union League Club member as well as founder, editor, and publisher of the Chicago *Daily News*, for more than four decades exerted his leadership for a better Chicago.

thus paying the money directly to Brundage instead of to the County Board or the court.

Attorney George B. McKibbin, a member of the Club's committee, said at a later day that the Board of Directors of the Club frowned upon this act, but as long as the committee was raising its own money, nothing was done about it. Club members Victor F. Lawson, owner of the *Daily News;* Julius Rosenwald, the merchant; and James B. Forgan, the banker, were among the heaviest contributors.

No sooner had the action of the Union League Club been announced than State's Attorney Crowe's office declared that such a procedure for financing a grand jury was illegal. But Justice McKinley told the grand jury to go ahead, stating that the Supreme Court had decided that "a judge has the power to call a grand jury for making an inquiry, and the attorney general, as an officer of the court, can be directed to pay the expenses resultant."

The special grand jury now settled down to investigate the so-called "expert fees" scandal of the Thompson administration. Many witnesses were called. Thompson, who was temporarily out of the mayor's chair at the time, having been defeated in April, 1923, by Judge William E. Dever, was himself a witness before this grand jury on November 28. He spent two hours detailing his complete ignorance of the internal workings of all the city departments during his two terms as mayor. He had no knowledge of "expert fees" or "gifts" to city officials from favored contractors, or fire department "slush funds," civil service violations, or "paving ring combines."

However, before the grand jury was dismissed in December, 1923, after having sat fourteen months, it indicted Michael J. Faherty, former head of the Board of Local Improvements; Percy B. Coffin, former president of the Civil Service Commission, and four others. These indictments were short-lived, as the Supreme Court in the early part of 1924 ruled that this special grand jury was an illegal body after its first month of service. The indictments were automatically quashed.

Coffin at once filed a libel suit for $500,000 damages against the individual members of the grand jury, charging them with slander. The Union League Club was too deep in this case now to withdraw. Co-operating with the Chicago Bar Association, the Club came to the defense of the grand jurors. Chairman Kelly of the Public Affairs Committee announced that Attorney William P. McCracken had been retained to represent the jurors. "Because they are being sued for performing what appeared to them as their public duty, the Union League Club does not want them to be put to any expense," Kelly explained to the newspapers. Two years later the Public Affairs Committee announced to its members that "in conformity with its original interest in this matter, the committee assumed expenses of successfully defending this suit." McKibbin, acting in behalf of the committee, was authorized to pay McCracken $400 as a fee.

The libel suit out of the way, the Club now sought reimbursement for the money it had advanced to further the grand jury investigation. This matter also was successfully resolved when on December 18, 1928, the finance committee of the County Board unanimously voted to pay back to the Club the money which had been put up five years before. The committee voted to reimburse the contributors pro rata after deducting 10 per cent for expenses.

The Union League Club had been able to salvage at least moral benefit from the case. Attention of the public had been called to the working of a special grand jury and how in many respects its operations were hampered and restricted. It was to further the public's education in this regard that fifteen years later, on November 24, 1943, the Club entertained the so-called October "Runaway Grand Jury" in a unique meeting in its Clubhouse.

This grand jury, investigating gambling—and especially the "big margin for graft" left in the alleged annual "take" of some $100,000,000 in and around Chicago—had worked harder and more conscientiously than most tribunals of this type. Its members had refused to take the word of the state's attorney's investigators but had gone out "to see for themselves," and had often met in all-night sessions. Hence the name "Runaway Grand Jury."

The luncheon meeting in honor of the members of this grand jury was attended by representatives of thirteen civic groups. The Union League *Bulletin* in reporting the affair labeled it, "The Grand Jury: Democracy in Action." The institution of the grand jury was extoled as the oldest bulwark of democratic popular liberties by Ernst W. Puttkammer,

Professor of Criminal Law at the University of Chicago Law School. Federal Judge George E. Q. Johnson outlined a plan for making municipal contracts public documents and creating a state bureau of audit and control, which, if adopted, "would go far to take the gravy out of public contracts." John T. Moran, vice-president of the Gunthorp Warren Printing Company, foreman of the grand jury, told of threats made to him and other members while serving on the tribunal.

As a public service, the results of this meeting were encouraging. Agitation resulted in a change of the law whereby local grand juries could sit sixty days if necessary, instead of thirty days as before. The Crime Commission had wanted a term of six months, such as afforded downstate tribunals, but was satisfied with the thirty-day extension granted.

To return to the Public Affairs Committee, in order to widen the scope of its civic activities and enlist a greater number of members in its work and to better realize its aims and objects, the Union League Club in 1924 engaged Edward M. Martin, former statistician and staff member of the National Institute of Public Administration and the Bureau of Municipal Research in New York City, as secretary of the committee. At the same time, it distributed questionnaires among the Club membership to discover the interests of members in the objects for which the Club was organized. From this information, the Public Affairs Committee set up nine subcommittees, numbering in all 144 members of the Club—the largest group ever engaged in this fashion. These committees were to investigate and carry on the work of the Club in nine fields: the administration of justice, city planning and zoning, conservation of natural resources, education, elections, military and naval affairs, public efficiency, race relations, taxes and public finance.

On December 8, 1925, the Club proposed a plan for a comprehensive investigation into civil and criminal justice in Chicago and Cook County, with a cost estimated at $150,000. In 1926, Chairman Kelly demanded a special state's attorney to investigate the gang killing of Assistant State's Attorney William H. McSwiggin, a prosecutor who had won a reputation for obtaining death penalty verdicts. "I have nothing against Crowe, but he is incapable of going into the beer racket," commented Kelly. The question of "Who killed McSwiggin?" was never to be answered.

The Union League Club had been a supporter of William McAndrew, a Dever appointee as superintendent of schools, whom Thompson had sworn to oust if re-elected for a third term. Thompson kept his word, and as one of his first acts on taking office, sought to fire McAndrew. Charles M. Moderwell, ex-president of the Board of Education, who two years later would be president of the Club, sought in vain to defend McAndrew on the stand against Thompson's charges that American history books used in the schools were tainted with the influence of King George of England. In the end McAndrew walked out of the trial and his job and never returned.

In 1928 the Union League Club was foremost in the demand for an investigation of the Sanitary District payrolls during the so-called "Whoopee Era." Three indictments eventually were returned, one naming Edward J. Kelly, who had been chief engineer of the sanitary district and who later was to be mayor of the city. This indictment was dismissed, however, and only one man was sent to prison. The presiding judge at the trials said testimony had revealed "hideous corruption prevalent in a public office created by the legislature."

The 1920's had been a busy decade for the Union League Club.

By the spring of 1930, Chicago found itself almost helpless in the grasp of a gigantic and highly organized band of criminals consisting of every type from lowbrow sluggers to soft-spoken gentlemen holding public office. Riding high on the illicit profits afforded by prohibition, crime had been organized with the efficiency of big business, or even big government, for it had established its own laws and arrogated to itself the right of life and death over its minions. Frank J. Loesch, as head of the Chicago Crime Commission, was later to admit before a meeting at the Union League Club that he had once called upon Al Capone to request him to use his influence to see that there was no violence at a certain election. Capone had graciously consented.

Now sensing an end to prohibition, the syndicate sought to broaden its powers and increase its profits. On February 4, 1930, there occurred what under any other circumstances would have been considered an insignificant shooting. Philip H. Meagher, building superintendent for the H. B. Barnard Construction Company, who was directing the work on the new Lying-In Hospital at the University of Chicago, was shot in the back by hoodlums. This shooting climaxed a long series of overt acts on the part of gangsters attempting to muscle in on legitimate business.

Three days after the shooting, Robert Isham Randolph, president of the Association of Commerce, announced that after a conference with State's Attorney John A. Swanson and Police Commissioner William F. Russell, a committee on prevention and punishment of crime had been formed to be known as the "Committee of Courage." Six men, leaders in civil and business life, would take up the task of "rescuing the city from the reign of gangsters, gunmen, and racketeers."

"The problem of law enforcement in the city of Chicago has reached a stage where representative citizens and business organizations must take personal and direct action," Colonel Randolph said. "The principal objective of the committee is to get the men who shot Meagher, but to do it we have to go into the whole situation."

The "whole situation" meant a confusing labyrinth of crime and racketeering which would lead up to the top men, or the top man, Al Capone. But the "Committee of Courage" would follow this devious path to the end, employing its own investigators and assembling evidence which would be given to the police and state's attorney. This would be done, too, with "no brass band and parade." The quotes are Colonel Randolph's.

No brass band was necessary, nor was a parade needed. The "Committee of Courage" leaped into newspaper headlines at the start, and soon thereafter, when a newspaperman tried to learn the personnel of the committee, Fred Ashley, publicity director for the Association of Commerce, said in an offhand manner, "Oh, just call it the Secret Six—the names of the committee are secret." So the Secret Six it became from that time until it went out of existence three years later.

Alexander G. Jamie, a former prohibition agent who had been chief investigator for the Secret Six, obtained his own charter for the organization in February, 1933, after the Association of Commerce had withdrawn financial support. Jamie claimed that during the career of the Secret Six it had handled 595 cases and had aided in 55 convictions, with sentences totalling 428 years. Fines of $11,525 had been paid, and recovery of $605,000 in bonds and $52,850 in merchandise had been made. The Secret Six had handled twenty-five kidnaping and extortion cases in which nine convictions had been obtained. Thus boasted Jamie.

Colonel Randolph, the only member of the Secret Six to be known, later admitted that the committee had not consisted of six men, but refused to his dying day to give the exact number or names of these members. Who were the Secret Six? This question has long been asked and long remained unanswered.

THE SPIRIT OF SEVENTY-SIX YEARS MAY STILL SAVE THE CITY'S GOOD NAME

Chicago applauded the spirited leadership of Union Leaguer Frank J. Loesch against Chicago's hoodlum politics.

Cartoonist McCutcheon comments on the campaign to clean up Chicago for the World's Fair of 1933.

It has now become known, however, that besides Colonel Randolph, others on the committee happened to be members of the Union League Club. Most directly interested in the shooting of Meagher was Harrison B. Barnard, president of the H. B. Barnard Construction Company. He had been a member of the Union League Club since 1915, and president of the Club in 1927–28. According to his son, Harrison Barnard, Jr., Barnard himself was one of the Secret Six. Edward E. Gore, president of Edward Gore & Company, a member of the Club since 1912, was president of the Crime Commission at that time. Budd Gore, his son, has said that his father told him he had been a member of the Secret Six.

The Secret Six, which may have been only three and not six, spent more than $1,000,000. When the question of finances came up at its first meeting, Samuel Insull, the utility magnate, arose and said, "Let's quit talking. I will match whatever amount is contributed here." Insull's initial effort in raising funds provided the committee with $450,000.

The Secret Six is credited by some with having contributed to the breaking up of the powerful Capone syndicate and especially with preventing it from moving in on legitimate business. It had an interesting sequel and that, too, involved members of the Union League Club.

When the Association of Commerce had withdrawn its support from the Secret Six, after a fight with Swanson, and State's Attorney Thomas J. Courtney had ordered the Secret Six investigators to surrender all deputy sheriff badges, a new crime-fighting agency "to replace the Secret Six," as the newspapers said, was formed. This group was headed by C. L. Rice, vice-president of the Association of Commerce. Other members were Charles R. Holden and Gerhardt F. Meyne of the Crime Commission; Bertram J. Cahn and Francis E. Brommell of the Citizens' Association; Joseph C. Belden and Thomas E. Donnelley

Frank J. Loesch is felicitated on his 76th birthday by Union Leaguers Bernard A. Eckhart, Julius Rosenwald, Benjamin F. Affleck, George W. Dixon, and Harry Eugene Kelly.

of the Employers' Association; and Robert Isham Randolph and George W. Rossetter of the Association of Commerce. This committee was called the "Co-ordinating Committee for Prevention of Crime and Civic Injustice." Its first function was to do something about the records of the Secret Six. Gerhardt Meyne, the contractor, a Club member since 1916, had this to say:

"I want it distinctly understood that I was never a so-called member of the so-called Secret Six. The Secret Six never fought crime, never brought about any real information that led to prosecutions, but did gather a lot of information which could be used for blackmail (if it ever fell into improper hands); but as far as prosecution was concerned, it had run the statute of limitations.

"I was one of those who together with Mr. Rice, Mr. Brommell, Mr. Joseph Belden, and Mr. Cahn maneuvered it out of existence and saw to it that all of its so-called information and records were burned and put out of harm's way. It is too bad that members of the Chicago Association of Commerce of that day did not recognize that they had an agency that was entirely fit to do just that job, but it did not and does not catch the imagination to stimulate hysteria. These things, if anything, are accomplished most if done quietly and credit given to the elected officials, even though they may have been pushed or driven into a corner where they are compelled to act.

"The Secret Six accomplished nothing in the purification of Chicago."

In spite of the difference of opinion as to the operations of the Secret Six, it must be conceded that it met a need and was effective, at least for a time, in its fight on organized crime.

Chapter Nineteen

A NEW CLUBHOUSE AND
A DEPRESSION

THE UNION LEAGUE CLUB JOINED ENTHUSIASTICALLY IN THE industrial and commercial pageantry of the boom years of the twenties by raising to the skies its four-million-dollar skyscraper building. It entertained with appropriate splendor, and then when the crash came and other clubs disappeared from the scene during the ensuing depression, the Club indulged in a laugh at its own financial troubles and those of its members by opening what was whimsically termed a "Million Dollar Room," papered with depreciated or worthless stock certificates and bonds.

The erection of the new and imposing Clubhouse had not resulted from an impulsive decision. During the first forty-odd years of its existence, the Union League Club had outgrown its housing facilities some half-dozen times. First it had moved from a room in the Sherman House to quarters in the Honore Block, and then into its own Clubhouse on Jackson Street in 1886. The annex was added a year later. In 1900 the Club purchased the lot south of the Clubhouse with the idea of erecting a new building some day, and two years later had acquired the ground upon which the Clubhouse itself stood. In 1916 another annex was added, and by 1922 the movement for a new building had crystallized, after some twenty years of dreams, discussions, and internal agitation by the more progressive members.

Under the presidency of Colonel George T. Buckingham in 1921–22, a Building Committee was appointed, with W. A. Illsley

The old Clubhouse shortly before its removal in 1924 to make way for the modern building.

as chairman. This committee had frequent conferences with the firm of Mundie & Jensen, the same company which, headed by Major William LeBaron Jenney, had built the old Clubhouse and the various additional wings. Sketches were submitted, "with the result that the fundamental principle has been adopted in designing the framework of the building which, while it will be perfectly adapted to the Club purposes, has also been designed as to permit the building for a moderate expense to be altered into a hotel or office building should it appear in years to come that the present site was no longer desirable for the home of the Union League Club." The Club was even then looking ahead to the future!

As the time drew near for the wreckers to invade the historic red brick building which had been the quarters of the Union League Club for more than thirty years, gloom settled over the lounge, the library, and the billiard room. Those at the tables in the dining rooms spoke in hushed voices.

On the last night, September 30, 1924, more than one thousand members gathered at a farewell banquet. President William J. Jackson was toastmaster, and four of the six living charter members of the Club were present—J. Frank Aldrich, Jacob Newman, Sidney C. Eastman, and James H. Moore. As these guests listened to speeches and stories of the past, the Club's oldest resident, P. H. Joyce, president of the Illinois Car and Manufacturing Company, was holding a wake in Room 302. But perhaps the man who wore the longest face and most sorrowful countenance was not a Club member, but John L. Enright, who for thirty-five years had been chief clerk at the Club. He had seen to it that every stick of furniture, every one of the collection

Recalling old times before the fireplace of the old Clubhouse are Congressman William J. Jackson, John E. Wilder, and Martin B. Madden.

of paintings (valued then at $300,000), everything movable, in fact, had been taken out or had been tagged for removal. "And the sight of such desolation was too much for the veteran clerk," one reporter commented. "He was Marius on the site of Carthage." Enright, then sixty-nine, predicted gloomily, "Things won't be the same."

As the walls crumbled under the wreckers' efforts, the 3,075 members took up temporary quarters at the DeJonge Hotel at 12 East Monroe Street, which was a former home of the Chicago Club. One hundred thousand dollars had been appropriated for moving, rent, repair, and equipment. So closely did the Building Committee figure, that at the end of the twenty months the Union League Club occupied this space the cost was $99,571.63!

Meantime, the Club *Bulletin*, which was revived in February, 1925, under the able editorship of Edward M. Martin, began to follow month by month the progress of the new building. The first issue of the *Bulletin* carried a picture of a hole in the ground, with the caption, "Watch It Grow!" It did grow. The May issue of the magazine showed ten stories of progress, and in November, 1925, it printed a picture of the building almost finished.

The twenty-two story building was formally opened and dedicated on Friday, May 21, 1926. Now a part of the skyscraper skyline of the city, it was designed for beauty and comfort and practicability. "The façades are an adaptation of the lighter Italian Renaissance period, its fenestration and detail giving to it as a whole the Colonial effect of the Georgian, essentially American," the architects said. "This characteristic feeling prevails in the refined simplicity of the interior, not too rigidly enforced to sacrifice the requirements for a downtown businessmen's club, a typical club home in the city, in style neither past nor present but for all time."

On the top floors were an ingeniously designed swimming pool, with overhead sky-lighting, and complete athletic facilities

Club presidents George T. Buckingham, Wyllys W. Baird, and William J. Jackson (left to right) at cornerstone ceremonies for the new Clubhouse.

Artist's impression of the Jackson Boulevard entrance of the new Clubhouse.

of all types, including a full-size gymnasium. There was a large main dining room, a somewhat smaller ladies' dining room, a grill room, numerous private dining rooms, and the lounge with its fireplace framed by a mantel of Tavernelle marble, bearing the Club motto: "Welcome to Loyal Hearts." There was a huge lounge running through two floors, a large and beautifully appointed library, as well as a billiard room, card rooms, barbershop, and 248 bedrooms and suites for members, including a "presidential suite" for distinguished visitors. Offices, bars, laundry and linen rooms, kitchens and pantries—nothing overlooked, everything in the latest and best of style. And the ladies! Their own entrance was on the side, on Federal Street as of old, for still no woman guest could pass through the sacrosanct main entrance. Women had their own reception room on the second floor, their own facilities and retiring room, with the fifth floor practically given over to them as a ladies' dining room.

After the building had been occupied for some months, use made evident the necessity for certain structural alterations, including the rearrangement of lavatory facilities and the moving of the reception desk from the second to the first floor. These changes were made, but on the whole, the building proved to be admirably adapted to its purpose.

There were six hundred guests at the dedication dinner when the new home was turned over to the members by the Building Committee. Harrison B. Barnard, vice-chairman of the committee, made the formal presentation, and President William J. Jackson accepted. He then relinquished his office, which he had held for two terms, to the incoming president, Harry Eugene Kelly. Guests ate with silver costing $30,500, and were conscious of the fact they were dining in a building that, without furnishings, cost 77½ cents a cubic foot; or a total, with everything complete, of $3,983,583.23.

The presidents of the New York, Detroit, Philadelphia, and

Aurora Union League clubs were present. It was a gala affair, well covered by reporters and photographers. The *Evening Post* was especially impressed by the Club's art collection. "First among the leading collections of works of art in clubhouses of this city is that of the Union League Club, which is being rehung in the new building," the newspaper said.

The next day, Saturday, the afternoon reception and open house and the Elizabethan costume party in the new building that evening drew some four thousand persons. The *Bulletin* reported: "The pomp, pageantry, and gaiety of Queen Elizabeth's Court characterized the celebration. . . . It was an evening of beautiful women in lace and ruffles, frills and puffs, and of courtly gentlemen, some in robes, others in hose and doublet." The role of Queen Elizabeth was taken by Florence Macbeth, prima donna of the Chicago Grand Opera Company.

The guests joined heartily in singing such songs as "Moonlight and Roses," "Sometime," "I Want to Be Happy," and "Always." There were dances of the Elizabethan period. Some of the costumes of the queen's ladies-in-waiting may have

Members congregate daily in the Main Lounge during the winter season to enjoy the glowing fire in the giant fireplace.

appeared burst at the seams, but this was not from the strain of dancing nor from too hearty laughing. When the costumes had arrived at the last minute, Miss Hilda B. Brown, in charge of the pageant, was chagrined to find that many were too small. Gerhardt F. Meyne, garbed as a purveyor of the *Acatrie* (provisioner), heard of the predicament, and setting down his huge tray upon which was a boar's head, went to the aid of the distressed damsels. Mr. Meyne was a large, powerful man—he still is. To alter the costumes, he simply grabbed them in both hands and pulled the seams apart at the places where they pinched. Miss Brown, who had not known Meyne until that moment, was so grateful that she rushed up and kissed him—or, to be more Elizabethan, bussed him. It was Meyne's turn to be overcome, and shortly thereafter he proposed to and was accepted by Miss Brown.

Florence Macbeth had been a charming queen at the opening reception. It was not long, however, before the Club was entertaining a real queen. On Tuesday, November 16, 1926, Queen Marie of Roumania and her entourage arrived at the women's entrance on Federal Street with the sirens of a police motorcycle escort screaming and wailing. Not even a queen could come through the main entrance, but her royal dignity was unruffled when she was greeted by George W. Dixon, chairman of the Reception Committee.

In the ladies' dining room, crowded with its three hundred guests, the Queen took her seat in an appropriate high-backed throne chair. Ira Nelson Morris, consul-general of Roumania in the United States, sat on her left, and Club President Harry Eugene Kelly on her right. As she calmly drew forth a long cigarette holder, adjusted a cigarette in one end and placed the other between her lips, there was a momentary lull in the conversation. Some watched with amused interest, others with astonishment. Never before had a woman publicly smoked in the Union League Club! Albert Pein, assistant maître d'hôtel, suddenly recovering from his state of frozen surprise, snatched up a silver tray upon which lay a white card and, conscious of his duty, advanced towards the Queen. This card bore the legend: *Please! Ladies are not allowed to smoke.* Some thoughtful member of the Reception Committee restrained Pein while Queen Marie accepted a light, drew deeply on her cigarette, and exhaled the smoke ceilingward with something of a sigh of satisfaction. Men smiled and women brightened hopefully, but Pein kept a stern vigil on the latter. The ladies no doubt prayed that the Queen's act would at last break the ban on smoking—but this was not to come until years later.

Alfred "Joe" Katz, then steward of the Club, who recently recalled the luncheon as "the greatest Club event" in his sixty-one years of service there, had gone to considerable trouble to prepare some native Roumanian dishes for the Queen. However, when the meal was served, it is said that her Majesty's plate contained the traditional chicken and peas—apparently all she had eaten at public events during her American visit. Who got the succulent Roumanian viands is not a matter of record.

The luncheon over, Queen Marie was escorted to the lounge where some four thousand persons gathered to see and hear her. Eager women stood on the seats and arms of the lounge chairs, as was evidenced later when the House Committee shook its collective head over the bill for repairing holes and rents made in the leather by high heels. Marie made what in everyone's opinion was a fine speech. She explained her visit by saying, "I have been asked why I came to this country and I shall tell you in your own words: I came to put Roumania on the map."

The visit over, Queen Marie was escorted to her waiting car in Federal Street, where she faced a bombardment of photographers' flash guns. Chairman Dixon was photographed standing beside the Queen and smiling brightly, but he closed his eyes at

Queen Marie of Roumania leaving the Club after the reception in her honor, escorted by Reception Committee Chairman George W. Dixon.

the wrong moment. It was with considerable relief that he saw himself in the picture as it later appeared in the *Union League Club Bulletin* open-eyed and alert, thanks to the expert hand of a retouch artist.

Other important guests came and went. There was Captain George B. Fried of the SS *America*, who had so heroically rescued the distressed SS *Florida;* President William T. Cosgrove of Ireland; President Pascual Ortis Rubio of Mexico; Dr. Hugo Eckener, intrepid commander of the dirigible *Graf Zeppelin*, and Chief Justice Charles Evans Hughes.

However, uncertain times were ahead. After the stock market broke in a wild panic on October 24, 1929, the black cowl of depression settled over the nation and continued through the first half of the thirties.

The depression brought its share of trouble to the Club in

several ways, the most serious of which was a badly depleted membership. Club memberships were one of the first things to be given up by men with greatly reduced incomes. "Under prevailing economic conditions, it is not surprising that our Club has suffered severely, not only in a high percentage of resignations, but in a decrease in the average expenditures of Club members," W. J. Dillon, chairman of the Finance Committee, reported in March, 1933. The Club had lost 761 members in a year. Dorothy Wilson, a key employee who has been the efficient overseer of the secretary's office in the Club since 1923, recalls that President Henry P. Chandler made almost daily visits to her office in that year and worried constantly about the steady flow of resignations. "I would tell him that something should be done about it," Miss Wilson says, "but it was very difficult to know what could be done."

Club President Benjamin F. Affleck (right) confers honorary memberships in the Club on Charles Evans Hughes and Frank J. Loesch at the annual meeting in 1929.

In 1933 John McKinlay, president of Marshall Field & Company, agreed to accept the presidency of the Club and to attempt to remedy the constant drain from resignations if he were given complete discretion. This was readily agreed to, and McKinlay began an energetic and vigorous membership program. Changes were made in initiation and reinstatement fees, and in the amount and terms of payment of dues. Some reductions were made. Wives, daughters, and other feminine relatives of members' families were encouraged to use the Clubhouse. It was during a Century of Progress, and as the house rules had been changed under President Chandler a year before, now for the first time in the history of the Club women were permitted to occupy sleeping rooms there. A special Membership Committee was appointed, and by 1935, when McKinlay's second term in office ended, Club membership showed a net increase of 313, bringing the total to 2,946—better, but still 926 below the total in 1930.

It was during McKinlay's second term in 1934 that the "Million Dollar Room" was created. One of the private dining rooms on the eighth floor of the Club was papered with stock certificates and bonds of a face value of more than a million dollars, which had been donated by members.

The "Million Dollar Room" became known over the nation and appealed to the public fancy. United States Senator Duncan U. Fletcher, in seeking to put through the Senate his stock exchange control bill, strengthened his remarks on the floor of the Senate by reference to the "Million Dollar Room" as an "evidence of what has been put upon the public in this country through these various enterprises."

With the beginning of financial recovery in the mid-thirties, the gold-and-green-bordered engraved certificates and bonds began to recover value. Members who had contributed them began to ask for their return. Fortunately the certificates had

Cartoonist Will E. Johnstone's reaction to the decommissioning of the "Million Dollar Room" in the New York *World-Telegram*.

Reclaiming stock certificates from the Club's famous "Million Dollar Room."

been so affixed that they could be removed from the wall, and by 1936 there were so many gaps that all were removed and given back to their owners. Some members waggishly suggested replacing the stocks and bonds with other types of "worthless material" such as "campaign promises of 1932" or "copies of the covenant of the League of Nations," but nothing came of this, and the room was redecorated in a more conventional manner.

It was unfortunate for the Club that the depression and attendant reductions in Club income came so soon after the construction of the new building. The building had been financed pursuant to a plan evolved by a good many astute business and professional men who were members of the Club, through the floating of two loans. A first mortgage loan was made by Northwestern Mutual Life Insurance Company. A second mortgage bond issue had been purchased by members of the Club, to some extent as a contribution to the building program, and with the knowledge that payment of the bonds would have to depend on continued Club prosperity. By 1935 it was apparent that principal and interest requirements on the two bond issues could not be met as they then existed and that a change in indenture provisions would be necessary. A committee was formed which obtained ready agreement from the bondholders to a reorganization program. On July 8, 1935, representatives of the Club appeared before Federal Judge Charles E. Woodward with an application for approval of a reorganization plan under Section 77B of the Federal Reorganization Statute. Seven days later the Chicago *American* announced that "The Union League Club set a record for settling 77B bankruptcy cases when the reorganization plan was approved by Federal Judge William H. Holly."

Club indebtedness consisted of a first mortgage of $2,350,000 and a second mortgage of $1,457,500, the latter held by some nine hundred bondholders, most of whom were Club members. Accrued interest on the first mortgage amounted to $340,000 and on the second mortgage to $218,000. The reorganization plan worked out by Club President Edwin C. Austin involved the waiving of past-due interest and the reduction of interest rates. Payments to second mortgage bondholders were to be deferred until principal of the first mortgage had been reduced to $1,000,000.

It appeared at the time of the reorganization that the settlement would result in a financial obligation which the Club could handle, and interest from that time was paid promptly when due and the principal of the first mortgage was reduced almost to the $1,000,000 figure. However, in 1948, consideration was given to the fact that principal of both mortgages would soon become due almost simultaneously and that refinancing would be necessary. President Frank C. Rathje appointed a Refinancing Committee under the chairmanship of Club member Homer J. Livingston, president of the First National Bank of Chicago, to work out a plan of refinancing. The law firm of Chapman and Cutler, of which Roscoe C. Nash and several other Club members were members, was retained as Club counsel. Nash was selected to handle the matter for the firm, and negotiations with the holders of the first and second mortgage indebtedness were commenced.

No difficulty was experienced in reaching an agreement with Northwestern Mutual Life Insurance Company as holder of the first mortgage, but it soon became apparent that only through the filing of a petition in the Federal Court for reorganization could a refinancing plan be made effective as to second mortgage bondholders. By reason of deaths of many of the original holders, the owners of about $100,000 of bonds of this issue could not be located, and any refunding plan could be made effective as to them only through court decree. A substantial additional amount of bonds had been purchased by non-members as speculations, and these persons were naturally interested only in obtaining the greatest possible profit on their purchases. With one or two rather glaring exceptions, Club members who still owned bonds readily approved the proposed refinancing plan. Under the tenure of George H. Redding as president, a petition was filed in the Federal Court on February 10, 1950, requesting approval of the reorganization plan. Judge Walter J. LaBuy recognized the importance of the matter to the Club and to Chicago in his appointment of Wilson Lampert, retired banker and former president of South Shore Country Club, and Club President Redding, as co-trustees. The plan for which the approval of the court was requested contemplated payment of principal in full over a period of twenty years and payment of interest semiannually until the retirement of principal. First mortgage interest was to be at a rate agreeable to the holders of the mortgage, and second mortgage interest at 5 per cent. All interest accrued on the second mortgage from the date of the prior reorganization was to be fully paid.

The plan was immediately approved by a majority of the holders of the second mortgage bonds, but a number of persons who had a speculative interest in the bonds caused a bondholders' committee to be organized. Negotiations with this committee dragged on for a great many months, although Club member John Dwyer, as chairman of the Members' Committee, devoted a total of many days of patient and effective service to carrying on the negotiations. Agreement on one question resulted in the raising of new objections. The committee finally requested not only the payment of interest accrued since the former reorganization, which the plan had contemplated, but also payment of a large amount of the earlier interest which had been cancelled by the court at the time of the first reorganization. This President Redding, and President Joseph A. Matter, who succeeded him, unequivocally refused to countenance. The question was argued in the District Court, which found in favor of the

The Main Lounge is popular with members for reading, visiting, or resting.

Club, and was then appealed by the committee to the United States Circuit Court of Appeals, which confirmed the finding of the District Court that there was no merit in the claim.

The press, of course, could not resist the opportunity to have considerable fun with the plush Union League Club during the reorganization period. STEAKS WILL BE SMALLER AT THE UNION LEAGUE CLUB, read one headline. In general, however, the newspaper accounts were very fair and it was recognized that the reorganization was not an attempt by the Club to avoid payment of any part of its indebtedness, but was instituted because it was the only available means of rendering effective the refunding of its two mortgages.

The Club was once again on a sound financial basis. During the presidency of Vernon R. Loucks, the membership of the

253

Club was restored to its legal maximum and Club income has since been gratifying. Florence M. Mulholland, Comptroller of the Club since 1933, has over that period been more responsible than any other person for the financial success of Club operations. Asked for her comments on the reorganization and the present status of debt retirement, she remarked that the reorganization period is one she will never forget, as the weeks turned into months and the months dragged into years—almost four years, until on January 15, 1954, the final decree was entered. As to the success of the reorganization she said in her comment:

"During all this time, the officers, directors, and members worked as one to bring the Club through to its present strength. Membership rose from 3,728 to 4,259. The operating profit for the last fiscal year was the highest in the history of the Club. The Club building is in excellent condition—the first nine floors completely air conditioned.

"We—I use the personal pronoun because the Club is a very personal institution—are very proud of the reduction of the funded debt in the last four years. In February, 1950, our funded debt of $2,737,122 consisted of a first mortgage in the amount of $1,037,500 and General Mortgage Bonds of $1,699,622. The balance sheet of June 30, 1954, shows the first mortgage to be $850,000 and the General Mortgage Bonds to be $984,275, a reduction in four years of more than $900,000.

"Payments into the sinking fund have been made to cover required payments almost a year in advance. Working capital is ample—Club equity of over two and a quarter million reflects a financial stability, and promises a future strong enough to carry on the fine traditions of the past seventy-five years."

With a brighter financial future of the Club in prospect, members began to look forward to the time when all of the net income of the Club could be devoted to the public work to which the Union League Club had dedicated itself.

Chapter Twenty

FIFTIETH ANNIVERSARY:
"I REMEMBER — "

THE TIME HAD COME TO CELEBRATE THE GOLDEN ANNIVERSARY. When 1930 rolled around, the Union League Club had been wedded for fifty years to the principles of encouraging, by moral, social, and political influence, unconditional loyalty to the Federal government, and to defending and protecting the integrity and perpetuity of the nation. It had promised to inculcate a higher appreciation of the value and sacred obligations of American citizenship, to resist and oppose corruption, to promote economy in public office, and to secure honesty and efficiency in the administration of national, state, and muncipal affairs. To a certain extent, it was satisfied with its past history in this regard.

Charles M. Moderwell, president of the Club at the time of its fiftieth birthday, summed up in his annual report: "During all these years the membership has been chosen from those citizens of Chicago who are concerned to make the city a better place in which to live. If one were to call the roll of the members of fifty years past, he would find there the names of the most distinguished citizens of Chicago and of the nation. The Club through its committees and its membership has had a part in every movement for the betterment of Chicago. . . . A half century in the life of an institution creates traditions, but also responsibilities. We may take proper pride in our ancestry, but we hope for better things from our posterity."

Celebration of the fiftieth anniversary of the Club had been considered by previous administrations, and elaborate plans had been suggested. But as the date approached, a new program was set up. Perhaps the stock market crash in the fall of 1929 had had something to do with the change in plans. Whatever the reason, after thorough consideration, the Board of Directors in 1930 decided to confine the celebration to the Club membership, "in the belief that the Club record for fifty years speaks for itself."

The anniversary was observed at a dinner in the new Clubhouse on Tuesday evening, March 25. In spite of the March blizzard which raged that night, the attendance was "more than remarkable," the Club *Bulletin* reported. President Moderwell was in the chair, which he would relinquish during the evening to the new president, John R. Montgomery. A special guest was

William H. Bates of Pekin, Ill., who in 1930 was the sole surviving member of the original council of the Union League of America.

William H. Bates, eighty-nine years old, of Pekin, Illinois, sole survivor of the original council of the Union League of America organized in June, 1862. Alfred E. Marling, president of the Union League Club of New York, sent a message that "we hope the best is yet to come in the progress and usefulness of your wonderful organization."

William P. Sidley, who had been president in 1911, reviewed the history of the Club, and stressed that "without conscious effort on its part, it has contributed, when needed, men and ideas and leadership to the service of the public." John Timothy Stone, pastor of the Fourth Presbyterian Church and president of McCormick Theological Seminary, drew applause when he said, "We have great problems in our city, and this Club was never organized to be in an easy chair." Dr. Stone, like Moderwell and others, beckoned to the future and hoped for even better things from the Club's posterity.

Fifty years was a long time. The total number of memberships during that period had been 6,084. Starting with 265 members the first year, by 1890 there were 1,263; in 1900 the total was 1,491; in 1910 it was 2,361; in 1920 still 2,356, and on the fiftieth anniversary there were 3,884 members. Members had come and gone, vacancies due to death had been 1,534, and those due to resignations and other causes had been 750. Now only two of the original members survived—J. Frank Aldrich and Sidney Corning Eastman. The latter was to die within the week of the fiftieth celebration. But of the group which had joined the Club in 1881 there still were seven left, and of those who had joined between 1882 and 1889 there were twenty-nine.

These old-time members and others were filled with memories of interesting Club activities. They recalled the good and the bad, the ups and the downs, some things serious and others amusing.

William H. Bates and
J. Frank Aldrich, special
guests at the Club's
fiftieth anniversary in 1930.
Sidney Corning Eastman,
the only other surviving
charter member besides
Aldrich, could not
attend the meeting.

There had been occasions when the Club membership did
not fully agree on certain issues, such as the one which resulted
in the Blaine-Cleveland split back in the 1880's. But no other
issue had so completely divided the Club into two hostile factions as an election of its own in 1920. The Reverend John
Timothy Stone had been nominated for Club president. He was
the first minister ever put up for election on the regular ticket—
or any ticket, for that matter. John Benham, of the newly
organized Public Affairs Committee, said at the time that Dr.
Stone's ability as an organizer and his sound business judgment
were the main factors influencing his nomination, and his relation to the church had not even been considered.

However, there was some sentiment among Club members
against the election of a clergyman, and a few expressed fear
that such an election would result in stricter Club regulations.

Some viewed Dr. Stone as a "prohibition man." He had been elected to resident membership in the Club by action of the Board of Directors on March 10, 1919—just a year before.

As the date of the election neared, George B. McKibbin, a young attorney just back from war, at the behest of Harry Monroe, Bernard E. Sunny, and others, suddenly set up headquarters in the Club and announced John Fletcher, vice-president of the Fort Dearborn National Bank, as the "members' candidate." In other words, Fletcher was to be the "dark horse" in the campaign. "We wanted a businessman because of the financial condition of the Club at that time," McKibbin explained recently. The contest was a heated one. Fletcher beat Stone by only twelve votes.

"For a time many members would not speak to each other because of their differences of opinion in this election," said McKibbin. "However, Fletcher made a good president. He at once assessed each member $300 to wipe out the debt incurred by the building of the annex in 1916. Some would not pay and resigned, but sufficient money was raised to liquidate the debt and thus the way was cleared for financing the new Club building."

This had been the third time in sixteen years that an opposition members' ticket had been put up against the candidate regularly nominated by the committee of the Board of Directors. The "Red" (opposition) ticket, headed by Charles W. Folds, had won just the year before.

In this contest there had been considerable "mud-slinging," and when Folds, the opposition candidate, was elected president, his opponent, F. Bruce Johnstone, an attorney, promptly resigned from the Club.

Some thoughts turned to the public reputation of the Club. Newspapers and historical writers had for the most part appreciated the sincere efforts of the Union League Club to carry out its principles, and with few exceptions everything written about the Club had been favorable. But there were exceptions. The Union League Club was a target of criticism from those who regarded it as a "rich man's club." Robert Shackleton in *The Book of Chicago* had stirred up the Club membership when he characterized the Union League Club as composed of "oldish men" of Chicago. Edgar Lee Masters, a lawyer, but better known for his *Spoon River Anthology*, seemed to have been personally embittered when at a later date in his *Tale of Chicago* he wrote:

Though gambling was continually denounced by the press and inveighed against by theologians, for many years gentlemen of the city, Federal Judges, contributors to the Civic Federation and Municipal Voters League, reform state's attorneys pledged to rid the city of sin, corporation lawyers taking occasion to flatter visiting Federal Judges with presents of whisky and by allowing them to win at poker, these and others of like disposition of mind associated themselves together in the rooms of the Union League Club, for the delight of mulcting a dull capitalist once a week of thousands of dollars, thereby adding drains to his purse already generous toward movements to suppress gambling, political corruption in the wards, prostitution and villainies of Yerkes. Around the corner from the Club on Sherman Court were bagnios, to which these hircinous [*sic*] spirits stole through the darkness. The next day across the street in the Federal building many young and industrious lawyers who had diligently prepared meritorious cases found themselves suddenly worsted at the instance of a United States Senator, or corporation lawyer expounding the law to a Federal Judge; while the judge by no expression betrayed the fact that the night before he had been handsomely entertained at the Union League Club. These powerful men soaked in hypocrisy, to whom the ward balls were unspeakable offenses, who were shocked by the song and joy of errant youth, and the unlicensed conduct of gay offenders in the Democratic populousness of the city, saw no inconsistency in their social attitudes.

Most Club members looked upon Edgar Lee Masters as a good poet.

The Hearst newspapers were particularly vigilant concerning anything out of the ordinary at the Club. Some contended at the time that the *American* and *Herald and Examiner* were seeking to ingratiate themselves with the labor unions, and in attacking a "rich man's club" they hoped to gain sympathetic readers among the working classes. Harry Reutlinger, who recalls those days and who is now managing editor of the *Herald-American*, smiles at such a thought and comments, "We only reported the news."

The newspaper attacks had been almost vicious in the early part of 1919, James M. Beck, former assistant attorney general of New York, had been scheduled to speak at the Club's Washington's Birthday celebration. The *American* bitterly assailed both Beck and the Club in column after column. Beck was characterized as "a defamer of President Wilson and foe of the plan to obtain six months pay for ex-soldiers." The Club was pilloried for inviting him. In the face of this opposition, Beck did speak. The *Tribune* reported next day that he had not attacked Wilson as expected, although he had done so at the Lincoln Day ceremonies in New York. Beck was to speak again under the auspices of the Club in 1936. It was on this occasion that the Club for the first time allowed women at the Washington's Birthday dinner in the Clubhouse.

Many recalled the excitement at the Club when Billy Sunday, the evangelist, was a guest in March, 1919. Frank J. Loesch had been one of the signers of the invitation which urged members to come "so that you can meet and talk to Billy Sunday." Mary Garden of operatic fame had been entertained in 1921 and was the first woman in the Club's history to be its guest of honor.

The Union League had been conscientious in observing

Judge Jesse Holdom, Club president and veteran Library Committee chairman, reminisces with Members Lessing Rosenthal and C. L. Speed.

all laws regulating the sale of liquor, but it was to learn the hard way in February, 1917, that cocktails mixed in bottles by Steve Kelley for members who wanted to take home his inimitable concoctions constituted "blended liquor," and that the Club was operating illegally because it did not have a $100 government rectifier's license. On the roster of the Club at the time was Charles F. Clyne, United States district attorney. Clyne found that the revenue agent who had demanded that the Club obtain the license was in the right, and the only thing Clyne could do if the money were not paid was to prosecute his own club for violation of the Federal statutes. He advised that a "cocktail license" be taken out, and it was.

A short time later, Bishop Thomas Nicholson, at the Des Plaines Camp Meeting, circulated a petition to ban liquor at the

Union League Club. He said that Frank J. Loesch, president of the Club at the time, was a signer. This precipitated a terrific row, which was amicably settled in time, and liquor still flowed at the Union League Club.

However, when prohibition reared its hydrant head during the first month in 1920, the Club faithfully removed the liquor from its shelves, eliminated the wine lists from its menus, and settled down to observe the law to the letter. But there were continual rumors that a nip was to be had here and there. Members were said to have their lockers crammed full of stuff "right off the boat." Harry Eugene Kelly, on becoming president in 1926, decided to put an end to this sub rosa imbibing. George B. McKibbin remembered the punitive expedition, as he went along in the capacity of second vice-president. Locker after locker was broken open and searched. "It was slightly embarrassing and, as I recall, rather unproductive," McKibbin remembered. "We got only a few bottles. But Kelly was that kind of man—he insisted on carrying out the Union League Club's commitment of unqualified loyalty to the government. In this way he was an idealist."

One rugged individualist was Ferdinand W. Peck, the man who brought grand opera to Chicago, and who had been president of the Club during the Columbian Exposition. Commodore Peck, who was living at the Club when prohibition came, incurred the displeasure of the House Committee when he appeared one day with an armload of filled bottles. He set them down in the lobby of the Club and invited all and sundry to partake. It was not long after this that the Commodore, feeling compassion for members of a girls' band which was tooting away in the chill air at Jackson Boulevard and Dearborn Street as part of a William Hale Thompson ballyhoo campaign for mayor, went out and invited them all into the Club for warmth and good cheer. This did it. The House Committee at once demanded Commodore Peck's room, and the Commodore promptly moved over to the Chicago Athletic Association. One member sympathized: "We had a tough president that year."

While there had been dancing in the Clubhouse on the occasion of the opening in 1886, it was not until three years later that this form of diversion was tolerated regularly in the Union League Club. J. Fred A. Halbach recalled that Albert E. Glennie, as manager of the Club, "was one of the first to introduce dancing in the old Union League Clubhouse, and the first event created a good deal of excitement." Halbach said all carpeted floors were covered with canvas "and after the New Year's dinner and reception the guests danced." Newspapers seemed to think that the dignity of the Union League Club was encroached upon, and next day one reported, ". . . and they even *danced* in the Union League Club!"

Chapter Twenty-One

KEEPING STEP TO THE MUSIC
OF THE UNION

DURING THOSE TROUBLOUS AND ANXIOUS YEARS WHICH USHERED in the second World War, the Union League Club experienced a resurgence of that spirit which had actuated its ancestral prototype—the Union League of America—to uphold Lincoln in preserving the Union. America had been dealt a terrific economic blow in the depression years, and now it found itself inevitably drawn into the maelstrom of international strife. By various means it was trying to find itself. Social analysts and economics statisticians were busy throughout the land, examining the condition of the people and the times.

The Union League Club was also to re-examine itself in soul-searching fashion. Once again the Club turned back to those patriotic motives which had inspired its founding. There was now a reaffirmation of its principles, followed by a vigorous defense of the Federal Constitution, and later there was a forcible restatement of its primary objects which preceded an inspiring crusade marked by the slogan, "America, Wake Up!" The Club's Washington's Birthday ceremonies took on new significance, and the Club now was also celebrating the birthday of Abraham Lincoln.

Members began to notice and re-read the primary credo of the Club engraved on the mantel over the fireplace in the lounge: *Welcome to Loyal Hearts. We join ourselves to no party that does not carry the flag and keep step to the music of the Union.*

The Union League Club had been founded in a sentiment of patriotism, and the Club president, Harry P. Chandler, struck the keynote in 1933 when he said: "Patriotism today calls for an intelligent participation in the affairs of government, which is a larger factor than ever before in the lives of the people."

Winston Churchill, then without cabinet post, was the first of a long list of speakers who would keep Club members well posted on current events. Churchill, who was in this country on a mission to persuade the United States to join England in repudiation of the gold standard, spoke before the Club on the evening of February 2, 1932. This was one of the Club's ladies' nights, and there were 1,720 in attendance: 1,200 in the dining room and 500 in the lounge, where they heard the address over the loud-speaker. This was one of the largest attendances recorded in the history of the Club to that date.

Rt. Hon. Winston Churchill was guest speaker at the Club in 1931. With him is Consul General Haggard.

Churchill had special praise for the reappointment of General Charles G. Dawes, former Vice-President and now on the honor roll of the Club, to head the Reconstruction Finance Corporation. In connection with this Churchill said: "All world accomplishments have been made not by politicians and parties, but by great men. The world today is ruled by harassed politicians, absorbed in getting into office or turning out the other men, who have not much time left for determining great issues on their merits."

Franklin Delano Roosevelt was elected to the Presidency of the United States in 1932. Although he was a nephew of Frederic A. Delano, who had been Club president in 1906, there was no rejoicing among most of the Club members. The Club as a whole had been strongly in favor of Herbert Hoover, an honorary member. As time went on, the Club built up a strong opposition to both the President and his New Deal. Although Grover Cleveland and Woodrow Wilson, both Democratic presidents, had been made honorary members, Franklin D. Roosevelt never was placed on the Club's honor roll. However, the Club in 1933 elected its own fourth Democratic president. This was John McKinlay, president of Marshall Field and Company. When elected for a second term in office in 1934, McKinlay told Dr. Edward M. Martin, director of public affairs, that this had come about "in spite of my being a Democrat."

Edwin C. Austin, who became Club president in 1935, expressed concern about the general attitude of the Club membership towards the Roosevelt administration. In his annual report in 1936 he stressed that in the matter of civic endeavor the Club had passed through a year in which attitudes ordinarily patriotic might have been termed partisan. "This fact did not warrant the Club in withdrawing from civic affairs and standing mute on the burning issues of the time," Austin admonished.

Austin appointed a Ways and Means Committee, one of

whose members was Dwight H. Green, later to be governor of the state. This committee joined with the Public Affairs Committee in presenting to the members a "Reaffirmation of Principles" at the pre-Constitution Day dinner on September 16, 1935. In the reaffirmation of principles the background, genesis, and history of the Union League Club were outlined to show that "the Union League Club is more than a Club—it is an institution upon which devolves a duty when sinister forces seek to destroy, or to undermine, the basic concepts of the American system of government. Its duty is to megaphone to the world that it stands, as always, *foursquare* for the Constitution." It further admonished that members of the Club "at this critical period, solemnly affirm that the *Union* of States, created by the Constitution, is the most successful experiment in the long history of government, and that upon its sure foundation successive generations of Americans have built up a civilization, cultural and material, which is the outstanding achievement of the ages." In view of this, it denounced as unpatriotic any and all efforts to substitute for the Constitution "any system of dictatorship, under whatever guise it masquerades."

Constitution Day had been observed as a result of the efforts of one of the Club members, Harry F. Atwood, former assistant state's attorney and president of the Constitution Anniversary Association. It had been said that whatever revival of reverence for the Constitution had taken place during this century was due more to the efforts of Atwood than to any other individual. He had organized the Constitution Anniversary Association in 1922 and had written many books and pamphlets on the subject.

Meanwhile, the pace of aggression had been stepped up in Europe and Asia. Italy penetrated Ethiopia in 1935 and Hitler moved into the Rhineland the year following. Japan had gone into Manchuria several years before. In a significant speech delivered in Chicago in October, 1937, President Roosevelt shouted that aggressors must be quarantined. That same year both Hitler and Mussolini were aiding Franco in the Spanish Civil War, and Japan attacked China. On April 30, 1937, Club President E. L. Hartig warned that the "enviable tradition" of the Union League Club must be maintained.

The Union League Club now became more than ever concerned with patriotic education. The Club's annual competitions for high school students to commemorate the birthday of George Washington were augmented by offering individual medals to winners in divisional contests, and university scholarships to first and second place winners in the finals of public speaking contests. Speakers like Colonel Frank Knox, publisher of the Chicago *Daily News* and Republican candidate for Vice-President in 1936, Bainbridge Colby, and Herbert Hoover appeared under Union League auspices.

The continued upholding of the American principle and the American way of life was put squarely up to the Union League Club membership by President Nicholas J. Conrad in calling for a referendum by mail on the restatement of the Union League Club principles in 1938. This restatement of principles was approved by the Club by a ratio of 24 to 1 and was formally adopted by the Club at a special meeting on January 30, 1938. From this spiraled a movement called the "America, Wake Up!" crusade. Newspapers and other publications throughout the nation were at once enthusiastic about this movement. The New York *Times* on February 13, 1938, carried a long story under the headline: WAKE UP! WARNS THE UNION LEAGUE CLUB.

With Conrad as chairman of the steering committee, the crusade was carried on through two more years in an effort "to preserve the fundamental principles that have made this nation great." Many noted speakers, including General James G. Harbord, Dr. Eduard Benes, former president of the Czechoslovak Republic, and General Charles P. Summerall, came to Chicago

Cartoonist Ernest C. Wilbur depicts the Club's plan for an "America, Wake Up" crusade through press, radio, and forum.

to address meetings. The committee spent almost $30,000, and among other things printed and distributed more than one-half million "Horse-and-Buggy Sense" pamphlets. Pamphlet No. 10 of this series urged every citizen to "support men for office who are American to the core," and to "check every candidate as if you personally were hiring him and entrusting him with all you hold dear."

The outbreak of World War II in 1939 created new problems in both foreign and domestic policies. Fearful that certain bills before Congress "embodied encroachments dangerous to American liberty and the American system of government," the Club in 1940 initiated a statement of national policy which recognized the necessity of concentrated power in the executive in the time of emergency and of unity in the successful prosecution of the preparedness program. This statement further urged that Congress "should not surrender its power and duties, and that the present emergency can be met without endangering the liberties upon which our government is founded." It also urged that President Roosevelt should not be given unrestricted powers and that Congress should remain in continuous session during the grave situation, and "thereby preserve supervision over governmental policies vested in it by the Constitution." This statement of national policy had been submitted to the Club membership, and with 54 per cent of the total of 2,500 membership voting, including members in twenty-five states, had been approved by 86½ per cent.

France collapsed in June of 1940, and in the autumn of that year the United States military draft went into operation. By 1941 this country was in a state of undeclared war with Germany, and Kenneth E. Rice, as president of the Union League Club, felt that "in these dark and troublous times" members would do well to reread and study the primary credo of the Club engraved on the mantel over the fireplace in the lounge. "It is well, indeed," his annual message read, "in times of turmoil and hysteria, when nations are attempting to devour each other, when men are being set against men, to reinvigorate our thinking by considering this sound fundamental principle, and when the issue is fully resolved, regardless of whether we think it right or wrong, every Union League Club member will be following it, wherever it is unfurled. Less than that we could not do and be true to the Union League principles and tradition."

Just a short time before, on February 14, 1941, the Chicago *Daily News* carried a story that "The Union League Club Sends First Private to the Army." W. O. Schilling, Jr., executive of the Fidelity & Guaranty Company, volunteered through Evanston Draft Board No. 5. He was twenty-seven and a graduate of the University of Wisconsin.

On the evening of November 19, 1941, former President Herbert Hoover, distinguished honorary member of the Club, spoke before a dinner audience of 681 in the Clubhouse. His speech, "Shall We Send Armies to Europe?," was broadcast from coast to coast. Hoover appealed for tolerance, understanding, and unity at home, and preservation not only of the Four Freedoms but of the "Fifth Freedom"—Free Enterprise—as well.

"If this becomes a war of expeditionary forces," he said, "it will be so long a war that vested interests, vested habits, the power of those who would destroy the Fifth Freedom will forge so permanently the totalitarianism of war that we can forget the Four Freedoms, and the Fifth Freedom as well.

"The destruction of freedom will come to America from within our borders, not from overseas. Our people are sadly divided and confused. The first need of this nation in the presence of danger is more unity of purpose. The task of statesmen is to find that common ground. . . .

"I therefore suggest that the attempt at artificial conditioning of the American mind for war should stop. Democracy will live on truth alone. The country needs assurance that no preparation or moves in that direction will be taken without prior authority of the Congress.

"Nations can blunder into war. But they cannot blunder into lasting peace. . . . Surely if we ceased to fan hate and fear, if we have labor peace, if we definitely act to preserve the Fifth Freedom, if our people are definitely assured that we are not going to send our armies to Europe without the authority of Congress, that we have a practical plan to preserve peace after the war—then we could summon far greater unity. Then also we might summon the whole world to reason."

Prior to Pearl Harbor, the Public Affairs Committee had devoted its attention to formulating a program which would express the attitude of the Union League Club toward the rapidly developing international situation and at the same time direct attention to the necessity of preserving free enterprise

Charles Gates Dawes, Herbert Hoover, and Club President Ferre C. Watkins at the Club's dinner meeting in 1941 when Mr. Hoover spoke on "Shall We Send Armies to Europe?"

as a basic factor in the so-called American way of life. After Pearl Harbor, the committee co-operated with Club President Ferre C. Watkins and the Board of Directors in organizing the Club's War Service Committee.

Founders' Day had come on December 19 that year, twelve days after Pearl Harbor, and at this time the Club adopted resolutions pledging its members to do their utmost in behalf of the war effort and urging individual members to assist to the greatest extent in the nation's efforts for victory.

This War Committee, headed by Lanning Macfarland, soon found that the government and its semi-official agencies were covering practically all civilian war service efforts. Those things which had been done by the Club's War Committee in World War I were now being done by the government.

The War Service Committee therefore decided that the

273

Club's most effective function at the start would be to "keep our members informed as to the various avenues of war service available, and assist them to find roles for individual service where they would be most effective." A war service office and information bureau was at once opened in the Club, with Mrs. Nita Huckins Herczel as secretary. Information regarding enlistments in the different branches of the service was provided, and appointments were made for members and others to donate blood to the Red Cross blood bank. Victory gardens and Salvage for Victory campaigns were sponsored. A speakers bureau was established, and protective measures planned in the event of air raids. The committee loaned a billiard table to one of the railroad station lounges for troops in transit. It aided in all the so-called "drives" and official programs. The Fathers of Sons in Service group contributed money to the Red Cross for use in behalf of American prisoners in enemy hands. This group numbered 278 members in 1943 and was headed by Judge Warren H. Orr as chairman. That year it gave substantially to the Red Cross.

Many individual members did their share, too, in acts of kindness and consideration to service men. A striking illustration of this was revealed after the war, when the Club received the following letter from Jim Hart, former captain of infantry of Louisville, Kentucky:

Shortly after Christmas of 1944, two other officers and myself were passing through Chicago on our way to Burma. We had but a few hours to spend in your city between trains. In the station a gentleman whose name I've forgotten introduced himself and took us to the Union League Club where we were immensely refreshed by a steam bath and a shower.

As we were leaving the Union League Club, an elderly gentleman of Swedish extraction asked if we were going overseas. We told him we were on our way, and he expressed his regrets that he didn't have time to entertain us. Later we found that he had surreptitiously slipped a fifty dollar bill into an overcoat pocket of each of the three of us. It was a kind act, and we appreciated the spirit more than the money. The three of us often spoke of that gentleman and remembered him with a great deal of warmth. In the jungles of Burma it was something nice to look back upon and know that was the kind of folks we were fighting for. Each of us got a Jap for him. . . . You can tell him for me that when he gets to Valhalla he will find the doors open and a noisy welcome from two soldiers he singled out of the busiest city in the world for a pat on the back and a word of encouragement. It was little things like that that kept the war on the road.

Hart's two buddies had been killed, but before they died they made him promise, if he survived, to bring back a Japanese battleflag to be presented to the "elderly gentleman of Swedish extraction." The Club member turned out to be C. E. Wickman, founder and president of the Greyhound Bus Lines.

A Club Roll of Honor for World War II was kept in the lobby. As of May 1, 1946, this roster contained the names of 121 members, 1,002 sons, 20 daughters, and 75 grandchildren of members in the armed forces. There also were 39 Club employees and 812 young men from the Union League Boys' Clubs in the services, making the grand total of 2,069, according to the report of the last chairman, George H. Redding. During the fifty-one month period of the War Service Committee's existence, a large sum was contributed by members to defray the expenses of the Club's special war service program. The unexpended funds existing when the committee was dissolved were authorized by the Club to be used in making provision for placement and vocational training of returning veterans.

Chapter Twenty-Two

CLUB SERVICE – ORDINARY
AND EXTRAORDINARY

THERE HAS NEVER BEEN ANY PROVISION IN THE BY-LAWS OF THE Union League Club which even vaguely hinted that a member might be asked to ride a coal truck, run an elevator, or be responsible for the removal of the garbage. Certainly there has been nothing in the house rules that suggested a Club member should wind the lobby clock, put out the Club cat, or bed down the furnace for the night. Members of the Club have relied on three hundred or more employees who could be depended on to do everything necessary for their convenience, comfort, and pleasure. These employees have been paid more than $1,000,000 annually to perform every type of duty from managing the Club to the picking up of a burnt match on the lobby floor.

During all its history the Club has maintained cordial relations with its employees, with one or two exceptions when there were clashes with the labor unions. The late Judge Jesse Holdom liked to tell about what he termed a "revolution" in the Club.

"Those were days (1918) when union waiters, chefs and cooks served the Club," he was wont to recount. "The inevitable strike came, and every waiter in the Club, including the head waiters, the chefs, cooks, and other kitchen mechanics walked out. All had been harmonious to that time. The pretense for the *causus belli* was a demand for a closed shop in which none but union men would be employed. To this demand the Club management had refused to yield, maintaining among other things that a Club was a man's home and the closed shop principle was not applicable to the home." The result of this strike was a disruption of restaurant service, and for weeks the restaurant remained closed. Finally, waiters and a crew to work in the kitchen were engaged and the open shop idea prevailed. Then, in the spring of 1918, under new Club management and with a drastic change in policy, waitresses were employed for the first time.

At that time Club members had been inconvenienced, but some thirty years later, when the Club again experienced labor trouble, the situation was met in a more serious fashion. The closed shop became the issue again, and once more the Club took a determined stand. This strike began on February 21, 1948, when, as the result of disagreement between the Club and the Elevator Operators' and Starters' Union over questions involving the closed shop and other matters, the union called out the Club's elevator operators on strike. Although the Club had always insisted on the right to hire and dismiss its employees as it saw fit, without regard to union membership, there had been no discrimination against union members, and at the time there were a number of union members working as engineers and in the kitchens. Wartime labor shortage had resulted in the temporary employment of girls as elevator operators. The girls were not union members at the time of their employment, but were organized by the union during their employment by the Club.

The strike of the elevator operators was ineffective, since operation of the elevators by other Club personnel was easy. Accordingly, without discussion of any kind with the Club, the union then called out the engineers and the cooks on a sympathy strike and established a picket line around the Clubhouse.

A special meeting of the Board of Directors was called late in the afternoon to consider what should be done. President

UNION LEAGUE-UNION BUSTER

Exclusive Club of the Rich Refuses To Recognize Elementary Rights of Its Underpaid Employees.

Sixteen (16) elevator operators join a union for the simple right to bargain collectively!

2,500 rich Union Leaguers said: "We are the bosses here. We refuse to recognize a legitimate Labor Union."

Sounds fantastic in the year of 1948, doesn't it? But that is the actual fact. This ultra-exclusive club of millionaires and billionaires is so incensed that sixteen elevator operators have joined Local 66, Elevator Operators' & Starters' Union that it has actually fired four girls for the sole "Crime" of signing a membership card! It has imported a professional strike-breaking agency to bring in strike-breakers from Kentucky and elsewhere! It has used its power and influence to circumvent and violate several city ordinances. These violations of the law and these shady practices don't seem to bother the conscience of the Union Leaguers for they are the fat over-stuffed bosses, they rule the land, and nobody can tell them what to do.

Local 66 is picketing the Union League Club day and night. We are merely asking for the workers the same terms and rights we have gained for 4,000 workers in hundreds of other buildings!

Is that unfair? The law, and all sense of justice, provides that Employers shall bargain collectively with any Union that represents a majority of its employees. Local 66 represents not a majority but 100% of the Union League elevator operators. This big club of the rich, however, refuses to recognize the rights of its employees.

We have no alternative but to fight back. And we shall continue to fight no matter what the cost, no matter what the sacrifice, until we have won for these 16 workers the same rights and the same privileges enjoyed by 50 million other American employees.

ELEVATOR OPERATORS' & STARTERS' UNION, LOCAL NO. 66

AMERICAN FEDERATION OF LABOR

"To see ourselves as others see us." Handbill issued during the elevator operators' strike of 1948.

Frank C. Rathje was out of town and First Vice-President Robert W. T. Purchas presided. Joseph A. Matter, who was present as Club secretary, later said about the meeting: "A serious decision had to be made. The board was told during the meeting that the engineers and firemen had all left the Club-house, that steam was decreasing in the boilers, and that by mid-night the Club would be without heat.

"Vital club machinery also was dependent on engineering

operation. The day was cold, and as the board's deliberations continued, the boardroom became less and less comfortable. Vice-President Purchas expressed the view that he and the board members had been put in office to keep the Club open and not to close it. However, the general feeling on the part of the board members was that an issue was at stake which the majority of the members of the Club would wish the board to sustain. It was felt that the Club, as a private institution, should be permitted to hire and dismiss its employees without outside interference. On the question of whether the Club's officers or the union was to run the Club, the principles on which the Club was founded seemed to leave little room for compromise. It was determined to refuse to give in, and to do everything possible to maintain normal Club services, but if necessary to close the Clubhouse until necessary operational arrangements could be made."

After this decision of the board, Vice-President Purchas, who was a graduate engineer and who was living in the Clubhouse, went at once to the engine room with Taylor Hay, the manager. Here they found that the coal supply was low, hardly sufficient to last through the night, but they were concerned just then with heating the Club. With considerable difficulty, engineers were found to operate the boilers and the engine room. The next problem was to obtain coal, since no Chicago dealer could deliver fuel through the picket lines. Two truck loads were brought to the Club the first night, but only one was successfully unloaded. The Club then adopted the expedient of purchasing its own coal outside the state and bringing it to the Clubhouse in trucks rented by it and manned by drivers hired for the purpose.

These drivers were subjected to considerable abuse by the pickets, and in order to bolster their morale and assist them through the picket lines, a number of members of the Club volunteered to meet the trucks some distance from the Clubhouse and to ride with the drivers the remainder of the distance. Probably between sixty and one hundred members of the Club helped in this manner, riding trucks, shoveling coal, and doing whatever else was required to effect the deliveries. Karl E. Seyfarth, a lawyer living in the Clubhouse who was particularly active in assisting the deliveries, recalls that one very cold night he saw Vice-President Purchas, "a dapper sort of fellow, wearing a Chesterfield overcoat with velvet collar, and black derby, in the alley on top of a truck load of coal, shoveling away with all his might." The truck was the type that did not automatically unload, and its contents had to be unloaded by hand.

When it became apparent that coal was being obtained by the Club in sufficient quantities, city police began arresting the Club's drivers for not having city sealer's weight certificates. It was argued that such certificates were necessary under an ordinance which had been passed to discourage out-of-town dealers from delivering coal in Chicago. The certificate was required to give the weight of the truck loaded and unloaded, and as a result, out-of-town drivers would have to pull into a weighing station at the city limits, unload their trucks and have them weighed, and then reload them for another weigh.

Although the Club maintained that the ordinance was obviously not applicable to coal brought into the state by its owner for his own use and in his own trucks, police continued to arrest the drivers. In all, a total of twenty-nine arrests were made, after each of which a representative of the Club would go to the police station with the driver and post the necessary $200 bail. Litigation instituted by the Club, which was handled for the Club by Member Paul R. Conaghan, was carried to the Illinois Supreme Court, which ruled that the ordinance did not apply to the Club's coal deliveries.

It should perhaps be mentioned that the arrests of the Club's truck drivers were not made by members of the police detail assigned to maintain order during strikes. This detail, under the supervision of Captain George T. Barnes, was on duty on the outside of the Clubhouse throughout the strike and maintained strict impartiality. Many times during the progress of the strike, Club officers expressed appreciation of the effective and fair work done by Captain Barnes and his men.

During the period of the strike, unanimous support was given the Club by its members. All inconveniences and the austerity of the restaurant menu were accepted with cheerful resignation. Club employees helped out in the kitchen and dining rooms. Miss Leah Foster and Miss Nell Huey of the reception desk went up to the Wigwam and served coffee and sandwiches. Miss Dorothy Wilson, assistant to the secretary, with Miss Anne Mulvihill and Miss Mary Peifer, worked in the kitchen. "I never baked so many pies in my life," recalls Miss Wilson. She said she and her helpmates turned out some eighty pies a day. Mrs. Herczel, on her way to work each day, would stop at Piper's Bakery, on North Wells Street, load a taxicab with bread and bring it to the Club. Meat was delivered through the front door by parcel post.

Florence Mulholland, Club comptroller, and Alberta Lund, her assistant, remember the reluctance of the old employees of the Club to leave when the union insisted that they do so. One employee, unable to trust himself to come for his back pay without breaking down, sent his wife. Many had tears in their eyes as they left the Club.

There was a truce during the strike on April 8 when the Club held a dinner in honor of Archibald Clark Kerr, Lord Inverchapel, retiring British ambassador to the United States. As he represented the Labor government in England, his Lordship did not deem it exactly cricket to walk through a picket line. So when Lord Inverchapel arrived at the Club, the pickets were temporarily withdrawn. While Lord Inverchapel stated that this had been arranged by William Green, then president of the American Federation of Labor, without knowledge of the British embassy, Martin J. Dwyer, president of Local 66 which had called the strike, recounted that hurried telephone calls had been made from the embassy in Washington to labor officials, and as a result "the ambassador's entry to the Club was then cleared by temporary removal of the pickets." A gentleman's agreement was made, the Club promising not to take advantage of the absence of pickets, but as soon as the ambassador left town the pickets returned and the small war was resumed.

The Club's attitude was expressed by Club President Frank C. Rathje, who made his annual report before the strike ended: "Because of the nature of our organization, its objectives and its functions, the Board of Directors of the Club feel that we cannot tolerate a 'closed shop' or a 'union shop'; that we must, under all circumstances, insist on the maintenance of an 'open shop' with all the term implies." He said employment opportunities for qualified individuals, regardless of their affiliation with outside organizations, "is our aim." A. Pope Lancaster, chairman of the House Committee's subcommittee on food, reported that attendance in the Club restaurants had been down "less than 10 per cent during the strike." As union musicians would not go through the picket lines, the Friday night parties, known as "Nights of Fun," had been temporarily discontinued, but later a "turn-table was secured and records used to supply music for dancing." At this same time a city-wide printers' strike was going on, and Dr. Edward M. Martin, as editor of the Club's *Men and Events* magazine, had trouble maintaining his publishing schedule and some issues were omitted. John R. Thompson, chairman of the Publications Committee, reported that under the circumstances "a remarkable publishing job" had been done.

When it became apparent that the Club would not yield in its principles and that the strike had reached a point where its

John L. Enright, who
served the Club for
sixty-five years.

lack of effectiveness was harming the union, a settlement was
reached which left the situation exactly where it had been at the
start. The Club remained free to select its own employees without regard to their status as union members, but with the understanding that the Club would continue its existing policy under
which no discrimination was made against union members in
the hiring of employees.

The Union League Club has boasted many loyal employees.
John L. Enright, who went to work in the Club as a checkroom
boy in 1888, was one. At a dinner given by the Club to veteran
employees, Enright, then assistant manager, in responding to a
toast by Bernard E. Sunny, whose membership dated back to one
year before Enright came with the Club, said: "I've seen this
Club change from what they called an old man's club fifty years
ago to an organization of younger men. Our members of a half
century ago, I might add, were not as old as they looked, but
they wore whiskers and top hats, and had to live up to such
things."

Enright died August 15, 1953, in his room at the Club to

which he had devoted a lifetime of service—both ordinary and extraordinary. Dorothy Wilson recalls one time when Patrick H. Joyce, president of the Chicago and Great Western Railroad, learned by cable that his wife was seriously ill in London. Joyce was living at the Club at the time. He made hurried arrangements to leave for London. When he arrived at the entrance with his baggage he found Enright there, his own suitcase in hand.

"I'm going with you, sir," said Enright, in response to the questioning look on the face of Joyce. "That is going to be a long, hard trip, and if you will pardon me, sir, I probably can be of some help."

Enright went with Joyce. When they found that Mrs. Joyce was in no immediate danger, the two then toured Europe together for three months, after which they brought Mrs. Joyce back home. Later Enright explained: "It was just a part of the Club service."

The high regard in which Enright was held by Club members proved unfortunate for him on one occasion. Enright had handled the details of a banquet at the Club for bankers who met to consummate the merger of the Central Trust Company and the National Bank of the Republic into the Central Republic bank. As the bankers took their seats, Enright was invited to sit with them. They wanted to let him in on a "good thing," and Enright pledged his entire life savings of $10,000. But the new bank went broke, and being a state bank the stockholders were doubly liable—so Enright not only lost his $10,000 but had to pay off a debt of $10,000 more.

On June 9, 1938, the Club honored the white-haired, twinkling-eyed Enright for fifty years' service. Mayor Edward J. Kelly was one of the guests at the luncheon, and Club President Nicholas J. Conrad, before presenting Enright with a plaque and a gold-headed cane, told of an occasion when the

Board of Directors of the Club received a strange request from a member concerning Enright. "The Board was deeply scandalized when the host of a United States senator asked permission to administer a thrashing to this mischievous hat-check boy after he had donned the senatorial headpiece and paraded around the lobby," said Conrad. Only the intercession of the amused senator saved Enright from being discharged.

There was another occasion when members complained of Enright's squeaky shoes. So Enright cast aside his shoes and appeared in bright red carpet slippers. "He almost got the boot," recalled a member.

Steve Kelley, another veteran, was one of the most remarkable bartenders in the Union League Club, or any other club, for that matter. He never tasted "anything alcoholic," explaining thus: "My mother in Neenah, Wisconsin, was a temperance leader, and at an early age I had instilled in me the evil effects of alcohol. I can still remember the 'stomach plates' and other lurid bits of art they used to illustrate the temperance lectures. All of these depicted what a man's insides looked like when he took strong drink. I can say the interior decoration was not

Steve Kelley, head barman at the Club for nearly sixty-five years.

pretty. Then there were moralizing poems and plays and songs and faces on the barroom floors and little girls crying 'Father, dear father, come home with me now.' I came to the conclusion that liquor was good for—the other fellow."

When Kelley came to the Club in 1889 there had been a rapid turnover of wine clerks, as bartenders were euphemistically termed. "My immediate predecessor as a wine clerk always started the day by drinking gin sours, and by ten o'clock in the morning he was tired and sleepy. When I took the job I not only wanted to keep it, but I wanted to stay awake and see everything that was going on."

The House Committee gave a big party in 1939 signalizing Kelley's half century of service to the Club. Alex D. Bailey, committee chairman, presented an engraved watch to him as a token of the Club's appreciation. Steve fondly treasured the watch, keeping it in a chamois cover.

"What time is it, Steve?" his friends used to ask him, just to see him carefully, almost tenderly, take the watch out of its protective cover and answer each inquiry with a knowing smile.

There had been one clubman who got into trouble with the Board of Directors, and who explained to the "jury" that his fondness for double bacardi cocktails was to blame. "The 'jury,' or Board of Directors, first tried the man and then they tried the double bacardi cocktails—then new in Chicago," explained Kelley. "They grew very sympathetic with the man's case."

Kelley usually had a story about one or more of the famous Club members he had known. He liked to recall how Frank O. Lowden, then a young attorney, told him a conversation he, Lowden, had had with George M. Pullman, whose daughter, Florence, Lowden married. "Mr. Pullman explained that Florence had extravagant tastes and spent a great amount of money," Lowden told Kelley. "He said to me, 'I don't think you will be able to buy Florence flowers on the $3,000 a year you make.' 'No, I won't, Mr. Pullman,' I said, 'She will have to do without flowers.' And she did—for a long time."

New anecdotes about Kelley continually come up when Club members meet at one of the bars. There was the story of the Club member who was required to move to Europe for business purposes. He was gone for fourteen years. On his first day back in Chicago he went into the Club bar. Steve Kelley quietly asked him, "Will you have your usual, sir?"

One day Louis Jacoby, Chicago correspondent of The Chase National Bank of the City of New York, sat down at the bar in the Wigwam. In the course of his conversation with Kelley he said he had been trying to meet F. J. Sensenbrenner, founder and president of the Kimberly-Clark Lumber Company.

"Well, that shouldn't be hard," said Kelley. "I know you, and Mr. Sensenbrenner and I were classmates in Neenah, Wisconsin, many years ago."

A few days later Kelley introduced Jacoby and Sensenbrenner and some time after this the two closed a $100,000 deal. "Simple as manufacturing a pousse café or polishing a crystal glass," grinned Kelley.

On July 20, 1954, Steve Kelley retired as the Club's head barman, after nearly sixty-five years of service. He had tried retirement in 1941 and returned to his boyhood home in Neenah, but after sixty days he was back at work. This time, however, his retirement was on "doctor's orders," and he died only a few weeks after his last day on the job.

Chapter Twenty-Three

WITHIN THESE WALLS

WITHIN THE WALLS OF THE UNION LEAGUE'S TWENTY-THREE story Clubhouse daily occurs a veritable cavalcade of human activities which reflect the varied interests of its more than four thousand members. The Clubhouse is both a service center for its members and their guests and a focal point for its members' many contacts with the social, civic, cultural, business and professional life of Greater Chicago.

There are so many things going on at the Union League that it would be difficult to imagine any one member who could be interested in all its varied activities or who could take advantage of all its services and facilities. Such a member would have to be a composite of hundreds, and could be nothing less than a Superclubman. However, if there did exist such a Superclubman, endowed with superior qualities of all kinds as well as with ubiquity, let us examine the many things which might engross him.

First, our Superclubman would be interested in the fourteen civic committees and groups which make the Club such a vital force in the community. Through the work of these committees, the Superclubman—and all members of the Club, of course—is kept informed of current events and encouraged to suggest or take action on vital issues. These committees and groups embrace Citizenship, City Manager Plan, Civil Defense, Elections, National Defense, Public Administration, Public Finance, Rebuilding

Metropolitan Chicago, Schools, Senatorial Redistricting of Illinois, Traffic Safety, Foreign Affairs, Race Relations, and the Jefferson-Lincoln Junto.

The Superclubman would be a busy man when he fulfilled his duties in connection with another phase of Club activities: the Members' Activities Groups. These internal groups appeal to Superclubman's—and individual members'—avocations, business interests, recreations, civic interests, and varied studies. Superclubman would find that one of the most active of these is the Railway Supply Group, which holds regular meetings as a part of a comprehensive program designed to interest those in the railway supply industry. Superclubman would sit in with members of the group and their guests to hear noted leaders of the transportation industry at the Clubhouse on alternate Friday noons. At other times he would meet with similar groups organized for members in the fields of insurance and law.

Being, of course, a war veteran, Superclubman would often be seen in the "Dugout," the headquarters of Union League Post No. 758 of the American Legion on the nineteenth floor of the Clubhouse. He would attend the weekly luncheon meetings on Mondays in these headquarters and find satisfaction in the speeches of special guests.

Most certainly Superclubman would be enrolled in the two Great Books courses, which are open to members and their families and friends. He would meet with recognized leaders for reading and discussion in the eighteen two-hour evening meetings during the year. Then he might hurry to attend the Younger Men's Group, another active unit, known as the "get-acquainted center" for members under forty, where "grandfathers are excluded except by special arrangement." Superclubman would attend the monthly meetings where guest speakers talk on "topics of current interest," and the regular Wednesday luncheon round table in the Wigwam, and be on

A Members Activity Group for reading and discussing the Great Books.

hand for the summertime sessions in the pool, and be interested in the group's two investment trusts, the "Wigwam Trust" and its more speculative twin, the "Kennel Trust."

Again, Superclubman would find himself busy with various activities appealing to members' hobbies—the Camera Group, the Fin, Fur, Feather Fans, the Union League Round Table, the Chess Group, the Speakers' Forum, and the Christian Fellowship Group, initiated by Walker O. Lewis to afford members and their guests monthly opportunity for luncheon, followed by inspirational talks and discussion.

We have seen that Superclubman is blessed with omnipresence. He would need it to take full advantage of the affiliated services and facilities available to him—the barbershop, the card room, and the billiard room; the Cigar Department, the Theater

Ticket Desk, the Service Department, which "keeps things on the move," the Transportation Desk, the Valet Service, the Reception Desk, and the Housekeeping Department, which give round-the-clock service to the members and guests who occupy the 232 sleeping rooms in the Clubhouse.

To keep in touch with all phases of the Club's activities he would subscribe to *Union League Men and Events*, which under the alert editorship of Nita Huckins Herczel undertakes faithfully to reflect the interests and activities of the Club.

Our Superclubman would find much to interest him in the Athletic Department. Located on the top floors of the building, with the swimming pool on the twenty-first floor, the department is patronized daily by a large number of members who have taken out special annual memberships entitling them to unlimited use of all of the department's services. Superclubman would join other members for a noontime plunge, followed by luncheon at tankside. Or he would take a swimming workout at the end of the business day. Possibly he would want to set a record for distance, and would swim so many laps a day in an endeavor to outdo

Chess, also, has its ardent devotees among Club members. A close match always draws an interested audience.

E. D. Uhlendorf, who swam over three thousand miles in the pool during twenty-two years.

Every type of exercise and athletic activity is offered, with expert supervision and coaching from the Club's athletic staff under the guidance of Director John L. Gray. There is a regular schedule of organized play, in addition to every facility for individual workouts and exercise. The gymnasium is the scene of daily volleyball games, handball games, and contests on the badminton courts. There are individual exercise rooms, rowing machines, a mechanical horse, and a complete health department with showers, steam baths, hot rooms, massage, and sun lamps.

Teams of members have represented the department in inter-club competition in squash rackets, volleyball, and handball. Young athletes who received their early training in the junior gym classes conducted each Saturday by the department for sons and grandsons of members have won individual honors in swimming and football in collegiate competition.

The Athletic Department's periodic exhibitions of swimming, diving, and gymnastics are special features, particularly of the annual New Year's Day open house program. These attractions have included the men's and women's swimming champions of the Central A.A.U.; the gymnastic teams of the University of Chicago, and the Chicago Turnverein; Jess Willard, Jack Purcell, Hugh Forggie, and Ken Davidson, badminton champions; the Jesters Club Team from London and the Chicago champions —Jimmie Anderson, Dave Pope, and Charles Hoerger—in squash racquets; as well as champions Joe Platek, Lefty Coyle, and Ken Snyder in handball; and world champion Coleman Clark in table tennis. Jack Dempsey and Gene Tunney have worked out in the gymnasium, and the Yale University swimming team uses the Club pool to keep in practice when passing through Chicago.

The swimming pool provides its share of anecdotes concerning the Athletic Department. Judge L. A. Stebbins was in the

Hotly contested volleyball
matches are daily features
in the Club gymnasium.

Daily swims in the Club's
pool with luncheons served
poolside.

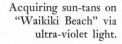

Acquiring sun-tans on
"Waikiki Beach" via
ultra-violet light.

habit of swimming in the raw until a change in the house rules specified that trunks must be worn. It appears that an Englishman, on being shown over the building, had been shocked when he saw naked bathers cavorting in the pool. The Board of Directors reacted by voting a taboo on nudity. Judge Stebbins responded in his own fashion. He appeared in the pool with his trunks on. But they were on, or around, his neck. The legal-minded jurist maintained he was abiding by the rule, as it did not specify where the trunks should be worn. Finally the house rules were changed again. Now it is optional whether swimmers wear trunks around their necks or anywhere else, or whether they wear what nature gave them.

Keeping the pool at the right temperature winter and summer is one of Director Gray's special tasks. Gray finds that most members like the water at a temperature around eighty degrees. In the unusually hot summer of 1942 it proved hard to maintain this temperature, so in response to a committee member's suggestion, cakes of ice were dumped into the pool. It took one ton of ice to lower the ninety thousand gallons of water one degree in temperature. This one degree of heat given up by the pool raised the atmosphere around it one degree. It looked as if he couldn't win, Gray thought. But his troubles were solved when a distressed chorus of yells came from the bar because of a shortage of ice there for highballs. The highball drinkers won.

The women in Superclubman's family would find that women of the Union League Club have their own department and their own programs. Available to them are such facilities as the Ladies' Lounge on the second floor, the bridge room on the fifth floor, and the cocktail lounge on the fifth floor, where men are admitted only as escorts. Women can also take advantage of breakfast in the Wigwam and luncheon and dinner service in the Main Dining Room. Provided for them, too, are private dining rooms for conferences, parties, bridge luncheons, re-

"Friday Nights of Fun" attract weekly quotas of merrymakers.

ceptions, and weddings. Regular parties for women are held
once each month. Lectures or book reviews are followed by
luncheon or bridge. Special family parties are held on Saturday afternoons, with educational features and motion picture
travelogues. The traditional open house on New Year's Day is
another event on the women's calendar, and the principal family
party is the children's annual Christmas party. The Union
League Club is one of the few private clubs which has guest-
room accommodations for women.

Of prime importance to Superclubman would be the Union
League Club cuisine, which has always been justly famous. A
list of the chefs who have been employed by the Club reads
like the Blue Book of chefdom. Although the many-course meals
with a different wine for each course which were the accepted

thing for banquets during the Victorian era are no longer in favor, and the use of table wines in this country has not been able to stage a successful comeback since the prohibition era, the Club still has available on its wine list 387 wines and liquors.

One pastry chef employed by the Club a few years ago had for many years been pastry chef at Buckingham Palace, where it had been his pleasant duty to make the fruit cakes which the King and Queen sent to favored subjects at Christmas. Fruit cakes made after this recipe are still made in the Club kitchens in large numbers each holiday season for purchase by members as gifts for their friends.

The old-timers will reminisce for hours about famous dinners held in the Club. Outstanding in the minds of many was the "game dinner" held in the Clubhouse on the evening of December 2, 1909.

The Grand Pacific Hotel had gained an international reputation fifteen years before for its annual game dinners, and now the Club sought to revive the custom. Some three hundred tuxedo-clad members attended at $7.00 a plate, and sat down to a wildwood repast consisting of game broth, fried brook trout meunière, breast of partridge en casolette, wild cherry ice, haunch of venison, canvasback duck Cumberland with wild rice and fried hominy, and "bear ice cream." The menu card was bound in simulated birchbark tied with beaded buckskin thongs, and the room was decorated with large leafy trees, which had been cut down and brought in for the occasion. On the tables were game groups molded from tallow. Over this sylvan scene hung an electrically-lighted "moon" which moved slowly back and forth overhead.

So successful was this game dinner, that after wiping their lips the Club members agreed it should be an annual affair. However, an inquisitive reporter found that certain of the game served was out of season. The case went before a judge. Frank O.

Lowden defended the Club, and on his argument that a man's club was his home and game could be served at any time in a man's home, the sympathetic judge dismissed the case.

Later the game dinner tradition was carried on for a quarter of a century by Member Luther M. Walter, who annually invited friends and associates to partake of moose, bear, and venison steaks from quarry shot by him in the Canadian wilds. More recently the Fin, Fur, Feather Fans have undertaken valiantly to continue the tradition.

Many dinners have been held at the Club which are notable for superior cuisine, gustatory delight, or epicurean exactitude. Many professional societies have held their monthly, quarterly, or annual meetings there for several decades. During the holiday season, in particular, the private dining room facilities are taxed to capacity with annual dinners, parties, or get-togethers for which accommodations are reserved a year in advance. Individual members have given select private dinners at the Club with charges for food and wine running as high as $60.00 per plate. An outstanding series of privately sponsored occasions during past years has been the dinner meetings of the Red Cross of Constantine, a Masonic society, whose members attend in full dress with decorations.

A dinner of more than ordinary interest was held at the Club on February 26, 1952. The Chicago chapter of the London Wine and Food Society selected the Club to serve the Society's annual Ladies' Night Dinner. The Society wished to duplicate in its entirety the state dinner served Queen Elizabeth of England, —then Princess Elizabeth—and the Duke of Edinburgh in Montreal during their Canadian trip in 1951. The Club duplicated exactly the seven-course dinner, although in order to do so it proved necessary to fly from Canada pheasant raised at the Oka Monastery, and to fly in from England a particular variety of sole. Especially noteworthy was the fact that, with only one

A corner of the Main Dining Room in the present Clubhouse, a favorite meeting place for members and their guests.

exception, each of the vintage wines served at the state dinner was available in the Club's own wine cellars.

Several years ago, when the Chicago Société de Chefs de Cuisine wished to stage a model buffet as an example to its members, the Union League Club was selected for the purpose. Some Chicago organizations use the Club regularly for their evening banquets. One of the most interesting of these is the Boswell Club of Chicago, a club of Chicago businessmen, each of whom has taken the name of a prominent literary figure of Johnsonian England, and who dine together once a month for good fellowship over food and wine and for round-table discussion of the personalities and literature of the Johnson-Boswell period.

Although less glamorous, the main business of the Club's

catering department is, of course, the daily serving of food and drink to its hungry members and their guests. An average day in the Club sees two thousand breakfasts, lunches, and dinners served in the Main Dining Room, members' grill, fifth floor buffet, and fifteen private dining rooms, all of which are air-conditioned. An average of 125 employees are engaged in the preparation and serving of food. Members' appreciation of the quality of the food and service is evidenced by the constantly increasing number of meals served.

Club members sometimes use the Club's dining facilities for rather unorthodox purposes. One member, of a quiet and retiring nature, would occasionally enter the dining room with a pretty girl and ask for "the most prominent table in the room." It developed that the girl was his secretary, and when he kept her working late he always took her to dinner. "The first time I took her out I went to a 'hide-away,' as I was afraid the circumstances would be misunderstood and I didn't care to have anyone else see us," he explained later, "but there were at least five of my friends in the so-called 'hide-away' and they subsequently made my life miserable. So now I find no one says anything when I dine my secretary in full public view." Another member, however, looked at the situation a little differently. A flashlight picture had been taken in the dining room one evening and he was so sure that he and his secretary were in the picture that he endeavored to buy the negative then and there.

Of course, not all members of the Club avail themselves of the dining rooms for their downtown eating. Many stories are told of Charles Gates Dawes, who became Vice-President of the United States, and who was among the last of the so-called "rugged individualists." One day a Club member was in a drug store near the Club getting a hurried lunch. He saw General Dawes on a stool beside him. "Why, what are you doing *here*, General?" he asked in some surprise. "Doing the same as you are," snapped the General. "Trying to save some damn money."

Federal Judge Kenesaw Mountain Landis was a frequent visitor at the Club during the years he held court just across the street. One day the Judge was presiding at a murder trial, but was not feeling very well, and before leaving court for lunch ordered a recess until the next day. He went to the Club for lunch, and a friend suggested that Steve Kelley (the Club's chief bartender) could probably prescribe some medicine for him which would fix him up. Kelley poured a tumbler full of whiskey for the Judge. The medicine was so effective that after finishing it Judge Landis went to the telephone and called his bailiff: "I feel much better and will hold court this afternoon. Bring in the defendant and jury. I'll find the defendant guilty and hang him." The Judge was of course speaking facetiously. When he returned to court he proved himself very jealous of the rights of the defendant, as was his invariable way.

Things occasionally go wrong in the culinary department, and many humorous stories are told of the complaints and "gripes" by members. A favorite anecdote of John Gould was about a member back in the nineties who did not like the kind of pie he got every day at lunch. He made several verbal complaints to Club directors and each time was told to follow the by-laws and "put it in writing." Finally one day, seated at a large table with his friends, he received the usual order of apple pie. He gazed at it, growing red in the face, then beckoned to the waiter for paper and string. He took out his card, wrote his complaint on it, placed it on the pie, wrapped the pie neatly in the paper, and then took it down and deposited it in the complaint box. "A new pastry cook was shortly engaged," said Gould.

One of the most popular social occasions of the Club is the annual New Year's Day open house. This is the one day of the year on which the entire Clubhouse is open to the ladies. The

Athletic Department stages an exhibition of swimming and diving in the afternoon, after which an elaborate buffet dinner is served in the Main Dining Room and dancing is available in the Crystal Room. The Club's chefs exert themselves in the preparation of items for the fifty-foot buffet table, and many of their innovations produced for these buffets have won prizes in the Salon of Culinary Art, competitions conducted annually by the International Association of Chefs. At one time no charge was made for the open house, and members could invite friends. J. Frank Aldrich, one of the founding members, pooled all his social obligations one year and invited two hundred guests. That day three thousand people attended the New Year's Day party!

The Club's Friday night buffets are also highly popular. The buffet table is varied and extensive, and after dinner there is entertainment and music for dancing. At one time these parties were enlivened by bingo. When, several years ago, the city staged a political crack-down on gambling and games of chance and the Club decided to support the crusade by abolishing its bingo games, the anguished cry went up of "What! No bingo?"

One interesting feature of the Club is the number of informal

Prize-winning entries in the annual Salon of Culinary Art conducted by the International Association of Chefs.

table groups which meet daily for luncheon in the Main Dining Room or the Wigwam. Members are attracted to the various groups either by a common avocation, personal friendship, or business or professional interests.

Some old-timers recall the "Here-Comes-Harper Table," which gained its name through a chance remark by Eugene Field, the poet. Franklin Head, Harry Selfridge, George Marshall, Charles Truax, William H. Gray, Field, and others had occupied this table in the southeast corner of the dining room of the old Clubhouse. On one occasion a member of the group had taken out his pocketbook and was examining its contents when Field, looking up, saw President William R. Harper of the University of Chicago approaching. Dr. Harper was already known as a money-raiser for the university and had had no little part in getting Rockefeller and Marshall Field millions. Eugene Field on seeing him shouted to the man with the pocketbook, "Put up your money, here comes Harper!"

Chicago and North Western Railway officials and their business associates met informally in the Club dining rooms for twenty-five years, a group which included F. W. Sargent, G. B. Vilas, H. H. Brigham, and others. Every variety of fire insurance man was claimed at the "Smoke and Cinder Table." H. G. Buswell was at one time "acting president" of the group. One of the greatest assets of this table was Edward J. Rogerson, who could be counted on to supply brook trout when in season.

Old-timers recall with nostalgia the luncheon sessions at the large round table in the Tower Room of the old Clubhouse. It had its regular coterie, and newly-elected Club members were invited to sit there as a means of getting better acquainted. Those in attendance were always well rewarded by hearing several good stories or important pronouncements by men of affairs, or a battle of wits over some current issue.

One of the liveliest table groups in recent years came together through the efforts of Member Frederick S. Moffatt. Here, too, one could always hear a good story, words of political wisdom, or a hot exchange over the latest news from Washington.

Other daily "regular tables" in the Wigwam are the Legion Table, where members of Union League Post dine to the accompaniment of good-natured banter and persiflage, the Interfraternity Table, the Transportation Table, the Volleyball Table, the Card Room Table, and the "Kickers' Table," so named from a humorous aspersion which stuck. Several of the groups which had been organized in the old Clubhouse were continued in the new building. One such group in the Main Dining Room was the "Judges' Table."

No less than three different groups have used "Round Table" in their title. In the 1890's the first Round Table grew up around

The Tower Room of the old Clubhouse was famous as a meeting place.

Member I. K. Boyesen, brilliant wit, able lawyer, and noted after-dinner speaker. The "Knights of the Round Table which is at the Union League Club," a group of members in the fire insurance business, have met daily at lunch since 1909 and annually hold a pre-Christmas "joust." There is also the Union League Round Table, monthly dinner group for members, organized in 1943 by Rousseau Van Voorhies with the collaboration of Joseph A. Matter as Library Committee Chairman.

"In 1890, when I joined the Club," Charles H. Coffin has recalled, "the Round Table had grown up around Boyesen—it was never incorporated, had no officers, no rules or regulations, but 'just growed.' About the only established custom of the Round Table was to send flowers at the death of a regular member. Sometimes resolutions were passed. Discussions at the table 'were always free, full, and sometimes hot.' Once one of the members burst into tears at some particularly poignant criticism. However, most of the jibes were taken good-naturedly.

"I also remember the keen wit and good comradeship of Jacob R. Custer. Probably the best-loved man at the table was Fred N. Clark, who used to entertain us once a year at the Midlothian Club. I well remember the sweet-tempered, kindly Thomas Dent, and Myron B. Beach, who was a master of the *bon mot*. In general, there was a great deal of bright talk, much valuable information, and amateur book reviews."

The "Knights of the Round Table" since 1909 have held their annual "joust" at the Club the first Saturday in December, and its worthies rally from far and near for the jollification. Each member bears the title of one of King Arthur's henchmen, and the presiding officer's symbol of authority is a shillelagh. Each knight serves an apprenticeship as neophyte and is advanced with fitting ceremony through stages of esquire and finally knighthood. A. F. Dean was the first moderator. Others who have served include A. F. Powrie and Wellington R.

"Knights of the Round Table" at one of their annual pre-Christmas jousts, with Knight W. R. Townley wielding the shillelagh.

Townley. The latter wrote a history of the order including "a constitution, by-laws, and moral precepts by which it is governed."

The formation of the Union League Round Table in 1943 established a new pattern of member-activity and became a factor in the Club's sponsorship, beginning in 1946, of groups to read and discuss the Great Books. The Round Table's evening meetings open with a period of good fellowship, which is followed by dinner. Then comes the guest speaker's discourse, after which debate, impromptu and unconfined, continues until the subject and participants are exhausted. Moderators, who are annually elected by the group, include Rousseau Van Voorhies, Joseph A. Matter, George E. Turner, Wilfred S. Stone, and John F. Sullivan, Jr.

Barbershop harmonizing at a members' "Western" stag party.

There have, of course, been many stories and anecdotes concerning all phases of the Club's activities. One is the story of the "man who reached for a star." It happened this way: On Christmas Eve each year the Club, following its long tradition, erected one of the largest Christmas trees that could be found. Standing on the lobby floor, it reached up through the stairwell to the third floor. On this particular occasion, a certain guest had been at a holiday party on the eighth floor and was making his way perilously down the steps. At the third floor he saw the Star of Bethlehem sparkling on the top of the tree. He was fascinated by it and sought to possess it. But he lost his balance and fell. Branch after branch broke his fall until he hit the lobby floor. Considering his bruises and other afflictions, it was thought best to place him in a guest room over night. By the next morning he had forgotten his desire to have the Star of Bethlehem, but did have a vague recollection of something else. "What happened when that basement boiler exploded?" he asked.

Chapter Twenty-Four

THE LIBRARY AND ART COLLECTION

It has been frequently said that the club's library today is surpassed by no other club library in the country. Its fifteen thousand volumes are housed in quarters occupying almost half of the fourth floor of the Clubhouse. In addition to works for the permanent collection, several hundred current books are purchased each year on publication, and upwards of one hundred current magazines and newspapers are available.

The Library Committee is one of the oldest standing committees of the Club. It was recognized by the founders of the Club that an adequate library would be of constant use and pleasure to its members, and work on the accumulation of a library was begun almost as soon as the Club was organized.

Many chairmen and members of the Club's Library Committees have contributed unstinting effort and time to the building of the fine collection of books and manuscripts which the Club enjoys today. One of the best-remembered committee chairmen was Judge Jesse Holdom, who headed the committee from 1908 to 1923. Judge Holdom often expressed the opinion that the library of the Union League Club of Chicago should be a "gentleman's library" in every sense of the word, and proceeded to do everything in his power to make it such. Many of the rare books, fine bindings, and works of art which are a prized part of the Club's collection today were donated to the Club by Judge Holdom.

In 1944, under the chairmanship of Joseph A. Matter, the Library Committee had the books in the library completely reclassified and catalogued. On the basis of an analysis of the works which would be needed to make it a completely well-rounded and comprehensive collection, the committee also compiled a printed "want-list" of several thousand books to be acquired for the library. This list covered not only the field of American and English literature, but included the principal works in Latin American, European, and Oriental literatures, as well as standard writings in the fields of art and architecture, economics, history, science, and sociology. Many of the books on the list were out of print, but successive committees under the chairmanship of Rousseau Van Voorhies, William S. Akin, and E. Richmond Gray have kept in constant touch with dealers in this country and in England and have succeeded in purchasing a substantial number of the desired books.

From 1917 to her death in 1948, Mrs. Bessie Frank served as Club librarian. Her friendly disposition, remarkable memory, and interest in the reading likes of the members of the Club endeared her to hundreds of users of the library and made her loss one hard to fill. Several librarians have served the Club since 1948. The size and complexity of the collection has grown until today the services of a professional librarian are required, and the post is being very ably filled by Miss Marian Jones.

During the early years of the Club, until the Art Committee was established in 1890, the Library Committee was also in charge of the organization and care of the Club's art collection.

The fostering and encouraging of art has been a tradition of the Union League Club since its founding days. As a collector of art the Club has assembled some three hundred oil paintings, water colors, etchings, lithographs, marbles, bronzes, and other items. This collection, in the judgment of experts, ranges from some of the finest examples of the work of very great artists to

A corner of the Club Library—a quiet retreat for reading or study.

items of mediocrity. In the opinion of George I. Haight, chairman of the Art Committee, this is fortunate. "It increases interest," he maintains. "Some of the humblest works of art speak with profound authority."

In the early days of the Club, without any definite plan or guidance other than the inherent esthetic sense of some members and the natural desire of all for harmonious Club surroundings, members from time to time presented the Club with engravings, paintings, and other art objects, mainly of historic value rather than artistic merit. As time went on, the Club maintained this liberal policy with reference to its acquisitions and finally appointed competent men to supervise the purchase of art works and their subsequent care.

It was in those formative days that W. M. R. French, director of the Art Institute of Chicago, was a member of the Club's Art Committee, serving from 1897 to 1899. J. Spencer Dickerson, chairman of the committee from 1904 to 1910, went on record as saying, "It is due, in no small degree, to his [French's] direction that the Institute has become one of the outstanding agencies for the encouragement and perpetuation of art production and the study of its processes. It was fortunate for the Club that early it had the benefit of Mr. French's judgment."

The first gift to the Club, a "likeness of Lincoln," was made in 1881, and was reported by the Library Committee. This committee made its first art purchase on March 14, 1882, when it voted to buy a crayon picture of Garfield. On October 12, 1886, a watercolor painting, "Cologne Cathedral," by Ross Turner, was presented by J. M. Thatcher—the first art gift by a member.

At the annual meeting on January 25, 1887, the Library Committee reported that during the year an oil painting of the president of the Club, J. McGregor Adams, had been presented by himself, and a color print of William E. Gladstone had been given by George F. Bissell.

Rollin A. Keyes on March 1, 1886, submitted reports and catalogues of the Art Association of the Union League Club of Philadelphia and suggested that a similar association be formed in the Club. The suggestion was referred to the Library Committee. In 1889 an addition was built to the Club, extending to the alley on the west, and the west side of the fifth floor was set aside as an Art Gallery.

An Art Committee was now necessary and was named in 1890. James W. Ellsworth was chairman, with Ferdinand W. Peck and Shea Smith as associates. This first Art Committee had charge of the Art Gallery "and all pictures and works of art belonging to the Club, and shall have exclusive management of all art exhibitions given under the auspices of the Club."

At a meeting of the Board of Directors held February 8,

1892, a change in the Club by-laws provided that 2 per cent of the annual dues be appropriated to the Art Committee for the purchase of works of art. As a result, by 1893 the Art fund had reached a total of $3,196.25, and the committee foresaw an "advantageous opportunity" during the next year to pick up bargains from the various Columbian Exposition collections. With funds so made available to an Art Committee composed of men of experience and good taste, some notable oil paintings, etchings, and sculptures were purchased during that period. To Judge John Barton Payne, chairman of the committee in 1895, is due the selection of a number of small oil paintings, particularly George Inness' "The Picnic in the Woods," one of this distinguished landscape painter's most typical and able canvases. Even today this painting is considered by some as the most noteworthy of the Club's art treasures and the most valuable in its entire collection. Some years ago it was appraised at $60,000.

About the same time, the Art Committee purchased for $600 the painting "Autumn," by Alexander Wyant, a contemporary of Inness. This picture was appraised at $15,000 in 1920.

In 1904, when Wallace Heckman was Club president, J. Spencer Dickerson was appointed chairman of the Art Committee. Dickerson served in this position for seven years, and during that time some of the Club's most admired paintings and sculptures were purchased. The excellence of the committee's selections was without a doubt due to Dickerson's enterprise and to the advice of such associates on the committee as Frank G. Logan, Frederic A. Delano, and Martin A. Ryerson, each a connoisseur.

Perhaps the most notable portrait obtained during this decade was Ralph Clarkson's "Lincoln." Painted from a rare photograph loaned to Mr. Dickerson by Charles F. Gunther, it is sometimes said to be the only portrait of Lincoln in which there is an evidence of a smile. It was unveiled in the Club's lounge on the occasion of the one hundredth anniversary of Lincoln's birth. On the same day, through the co-operation of Frank G. Logan, there was placed on view a number of his Lincoln relics, including a pearl-handled penknife seen in the hand of the President in the portrait. The knife is now on exhibition at the Chicago Historical Society.

By 1907 the Club had a collection of which it was justly proud. At that time a *Catalogue of Paintings and Other Works of Art of the Union League Club* was prepared by Miss Lena M. McCauley for the Art Committee, then composed of J. Spencer Dickerson, Frederic A. Delano, and W. Scott Thurber. In her foreword, Miss McCauley stated the time had arrived for shaping a definite policy regarding the increase of the collection, and offered suggestions for the guidance of future committees. "It would seem manifestly proper for an organization interested in public affairs to acquire paintings of historical subjects and the portraits of statesmen and men prominent in public life, and from its breadth of aims to exercise catholicity of choice in the various fields of art," she added.

Miss McCauley was of the opinion that the Club had within its power the means of influencing, and to a certain degree directing, local taste, "and with this in mind the selection of the best works of American art, with a particularly friendly attitude toward artists in Chicago, would not only awaken general appreciation, but encourage our national art production." She said it was the privilege of the Union League Club "to offer encouragement and patronage to municipal art advancement."

The Club is also proud of a marble bust of Daniel Webster by the American sculptor Hiram Powers, and the bronze, "Man Carving His Own Destiny," by Albin Polasek. "The Blessing of the Boats," by Robert Reid, is the largest canvas in the Club's collection, measuring 72 x 90 inches. Two choice items are from the brush of James A. McNeill Whistler, "Winter Scene" and

"The Spirit of the Union League Club," a heroic-size mural, and the bronze statue of "Man Carving His Own Destiny," two notable items in the Union League Club's art collection.

"Venice." When Paul Schulze became chairman of the Art Committee in 1929, many etchings of Chicago scenes and famous American statesmen were added to the collection. Many were the works of Chicago artists, one of whom was Otto Schneider. His portrait of Theodore Roosevelt is highly regarded. Familiar to every member, too, is the mural by Edwin Howland Blashfield, "The Spirit of the Union League Club," above the fireplace in the Main Lounge.

Besides Thomas Buchanan Read's painting, "Sheridan's Ride," depicting an incident in the Civil War in the Shenandoah Valley, the Club also has the poet-painter's manuscript poem by the same title. Read's picture of "Sheridan's Ride" is one reduced by himself from his life-size canvas. The Club, however, possesses

313

Louis Betts' portrait of Luther Laflin Mills is viewed by Art Committee Chairman George I. Haight and son Matthew Mills.

the life-size study sketch of the head of Sheridan.

Among paintings of charter members of the Club is one of Luther Laflin Mills, painted in 1898 by Louis Betts. An interesting story is told of how the Club came into possession of this portrait. Chester M. MacChesney, chairman of the board of directors of Acme Steel Company and president of the Chicago Galleries Association, was walking on the Chicago campus of Northwestern University one day when he noticed a group of boys burning trash and papers removed from one of the buildings. He rescued the painting just a few minutes before it was to have been tossed into the fire. MacChesney wrote Betts, who identified it and said he had painted it for the Chicago Press Club. In 1952, at the suggestion of Matthew Mills, Club member and son of the subject of the portrait, MacChesney gave the portrait to the Union League Civic and Arts Foundation.

In the collection are three portraits of distinction, both historically and artistically, by G. P. A. Healy, one-time resident of Chicago. These portraits, all painted from life, are of General Frémont, Stephen A. Douglas, and Daniel Webster.

Another portrait which the Club values is that of Melville W. Fuller, a resident of Chicago, who later became Chief Justice of the United States Supreme Court. It hangs in the Club library. When Willard King's biography of Fuller was published a short time ago, the publisher declared this to be the finest existing portrait of the Chief Justice and borrowed it from the Club for use in preparing the jacket for the biography.

Another interesting portrait is that of General Ulysses S. Grant by William Coggswell, one of the few painted from life. General Frederick Grant, when stationed in Chicago in charge of the Department of the Lakes, told William B. Mundie that

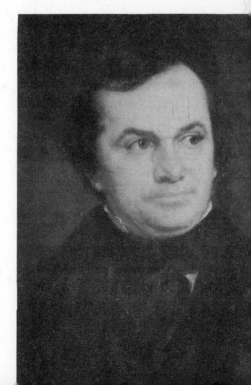

Portrait of Stephen A. Douglas
by G. P. A. Healy in the
Club's art collection.

Robert Hinckley's portrait of Chief Justice Melville W. Fuller.

"it was the one portrait the family liked and considered the best."

Mundie later wrote a chapter entitled "Art in the Union League Club" for *The Spirit of the Union League Club*. Here he recounts an interesting story of how the Club acquired a portrait bust of George Washington, made by the famous sculptor-potter of England, Josiah Wedgwood. The bust was modeled by Houdon, noted French sculptor, who visited this country to execute the statue of Washington direct from casts made of the living figure. The original now stands in the state capitol building in Richmond, Virginia. Washington in his diary of October 7, 1785, wrote: "Sat this day in Mount Vernon for Mr. Houdon."

Wedgwood and Houdon were friends and students in Paris and were often together. Wedgwood modeled his bust from Houdon's cast and made it in that famous black basaltware unique with him at that time. He made ten of them from this mold, only three of which are known to be in existence. One is in London, another in the Boston Museum, and the third was purchased by the Union League Club fifty years ago for $100.

Mundie wrote that in the Club "no rigid standard has prevailed." He said that the effort had been to maintain a broad viewpoint, to include merit, and "to accept others as may be because of historical association, deeming it proper for a club interested in public affairs, and within its function, to lend both patronage and encouragement to Art, ever seeking for better things, which may give to its members the satisfaction that comes from association with objects of beauty."

This is what George I. Haight later termed "art for laymen." The scope of such art would necessarily be large and would include everything from the finest paintings to the sets of rare and decorative English sporting prints—among the Club's latest acquisitions—which adorn the walls of the Wigwam and the Rendezvous. But also noteworthy of such "art for laymen" is the Municipal Art League's collection of forty-one paintings which were displayed in part in the Main Dining Room of the Club, and which the Union League Civic and Arts Foundation subsequently purchased. Assembled by the Art League through the awarding of annual purchase prizes to Chicago artists over a period of more than half a century, the collection is distinctively and uniquely representative of Chicago and Midwest art.

During 1928 and 1929 prize competitions among Chicago artists under thirty years of age were conducted by the Public Affairs Committee as a means of getting original paintings to be given to the high schools as prizes for their representatives who won awards in the Club's public speaking and poster design competitions. Five $100 purchase prizes were given each year. The paintings entered by the artists were displayed for short periods on racks set up in the Main Lounge. The awards were

"One Winter Afternoon," by artist Frank V. Dudley, one of the paintings acquired by the Union League Civic and Arts Foundation from the Municipal Art League.

selected by a committee of Chicago artists, including R. Fayerweather Babcock, Pauline Palmer, and Percy B. Eckhart.

In order to provide additional stimulus and financial encouragement to artists in Chicago and vicinity, the Club arranged a competition and exhibit as part of its seventy-fifth anniversary program in February, 1955. All artists in and within one hundred miles of Chicago were invited to submit pictures in oil, water color, and other media. A number of purchase prizes in substantial amounts were made available by the Club, the Union League Civic and Arts Foundation, and individual members. A jury composed of Chicago artists selected from the pictures submitted the ones exhibited and awarded the prizes.

Chapter Twenty-Five

THE UNION LEAGUE CLUB:
AN INSTITUTION

CHICAGO WAS INCORPORATED AS A CITY IN 1837. BUT CHICAGOANS like to think of their city as having been founded in 1833, the year to which the earliest record of the city seal can be traced.

Similarly, the Union League Club of Chicago was incorporated in 1879, and held its first meeting in 1880, but Club members like to think of the Club as having been conceived in the spirit of 1862, at the time the Union League of America sprang into existence. This is a reasonable proposition, since the Union League Club has carried on the patriotic principles and ideals of its progenitor.

But the point to be made is this: Chicago as an incorporated city is 118 years old in 1955. The Union League Club of Chicago as an incorporated club is 75 years old. Thus the life of the Club is almost three-quarters that of the life of the city. It can safely be said that no faithful history of the city of Chicago can be written unless it includes as well the history of the Union League Club of Chicago.

Much credit for the continued existence and prosperity of the Union League Club is due those members who, in the year of the Club's founding, diverted what might have been merely a political club into an organization which would faithfully further its primary objects: "To encourage and promote by moral, social and political influences, unconditional loyalty to the Federal Government, and to defend and protect the integrity and perpetuity of this nation." From that time on it became evident that the Union League Club was not a "party club," but one wholeheartedly interested in obtaining that which would prove best for the community, state, and nation.

Credit is due also to those foresighted members who from time to time enlarged the scope of the Club so that it has become inseparably identified not only with Chicago's civic development but with the city's social and cultural life as well. In this regard, in the words of George T. Buckingham, the Union League Club is more than a Club—it is an institution, and an all-embracing one, at that. It has been termed "the most diversified and representative club in the Middle West." Though one of the oldest clubs in Chicago, it is modern and up-to-date in every respect, and no other club has a clubhouse so large, so well appointed, and so adequate for the many activities that go on there.

Year after year since its establishment, its membership has included the business and professional leaders and the most representative men of the community. Its members, almost without exception, are men who do things in their businesses and professions—in the city, in the state, and throughout the nation. Thus, the name of the Union League Club of Chicago has become a symbol of responsibility, accomplishment, patriotism, and loyalty. At many critical times in Chicago's development the Club has put the force of its leadership into the cause of a greater city. Nor has it ever shirked its duty in national affairs. Politics have played no part. The Union League Club is neither a Republican nor a Democratic organization. While the majority of its presidents, for instance, have been Republicans, there have been four who were Democrats—Frederic A. Delano, 1906; Frank H. Scott, 1918-19; Henry P. Chandler, 1932-33; and John McKinlay, 1933-35.

The Club is nonpolitical, conservatively progressive, and so

Governor Adlai E. Stevenson signs the Illinois City Manager Enabling Act in 1951, climaxing a movement initiated by the Club in 1931.

organized as to take effective action in vital nonpartisan matters through its Public Affairs Committee. Its accomplishments in behalf of improved public affairs have been distinguished by a grasp of realities and a determination to accomplish what it undertakes.

The Union League Club's spirit of civic service, which in 1919 found expression in the promotion of the Union League Foundation for Boys' Clubs, again took special form in 1949 in the establishment of the Union League Civic and Arts Foundation. Incorporated under the Illinois Not-for-Profit Corporation Act, this Foundation was organized to give practical expression to the cultural and civic objectives of the Club's Art, Library, and Public Affairs committees, but without conflicting with the established pattern of Club committee action or Club policy.

The inception of the idea for the Foundation dates back to numerous incidents, many of which seem unrelated. In many instances the Club, through its Public Affairs Committee, had conducted different types of activities, such as essay and public speaking contests for high school pupils, public commemoration of patriotic anniversaries, awarding prizes for paintings by young Chicago artists, and conducting conferences for public school and other groups, which it had been suggested should be put on a continuing basis.

Oscar A. Kropf, as chairman of the Public Affairs Committee in 1927-28, proposed that a permanent fund should be established to finance an annual public lecture on citizenship to continue the annual Washington's Birthday observance which began in 1887.

The definite plan for the Foundation, however, was given initial impetus of Joseph A. Matter. As chairman of the Library Committee, he issued a special request to the membership of the Club for gifts of specific books. Encouraged by this experience, he then proposed to the Board of Directors the plan of organizing a special purpose agency to foster cultural, civic, and related activities, contributions for the support of which could be made by Club members on a tax-deductible basis. In the meantime, several committees of the Club independently developed projects which would logically fit under a plan of special sponsorship.

Carl V. Wisner furthered the idea by urging the publication of special textbooks for use of schools and civic classes. Research by him disclosed that out of several hundred educational foundations only one implied civic education in its title, and that one agency was no longer active.

In December, 1947, Matter, who had been elected secretary of the Club and a member of the Board of Directors, was invited by President Frank C. Rathje to re-open his proposal of the Foundation. This was discussed informally at several meetings, and at its May, 1948, meeting, the board authorized the appointment of a special committee to formulate a plan and recommendation concerning the proposed Foundation. The members of this special committee were: Joseph A. Matter, chairman,

George I. Haight, George H. Redding, George E. Turner, and Carl V. Wisner.

A comprehensive memorandum was submitted to the Board of Directors on November 3, 1948, and the plan of the Foundation was approved in principle by the Board of Directors at its November 9 meeting.

On January 6, 1949, another detailed report was submitted to and approved by the Board of Directors. On January 19, 1949, the Illinois secretary of state issued incorporation papers to the Union League Civic and Arts Foundation under the Illinois Not-for-Profit Corporation Act. Joseph A. Matter, George I. Haight, and George H. Redding were the incorporators, and joined with Matthew Mills, Harrison B. Barnard, Frank C. Rathje, and Erwin W. Roemer as directors.

The objectives of the Foundation are: (1) to aid civic education and improve government at both local and national levels through research in the principles underlying effective citizenship, and preparation of educational materials furthering those principles and encouragement of the use of such materials by schools and civic groups; (2) to aid historical research through the collection and preservation of historical Americana, the encouragement of historical research in Midwest history, the granting of scholarships and aids to historians, writers, and students, the collection of pertinent materials and documents, and the encouragement of young writers through the making of awards and prizes; and (3) the encouragement of music and the arts in the Midwest area through the fostering of talent, the awarding of prizes, the purchase of works of art, the sponsoring of discussion forums, and the encouragement of writing.

At its initial meeting, held March 2, 1949, the Foundation's board of directors adopted a constitution and by-laws which provide for a board of directors, corporate officers, and four types of membership based on contributions. Officers, directors, and members of the Foundation must be either members or privilege holders of the Union League Club.

The first officers of the Foundation were George I. Haight, president; Joseph A. Matter, Percy B. Eckhart and Robert Hall McCormick, vice presidents; Matthew Mills, secretary; Richard E. Pritchard, treasurer; Edward M. Martin, executive director.

The officers of the Foundation during 1954-1955 were: George I. Haight, honorary chairman; Joseph A. Matter, president; George H. Redding, George L. Seaton and Lyman M. Drake, Jr., vice-presidents; William H. Ganley, secretary; O. D. Bast, treasurer; Edward M. Martin, executive director.

Meanwhile, the relationship of the Foundation to the Club was established by a working agreement approved by the Club's Board of Directors February 15, 1949, assigning Room 402 as the Union League Civic and Arts Foundation Room for use as library and research headquarters. At the annual meeting of the Club, May 24, 1949, the members adopted the following amendment to the by-laws of the Club:

> The Union League Civic and Arts Foundation, an Illinois corporation not-for-profit, the object of which is "furthering education and progress of civic, literary, historical and artistic fields," may have its principal office in the Clubhouse and may solicit subscriptions to its treasury from members, but on such terms and under such conditions as from time to time may be prescribed by the Board of Directors of the Union League Club of Chicago; provided that the Board of Directors of the Foundation shall always be composed of members or privilege holders of the Union League Club of Chicago.

The United States Treasury Department in a ruling dated August 30, 1950, declared the Foundation to be an educational agency, thus making it possible for Club members to contribute financially to support the Foundation's activities and receive full income tax credit for such contributions.

The Foundation has donated prizes in competitions for new writers conducted by the Midwest Writers' Conference, awarded grants for historical research concerning loyalist movements in the North during the Civil War, provided annual Civic Leadership Awards to four Chicago high school pupils in contests sponsored by the Vocational Conference for Chicago High Schools, and assisted in the historical research for a publication concerning the role of railroads as a strategic factor in the Civil War. It has organized the George Ade Society as a means of encouraging research in Midwest Americana, and received from James D. Rathbun a collection of valuable books, manuscripts, and mementoes of the famous writer. The Foundation also has invited students and faculty from thirty-one Midwest colleges and universities to make use of its research materials.

The Foundation, further, has provided tuition scholarships at Northwestern University for traffic safety instruction for police officers from the city of Chicago and the Chicago Park District; research reports, now in preparation, will discuss the unique contributions of the city-manager plan in Illinois municipalities which have adopted that plan of administration, and also the operation of the community caucus system as a means of securing nonpartisan nomination and election of candidates in municipal elections.

As encouragement to art, the Foundation acquired the art collection of forty-one paintings by Chicago artists owned by the Municipal Art League of Chicago, thus permitting that League to extend its activities for the recognition and encouragement of Art in the Chicago area.

The Foundation also initiated and co-sponsored with the Club an art exhibit and presentation of awards for Chicago artists in commemoration of the seventy-fifth anniversary of the founding of the Club, and initially proposed and assisted in the preparation of this history of the Union League Club.

Famous art collection changes ownership. Union League Foundation President George I. Haight hands final payment to Municipal Art League President Paul Schulze.

On the honor roll of the Union League Club are the names of many of the Presidents of the United States. As honorary members, James A. Garfield, Chester A. Arthur, Benjamin Harrison, Ulysses S. Grant, Rutherford B. Hayes, Grover Cleveland, William McKinley, Theodore Roosevelt, William Howard Taft, Calvin Coolidge, Herbert Hoover, and Dwight D. Eisenhower have aided in fostering and diffusing the spirit of the Union League Club of Chicago.

Two Vice-Presidents of the United States have been honorary members: Levi P. Morton and Charles Gates Dawes. The Club contributed a Secretary of State under Cleveland, Walter Q. Gresham; a Secretary of War under McKinley, Russell A. Alger; a Secretary of the Treasury under McKinley, Lyman J. Gage; a Secretary of the Interior under Coolidge, Roy O. West, and a Secretary of Commerce under Herbert Hoover, Robert P. Lamont. The list of its members who have been United States senators includes the names of John A. Logan, Charles B. Farwell, Shelby M. Cullom, Lawrence Y. Sherman, William B. McKinley, Charles S. Deneen, Medill McCormick, Otis F. Glenn, Albert J.

Hopkins, and Homer E. Capehart. Since 1875, when William Aldrich became a member of the Forty-fifth Congress, many of the congressmen from the First District of Illinois have been Union League Club members, among whom were Rensom W. Dunham, George A. Taylor, J. Frank Aldrich, James R. Mann, Martin B. Madden, and Morton D. Hull.

Many times members have pondered over the question of just what it was that prolonged the existence of the Union League Club and made it greater and more important in the life of the community each year. Many Club presidents have considered this question in their annual reports, but possibly Judge Christian C. Kohlsaat, as retiring president in 1897, expounded this thought with more vigor and clarity than any other. The sentiment he expressed is as fitting today as it was fifty-eight years ago:

"Much, however, as the business affairs of the Club demand our careful attention, we must not for a moment lose sight of our real and more important duties. The one is but the pregnant basis for the other. Surely the greatest usefulness of the Union League Club is before and not behind us. No one in all this great city and its tributary regions misunderstands our purposes. Our flag, once hauled to the masthead, will never be lowered. Those who declared the principles which henceforth have been our charter brought to their task no political creed, save the greatest good to the whole country; no religious test save the welfare of humanity. We have carved a welcome to loyal hearts above our hearthstone, and writ fealty to our nation's flag over the arches of our doors. As Daniel of old prayed with his window open toward the beloved Jerusalem, so our eyes, our hopes, our service, our prayers are all for our country. To hold the position so readily accorded us, we shall need to do more than thus protest our patriotism.

"We cannot accomplish much in excess of the sum of the purposes of all our members. Each of us should continually meditate upon the evils to be remedied and the methods to be applied. The constant desire to reform abuse and wrong should be the aggressive element of a Union League man's mind— a divine unrest. Our uncomfortable activity may not in the future, as it has not done in the past, attract to our practical life the association and assistance of the very rich or pleasure-seeking classes, but notwithstanding, those same classes take comfort in our existence and influence. It is often a source of strength to know that others expect great things of us and depend on us. This source of strength we have. There is, in this city, no other organization with such opportunities and powers for good. If we fail to make use of them we cannot prosper. So very true is this that every member should continually and anxiously bear it in mind.

"Gentlemen of the Club, we congratulate you, as well we may, upon your prosperity; we felicitate you upon what you have achieved; we extol your power for good; we declare your responsibility. Shall we be equal to it?"

It has been the determined will of each member of the Club in the past, and will be the determined will of each member of the Club in the future, so to answer Judge Kohlsaat's question as to make certain the truth of Herbert Hoover's prediction in his foreword to this history: "With these foundations in purpose and service, the Union League Club of Chicago will live to celebrate its 150th anniversary."

APPENDIX

Membership reaches 1,000, March.

Stockholders of Columbian Exposition hold first meeting in Clubhouse, April 10; Club endorses World's Fair, July 22.

1891. Discussion: "Should Foreign Languages Be Taught in Chicago Schools."

Organizes corporation to fight smoke nuisance.

Reception to Mr. and Mrs. Henry E. Stanley, January 19.

Membership reaches 1,200, December 31.

1892. Votes to appropriate 2% of annual dues for purchase of art.

1893. Edward Everett Hale, Washington's Birthday orator.

Breakfast and reception honoring Duke of Veragua, May 6.

Reception to Sir Richard Webster, Royal British Commissioner to Columbian Exposition, September 29.

1895. Champions the adoption of the Chicago Civil Service Act.

1896. Col. Theodore Roosevelt, Washington's Birthday orator.

Banquet for mayors at Better Government Conference, December.

1897. Reception to delegates of the Congress of American Nations.

1898. Reception to President and Mrs. Sanford B. Dole of Hawaii.

President Benjamin Harrison, Washington's Birthday orator.

Endorses action of Congress in declaring war on Spain, April 22.

Celebrates Peace Jubilee Week commemorating end of Spanish-American War; President McKinley reviews parade from grandstand in front of the Clubhouse, October.

1899. President McKinley and other distinguished personages are guests of the Club at ceremony for laying cornerstone of Federal Building, October.

1900. Washington's Birthday exercises held in 46 schools, February.

Initiates purchase of Clubhouse site, April 10.

Discussion: "The Consolidation of Municipalities of the City of Chicago," April 10.

Dewey Day parade and reception to the admiral, May 1.

Club delegation attends Illinois Day at Omaha Exposition as guests of C. & N.W. Ry.

Launches movement for State Civil Service Law.
Discussion: "Non-partisan Control of State Institutions."

1901. Elihu Root, Washington's Birthday orator, February 22.
Initiates plan to improve caliber of legislative candidates.

1902. Senator Albert J. Beveridge, Washington's Birthday orator.
Completes purchase of Clubhouse site, October 14.

1903. Senator George F. Hoar, Washington's Birthday orator.
Membership limit fixed at 1,500, October 12.

1904. Discussion: "Necessity for City Charter Revision," April.
Reunion of "Class of '80," May 24.

1906. William Howard Taft, Washington's Birthday orator.
Subscribes $7,077 to San Francisco Earthquake Relief Fund.
Advocates doubling city licenses for saloons. Pamphlets distributed on *Municipal Revenues* and *Municipal Ownership*.

1907. Reception to President and Mrs. Cleveland, February 21.
President Cleveland, Washington's Birthday orator (his last
public appearance).
Discussion: "Is Smoke Prevention in Chicago Practical?"
Favors adoption of new Chicago charter, September 4.
Discussion: "A Rational Method of Dealing with Delinquents."
Favors extension of Sanitary District channel to Joliet.

1908. Charles Evans Hughes, Washington's Birthday orator.
Discussion: "Deep Waterways to the Gulf," October.
Co-operates in selection of Chicago post office site.

1909. Creates "veteran membership" classification, April 13.
Co-operates in conducting a secret investigation of the Chicago Police Department.

1910. Americanization mass meeting at First Regiment Armory.

1911. Theodore Roosevelt, Washington's Birthday orator.

1912. Ambassador Jean Jules Jusserand, Washington's Birthday
orator.

1913. Resident membership limit raised to 1,800, February 28.
William Jennings Bryan addresses annual meeting.

1915.   Club contributes $1,000 to Eastland Disaster Fund, July 26.

1916.   Athletic Department opened, October 5.

1917–18.   War Committee issues booklets on "Why We Fight."

1917.   Adopts resolution recommending enactment of universal and compulsory military training law, March 27.

1918.   Governor Frank O. Lowden, Washington's Birthday speaker.
Reception for M. Viviani, Marshall Joffrel, and members of the French War Mission, May.
Peace Jubilee Dinner, November 14.

1919.   Merges Committee on Political Action and War Committee into Public Affairs Committee; advocates reorganization of Chicago government; endorses Constitutional Convention plan; endorses legislation for "citizen army" and "system of universal training of young men."
Union League Foundation for Boys' Clubs incorporated.

1920.   Sponsors Chicago Zoning Conference and urges adoption of zoning legislation, February 28.
Union League Boys' Club No. One dedicated, May 29.
Initiates publication of *Union League Bulletin*, July 1.
Sponsors Central States Forestry Conference.
Governor Lowden appoints Club members on Chicago Commission on Race Relations.
Supports legislation to establish state police; reorganization of Illinois National Guard and "United Americans."

1921.   Entertains Mary Garden.

1922.   Herbert Hoover delivers Washington's Birthday address.
Albert J. Beveridge orator at John Marshall dinner.

1922–23.   Forms committee of 125 to "Save Great Lakes."
Raises fund to prosecute offenders in Herrin massacre.
Places St. Gaudens bust of Abraham Lincoln in Hall of Fame.
Organizes conference to advocate reassessment of Chicago realty.

1923.   Conducts Memorial Service for President Warren G. Harding in Orchestra Hall, August 10.

1923–24. Organizes Illinois Forestry Association.
Raises special fund to finance grand jury investigations.
Donates $1,000 to Japanese Earthquake Relief Fund.
Co-operates in formation of Joint Committee on Schools.

1924. Conducts survey of Chicago Civic Agencies.
Club moves to temporary quarters at 14 East Monroe Street.

1925. Public Affairs Committee re-instates *Union League Bulletin*.
Lays cornerstone of new Clubhouse, October 12.

1926. Publishes *Directory of Chicago Civic Agencies*, January.
Opens and dedicates new Clubhouse, May 21.
Reception to Queen Marie of Roumania, November 16.

1927. Opens Union League Boys' Club No. Two, April 2.
Conducts competition among young Chicago artists.
Organizes Citizens' Public Education Commission, April.
Organizes Chicago Civic Conference, October.

1928. Entertains President William T. Cosgrove of Ireland.
James M. Beck speaker at Constitution Day dinner.
Sponsors Chicago meeting of Conference on Government.

1928–29. Contributes $2,450 to special grand jury fund.
Conference held to "stabilize Chicago zoning ordinance."

1929. Confers honorary memberships on Charles Evans Hughes
and Frank J. Loesch, March 26.

1930. Fêtes President Pascual Ortis Rubio of Mexico, January 4.
Celebrates Fiftieth Anniversary of founding of the Club.

1930–31. Contributes fund to finance study of citizenship training.
Urges calling of Illinois Constitutional Convention.
Adopts policy of supporting Chicago Bar Association's
recommendations on judicial candidates.

1931. Mayor Russell Wilson of Cincinnati delivers address on City
Manager Plan, November 19.

1931–32. Urges reorganization of Chicago's government.
Address by Rt. Hon. Winston Churchill.

1933. Entertains Dr. Hugo Eckener and Ambassador Hans Luther.

1933–34. Special fund raised for "Honest Ballot."

Awards Citizenship Medals to high school pupils.
Co-operates in publication of *Merit System in Illinois.*
Publishes report of Advisory Commission on Civic Education.
Sponsors addresses by Hon. Murray Seasongood and Henry
Bentley of Cincinnati on City Manager Plan.

1934. Raises special fund to prosecute vote frauds and convict
offenders; resulting publicity helped to enact Permanent
Registration Act for Chicago.

1935. Adopts "Reaffirmation of Principles" at special dinner.
Urges adoption of drivers' license legislation.
Opposes creation of "Coney Island" on lake front.

1936. Recruits poll watchers to prevent fraud in November election.
Helps to organize Joint Committee on Voting Machines.
Co-operates to form Chicago City Manager Committee.
Address by Senator Arthur H. Vandenberg.

1937. Publishes pamphlets: *Traffic Control,* by William F. Sloan;
Civil Service—Nation's Biggest Business; and *Civic Plan for
Chicago,* prepared by General Frank Parker.
Initiates "America, Wake Up" crusade; adopts "Restatement
of Union League Principles."
Address by Herbert Hoover: "The Supreme Court."
Address by Clarence A. Dykstra, city manager of Cincinnati.
Endorses legislation for adoption of voting machines.

1938. Co-operates in voters' registration drive.
Co-operates in forming Illinois Council-Manager Conference.

1939. Address by Dr. Eduard Benes: "Is European Democracy
Going to Collapse?"
Issues *Horse-and-Buggy Sense* pamphlets as part of "America,
Wake Up" crusade.
Urges adoption of City Manager enabling act.

1940. Collaborates in circulating state-wide City Manager advisory
referendum petition.
Collaborates in formation of Joint Civic Committee on
Elections.
Address by Senator Robert A. Taft: "Planned Economy
without a Plan."

334

1941. Endorses Walter-Logan Bill.
Conducts club-wide advisory referendum against control of the Congress by the Executive.
Opposes repeal of Illinois Civil Service Act.
Issues report urging state supervision of local finance; re-endorses City Manager Plan enabling legislation.

1942. Establishes War Service Committee.
Initiates vocational conferences for Chicago high schools.
Recruits poll watchers to prevent ballot thefts in First Ward.
Organizes Advisory Council on Farm Placement.

1943. Creates special Committee on Post-War Reconstruction.

1944. Address by Governor John W. Bricker of Ohio.
Urges settlement of Chicago traction problem.
Co-operates in recruiting 2,500 poll watchers.

1945. Urges adoption of plan for congressional redistricting.
Re-endorses City Manager Enabling Act for Illinois.
Establishes Vocational Counseling Service for veterans.

1946. Endorses Gateway Amendment and referendum on voting machines for Chicago.
Issues report on National Security.
Endorses legislation for reorganization of Chicago school superintendency and Crime Commission bills.
Tribute to members and their sons in World War II.
Confers honorary membership on General Dwight D. Eisenhower and Admiral Chester W. Nimitz.
Address by Jan Masaryk: "Central Europe."

1947. Endorses Mundt-Nixon bill to curb communist activities.
Issues comprehensive plan for National Security Training.
Endorses Gateway Amendment legislation.
Advocates plan for building new Dunbar Trade School.
Endorses voting machine bond issue.

1948. Re-endorses Gateway Amendment proposition.
Endorses Judd bill concerning citizenship for Japanese residents.
Publishes history of communism by Walter L. Furbershaw.

1949. Collaborates in drafting City Manager enabling legislation.
Joins in court action to validate voting machine purchase.
Organizes Union League Civic and Arts Foundation.

1950. Endorses $50,000,000 school building bond issue.
Urges enactment of Congressional Redistricting Plan.

1951. Legislature enacts Illinois City Manager Enabling Act.
Club forms Illinois Commission on Government Personnel.
Collaborates in preparation of handbook on elections.
Contributes special fund to "Citizens of Greater Chicago."

1952. Co-operates in preparation and distribution of *Your Vote—
The Key to Good Government* and *Pocket Guide for
Voters.*

1953. Endorses proposal to amend the Judicial Article of Illinois
constitution, plan to create Chicago metropolitan services
commission, Reapportionment Amendment, commission to
reorganize Illinois merit system, and Bricker Amendment.

1954. Conducts activity in behalf of Reapportionment Amendment.
Sponsors conference on recommendations of Chicago Home
Rule Commission.

Officers of the Union League Club
1880–1955

PRESIDENTS

James B. Bradwell [1]	1880	William F. Hypes	1915–16
Lewis L. Coburn [2]	1880	Frank J. Loesch	1916–17
John C. Coonley	1881–82	Howard G. Hetzler	1917–18
Elbridge G. Keith	1883	Frank H. Scott	1918–19
J. McGregor Adams	1884–86	Charles W. Folds	1919–20
George W. Smith	1887	John Fletcher	1920–21
John L. Thompson [3]	1888	George T. Buckingham	1921–22
Franklin H. Head [4]	1888	Wyllys W. Baird	1922–24
George F. Bissell	1889	William J. Jackson	1924–26
Cyrus D. Roys	1890	Harry Eugene Kelly	1926–27
Franklin H. Head	1891	Harrison B. Barnard	1927–28
George E. Adams	1892	Benjamin F. Affleck	1928–29
Ferdinand W. Peck	1893	Charles M. Moderwell	1929–30
John P. Wilson	1894	John R. Montgomery	1930–31
John H. Hamline	1895	Guy A. Richardson	1931–32
Christian C. Kohlsaat	1896	Henry P. Chandler	1932–33
Thomas B. Bryan	1897	John McKinlay	1933–35
Alexander H. Revell	1898	Edwin C. Austin	1935–36
John S. Miller	1899	Ernest L. Hartig	1936–37
Eugene Cary	1900	Nicholas J. Conrad	1937–39
Volney W. Foster	1901	John L. Clarkson	1939–40
Robert Mather	1902	Kenneth E. Rice	1940–41
Edgar A. Bancroft	1903	Ferre C. Watkins	1941–42
Wallace Heckman	1904	Albion C. Cronkhite	1942–43
Alexander A. McCormick	1905	George I. Haight	1943–44
Frederick A. Delano	1906	Thomas E. Bond	1944–45
Charles S. Cutting	1907	Claude F. Baker	1945–46
Leroy A. Goddard	1908	Charles Z. Henkle	1946–47
Jesse Holdom	1909	Frank C. Rathje	1947–49
John E. Wilder	1910	George H. Redding	1949–51
William P. Sidley	1911	Joseph A. Matter	1951–52
Abram W. Harris	*1912–13	Vernon R. Loucks	1952–53
William H. McSurely	1913–14	Russell L. Peters	1953–54
Clarence S. Pellet	1914–15	Alex D. Bailey	1954–55

FIRST VICE-PRESIDENTS

William H. Bradley	1880	Ferdinand W. Peck	1891–92
Charles E. Culver	1881–82	John P. Wilson	1893
Charles M. Henderson	1883	Christian C. Kohlsaat	1894
John L. Thompson	1884–86	Charles H. Aldrich	1895
H. N. Higinbotham	1887	Melville E. Stone	1896
Franklin H. Head [5]	1888	Lester L. Bond	1897
George F. Bissell [6]	1888	George A. Follansbee	1898
O. S. A. Sprague	1889	Frederick A. Smith	1899
James W. Ellsworth	1890	Marvin A. Farr	1900

337

Bernard E. Sunny	1901
Alexander A. McCormick	1902
Frederic W. Upham	1903
O. B. Taft	1904
Jerome G. Steever	1905
Charles S. Cutting	1906
Andrew MacLeish	1907
Jesse Holdom	1908
William Holabird	1909
Francis T. Simmons	1910
Allen B. Pond	1911
William H. McSurely	*1912–13
Clarence S. Pellet	1913–14
Horace K. Tenney	1914–15
Frank J. Loesch	1915–16
Howard G. Hetzler	1916–17
A. D. Sheridan	1917–18
F. B. Johnstone	1918–19
William H. Winslow	1919–20
George T. Buckingham	1920–21
Fletcher M. Durbin	1921–22
William A. Illsley	1922–23
Britton I. Budd	1923–24
Harry Eugene Kelly	1924–26
C. W. Seabury	1926–27

Benjamin F. Affleck	1927–28
George W. Dixon	1928–29
John R. Montgomery	1929–30
Henry H. Hilton	1930–31
Thurlow G. Essington	1931–32
Francis X. Busch	1932–33
Carl R. Latham	1933–34
Ernest L. Hartig	1934–36
Edward J. Bullock	1936–37
James D. Cunningham	1937–38
John L. Clarkson	1938–39
Kenneth E. Rice	1939–40
Charles A. Bethge	1940–41
George F. Spaulding	1941–42
George I. Haight	1942–43
Thomas E. Bond	1943–44
Frank C. Rathje	1944–46
Alex D. Bailey	1946–47
Robert W. T. Purchas	1947–49
George L. Seaton	1949–51
Allin K. Ingalls	1951–52
Russell L. Peters	1952–53
John F. Mannion	1953–54
George R. Bailey	1954–55

SECOND VICE-PRESIDENTS

Edward A. Small	1880
Silas M. Moore	1881–82
J. McGregor Adams	1883
Byron P. Moulton	1884
Eugene Cary	1885–86
Albert L. Coe	1887–88
Edson Keith	1889
Albert L. Coe	1890
Porter P. Heywood	1891–92
Jonathan W. Brooks	1893
James H. Moore	1894
John S. Belden	1895
E. S. Conway	1896
Bernard A. Eckhart	1897
Hiram R. McCullough	1898
A. C. Bird	1899
Theodore W. Letton	1900
Andrew MacLeish	1901
Wiley J. Littlejohn	1902
Walter H. Wilson	1903
I. S. Blackwelder	1904
Charles P. Whitney	1905
Wallace L. DeWolf	1906

William P. Sidley	1907
Joseph Downey	1908
William B. Biddle	1909
Allen B. Pond	1910
George R. Skinner	1911
Clarence S. Pellet	*1912–13
Arthur C. Field	1913–14
George W. Dixon	1914–15
John A. Bunnell	1915–16
Rush C. Butler	1916–17
F. B. Johnstone	1917–18
Ralph H. Hobart	1918–20
David L. Goodwillie	1920–21
William A. Illsley	1921–22
Frederick P. Vose	1922–23
John V. Norcross	1923–24
Arthur H. Woodward	1924–26
George B. McKibbin	1926–27
George S. Ballard	1927–28
William B. Moulton	1928–29
Herbert H. Taylor	1929–30
F. O. Hale	1930–31
Francis X. Busch	1931–32

Samuel O. Dunn 1932–33	Matthew Mills 1945–46
J. Kibben Ingalls 1933–34	Herman O. Walther 1946–47
Marshall E. Keig 1934–35	George H. Redding 1947–49
Edward J. Bullock 1935–36	Fred M. Echoff 1949–50
Matthew Mills 1936–37	Joseph A. Matter 1950–51
William Marshall Ellis . . . 1937–39	Overton S. Chambers . . . 1951–52
George F. Spaulding 1939–41	B. Clifford Graves 1952–53
Alex D. Bailey 1941–42	George R. Bailey 1953–54
Allin K. Ingalls 1942–44	John P. Ballman 1954–55
Donald M. Wood 1944–45	

SECRETARIES

Philip A. Hoyne [7] 1880	Warren Gorrell 1915–18
E. Raymond Bliss [8] 1880	C. M. Trowbridge 1918–21
Robert S. Critchell 1881–82	Walter S. Ross 1921–22
Rollin A. Keyes 1883	George W. Springer 1922–25
Sidney C. Eastman 1884	William P. Reed 1925–28
Rollin A. Keyes 1885	George O. Fairweather . . 1928–29
George Driggs 1886	Charles Z. Henkle [9] 1929
Henry M. Bacon 1887–88	Howell W. Kitchell [10] . . . 1929–33
William H. Hubbard . . . 1889–90	Charles Z. Henkle 1933–35
Henry A. Knott 1891–93	John L. Clarkson 1935–37
Walter H. Wilson 1894–95	Ferre C. Watkins 1937–40
William P. Williams 1896–97	Harris E. Wilder 1940–42
Will H. Clark 1898	Douglas K. Huntress . . . 1942–44
Robert P. Walker 1899–1900	Robert W. T. Purchas . . . 1944–47
Frank R. Greene 1901–02	Joseph A. Matter 1947–50
Frederick Greeley 1903–05	Overton S. Chambers . . . 1950–51
David B. Lyman, Jr. 1906–08	Richard M. Lamport . . . 1951–52
Walter D. Herrick 1909–11	Lyman M. Drake, Jr. . . . 1952–55
A. F. Allen *1912–15	

TREASURERS

William Penn Nixon 1880–82	F. L. Hankey 1908–09
George M. Bogue 1883	Arthur Heurtley 1910–11
William V. Jacobs 1884	Albert W. Harris *1912–14
Walter B. Mitchell 1885	G. P. Hoover 1914–16
Rollin A. Keyes 1886–88	Henry S. Henschen 1916–18
William Moseback 1889–90	C. S. Castle 1918–20
William D. Preston 1891–92	Clifford Arrick 1920–22
Frederick T. Haskell 1893	Edwin F. Mack 1922–25
Edward B. Lathrop 1894–95	R. Frank Newhall 1925–27
Carl Moll 1896	J. Edward Maass 1927–29
John C. Neely 1897–98	Hugo A. Anderson 1929–31
Edwin A. Potter 1899	John W. O'Leary 1931–33
John McLaren 1900	Ernest L. Hartig 1933–34
D. A. Moulton 1901–02	Edward J. Bullock 1934–35
George F. Orde [11] 1903–05	Harold Eckhart 1935–36
F. L. Hankey [12] 1905	George F. Spaulding 1936–38
Frank G. Nelson 1906–07	William Day Truesdale . . . 1938–40

Lyndon H. Lesch	1940–43	Richard E. Pritchard	1949–51
Claude F. Baker	1943–45	Harold W. Lewis [14]	1951
Raymond J. Koch	1945–47	Richard E. Pritchard [15]	1951–52
John J. Geddes	1947–48	Charles M. Nelson	1952–54
Kent C. Childs [13]	1947–49	Orval D. Bast	1954–55

* Fiscal year changed to end last day of February instead of last day of December.
[1] Elected president of Board of Directors January 20, 1880.
[2] Elected president of the Club January 27, 1880.
[3] Elected president January 24, 1888, died on 31st day of same month.
[4] Elected to fill vacancy after death of President Thompson.
[5] Elected president, January 24, 1888.
[6] Elected to fill vacancy, January 24, 1888.
[7] Elected secretary of Board of Directors January 20, 1880.
[8] Elected secretary of the Club January 27, 1880.
[9] Transferred to non-resident.
[10] Elected to fill vacancy.
[11] Resigned May 6, 1905.
[12] Elected to fill vacancy.
[13] Elected acting treasurer June 18, 1947.
[14] Resigned December 18, 1951.
[15] Elected to fill vacancy.

HONORARY MEMBERS

Date of Admission

Ulysses S. Grant	1880
James A. Garfield	1880
Rutherford B. Hayes	1880
Shelby M. Cullom	1880
Philip H. Sheridan	1880
William T. Sherman	1880
Henry W. Blodgett	1880
Thomas Drummond	1880
Chester A. Arthur	1881
John M. Harlan	1881
John M. Schofield	1884
Walter Q. Gresham	1885
Alfred H. Terry	1886
Chauncey M. Depew	1888
George Crook	1888
Benjamin Harrison	1889
Levi P. Morton	1889
Melville W. Fuller	1889
Nelson A. Miles	1890
W. C. P. Breckenridge	1892
William McKinley	1894
David J. Brewer	1894
Henry B. Brown	1897
Joseph E. Gary	1898

Date of Admission

Peter S. Grosscup	1900
Christian C. Kohlsaat	1900
Theodore Roosevelt	1901
Thomas B. Bryan	1904
Grover Cleveland	1907
Lewis L. Coburn	1910
William J. Calhoun	1910
Albert B. Cummins	1916
Woodrow Wilson	1917
William H. Taft	1919
Herbert C. Hoover	1923
Calvin Coolidge	1926
Charles Gates Dawes	1927
John J. Pershing	1928
Charles Evans Hughes	1929
Frank J. Loesch	1929
Frank O. Lowden	1935
George T. Buckingham	1940
William P. Sidley	1940
Douglas MacArthur	1942
Dwight D. Eisenhower	1946
Chester W. Nimitz	1946
Franklin Bliss Snyder	1948
Robert Alphonso Taft	1952

HONOR ROLLS OF THE UNION LEAGUE CLUB

SPANISH-AMERICAN WAR HONOR ROLL

This Roll of Honor was prepared in 1922 by the Club's Service Roll Committee

Clifford Arrick
Fred Bennett
Alva L. Bournique
Taylor E. Brown
B. M. Chiperfield
William G. Dows

Milton J. Foreman
M. L. C. Funkhouser
Thomas Francus Howe
Nathan William Mac-
　Chesney
John Moore
Elisha Morgan

George M. Moulton
Harold L. Myers
Theodore Roosevelt
Richings P. Shand
Gordon Strong
Edward H. Young

WORLD WAR I HONOR ROLL

*The following Roll was prepared by the Club's Service Roll Committee in 1922
and is intended to include the names of all men who were members
of the Club during the period the Nation was at war—
April 6, 1917, to November 11, 1918.*

C. W. Alton
Bion J. Arnold
W. B. Ashby
Guilford C. Babcock
Harve G. Badgerow
Ralph J. Badgerow
Clarence J. Blaker
Christy Brown
Frederick A. Brown
J. S. Broeksmit
D. H. Burnham
Paul Butler
Julius W. Butler
H. M. Byllesby
Robert F. Carr
B. N. Carvalho
B. M. Chiperfield
Kenneth D. Clark
Will H. Clark
Duncan L. Clinch
Warren C. Corning
R. E. Cotton
Ralph Crews
Ray H. Davies
Charles G. Dawes
W. S. Dunham
C. G. Ellis
Lester L. Falk

Gilbert Fitz-Patrick
Milton J. Foreman
F. H. Gansbergen
L. R. Gignilliat
Melville Gillett
Arthur Gosline
W. B. Gray
Cecil D. Gregg
George H. Harries
Stanley G. Harris
Oscar H. Haugan
Henry H. Hilton
Ralph H. Hobart
William J. Hoppe
Roger B. Hull
Harry H. Hunter
William B. Jackson
Arnold Joerns
James B. Kaine
Marshall E. Keig
W. B. King
Edward N. Lake
Elwin W. Law
Albert J. Love
James A. Lounsbury
Nathan William Mac-
　Chesney
Franklin H. Martin
Hubert F. Miller

A. C. Moon
Wensel Morava
R. H. Morse
George B. Ogle
Troy L. Parker
P. F. W. Peck
M. Milton Portis
Wilbur E. Post
Charles H. Prindeville
Robert W. Richards
F. G. Robbins
A. L. Schoeninger
C. E. Schauffler
John S. Sensenbrenner
Irving Shuman
H. H. Spaulding, Jr.
C. J. Swan
Harold H. Swift
Kenneth S. Templeton
C. N. Thomas
Daniel G. Throne
Averill Tilden
Preston A. Wells
Thomas E. Wells
Milton Wilson
S. C. Woodard
James N. Wright
C. Van Deventer

WORLD WAR II HONOR ROLL

Members in Service from Declaration of War, December 8, 1941, to V-J Day, September 2, 1945.

William R. Abbott, Jr.
Benjamin S. Adamowski
Albert H. Andrews, Jr.
★John R. Bailey
Frederic H. Bassett
Harold R. Bechtel
Vernon W. Behel, Jr.
Maurice J. Bernet
Henry E. Billington
Edward F. Blettner, Jr.
Ellis G. Bovik
Henry H. Brigham, Jr.
Claude L. Brignall
Jewell V. Burk
Alfred Lee Burke
Irvin A. Busse, Jr.
Charles F. Butler
Samuel J. Campbell
Thomas D. Campbell
Robert E. Carroll
Thomas Cerny, Jr.
John L. Clarkson
Frank H. Collins
Corwith Cramer
Alfred W. Craven, Jr.
Ben F. Duvall
Lommen D. Eley
Benjamin H. Ernst
P. Wilson Evans
Wm. Harrison Fetridge
Robert S. Fisher
James C. Foster
Donald S. Funk
Walter L. Furbershaw
Robert H. Gardner
John H. Grace, Jr.
John P. Griffin
Frederick C. Hack, Jr.
Edward A. Haight
Robert E. Hallberg
Joseph R. Harmon

James Jay Harrington, Jr.
Thomas A. Harrington
Charles Z. Henkle
Edgar J. Higgins
Carlton Hill
Walter E. Hook
Walter Austin Horner
Samuel Insull, Jr.
Dugald C. Jackson, Jr.
Walter R. Jeffrey
Alexander L. Johnson
Kermit F. Knudtzon
Herman E. Lacy
Donald C. Lahey
Richard M. Lamport
John T. Landreth
J. Alton Lauren
Roger R. Leech
Jose M. Lenone
George Edward Leonard, Jr.
Orman I. Lewis
Ralph Bigelow Lourie, Jr.
William E. Lucas
Nathan William Mac-
  Chesney
Lanning Macfarland
Robert W. Manly
George L. Martin
Hardin W. Masters
Willard R. Matheny
Howard A. McKee
Miles F. McKee
William Benton
  McMillan
Alan H. Means
Graydon Megan
George S. Middleton, Jr.
Wells Miller
Fred C. Nonnamaker, Jr.
George G. Olmsted, Jr.
Wilmot C. Palmer, Jr.

Clyde L. Parsley
Bruce Parsons
Aubrey Peters
George E. Phelps
Robert C. Pierce
Cassius Poust
John R. Reilly
Frank W. Renwick, Jr.
William M. Roche
William P. Rock
Cyril J. Ryan
William O. Schilling, Jr.
Russell C. Schreck
Victor Hugo Schulze
Melvin H. Schwartz, Jr.
Newton P. Selover
John H. Sharp
Walter A. Sheaffer II
Frank S. Sims
Melvin B. Skinner
George F. Stahmer II
Aaron K. Stiles
Fred W. Strouce
Robert H. Swanson
John W. Taylor, Jr.
Herbert A. Vance
Robert M. Van
  Valkenburgh
George E. Victor
Logan A. Vilas
Edward K. Wait
Alfred R. Walker
Willett F. Weber
Nelson G. Wettling
James H. Wheat
Harris E. Wilder
Douglas Wilson
William E. Withall
Donald M. Wood, Jr.
Herbert N. Woodward
Carroll Q. Wright, Jr.

★ Killed in service.

Bibliography and Source Material
BOOKS

Addams, Jane. *Forty Years at Hull House.* New York, 1935.

Ahern, M. L. *The Great Revolution.* Chicago, 1874.

—— *The Political History of Chicago.* Chicago, 1886.

Andreas, Alfred T. *History of Chicago.* 3 vols. Chicago, 1884–86.

Andrews, Wayne. *Battle for Chicago.* New York, 1946.

Bennett, Fremont O. *Politics and Politicians,* Chicago, 1886.

Benton, Elbert J. *The Movement for Peace Without Victory During the Civil War.* Publication No. 99, Collections of the Western Reserve Historical Society, Cleveland, 1918.

Blair, E. T. *A History of the Chicago Club.* Chicago, 1898.

Bliss, E. R. *Beginning of the Union League Club of Chicago.* Chicago, 1916.

Buckingham, Col. George T. *The Projected Sack of Chicago.* Chicago, 1939.

Bross, William. *History of Camp Douglas.* Chicago, 1878.

—— *History of Chicago.* Chicago, 1880.

Castleman, John B. *Active Service.* Louisville, 1917.

Cochran, William C. *The Dream of a Northwestern Confederacy.* State Historical Society of Wisconsin, 1916.

Cole, A. C. *Centennial History of Illinois, Vol. 3.* Springfield, Ill., 1919.

Cook, Frederick Francis. *Bygone Days in Chicago.* Chicago, 1910.

Coyne, F. E. *In Reminiscence.* Chicago, 1941.

Critchell, Robert S. *Recollections of a Fire Insurance Man.* Chicago, 1909.

Currey, J. Seymour. *Chicago: Its History and Builders.* Chicago, 1912.

Dawes, Charles G. *Journal of the McKinley Years.* Edited by Bascom N. Timmons, Chicago, 1950.

Eastman, Sidney Corning. *A Letter to Members of the Union League Club.* Chicago, 1886.

Encyclopedia of Biography of Illinois, 1892.

Gale, Edwin O. *Reminiscences of Early Chicago.* Chicago, 1902.

Gibson, Guy J. *The Union League Movement in Illinois During the Civil War.* (Thesis). Urbana, Ill., 1953.

Glessner, J. J. *The Commercial Club of Chicago.* Chicago, 1910.

Goodspeed, T. W. *University of Chicago Biographical Sketches.* 2 vols. Chicago, 1922–25.

Granville, Austyn, and Knott, William Wilson. *If the Devil Came to Chicago.* Chicago, 1894.

Gray, Wood. *The Hidden Civil War: The Story of the Copperheads.* New York, 1942.

Hackett, Karleton S. *The Beginning of Grand Opera in Chicago.* Chicago, 1913.

Hamilton, E. Bentley. *The Union League: Its Origin and Achievements in the Civil War.* Illinois State Historical Transactions. 1921.

Harrison, Carter H. *Growing Up With Chicago.* Chicago, 1944.

Higinbotham, Harlow N. *President's Report of the World's Columbian Exposition.* Chicago, 1898.

Johnson, Claudius O. *Carter Harrison I.* Chicago, 1928.

King, Hoyt. *Citizen Cole of Chicago.* Chicago, 1931.

Kinsley, Philip. *The Chicago Tribune: Its First Hundred Years.* 3 vols. Chicago and New York, 1943–46.

Kirkland, Joseph. *The History of Chicago.* Chicago, 1894.

Leach, Paul R. *That Man Dawes.* New York, 1930.

Leech, Harper, and Carroll, J. C. *Armour and His Times*. New York, 1938.

Lewis, Lloyd, and Smith, H. J. *Chicago: The History of Its Reputation*. New York, 1929.

Linn, James Weber. *Jane Addams*. New York, 1935.

Lowden, Frank O. *Report of the Executive Committee Appointed by the Union League Club of this date*. April 22, 1898.

Maddock, Kathryn. *Joseph Medill: An Editor of the Old School*. (Thesis). University of Illinois, 1916.

McCauley, L. M. *Catalogue of Paintings, Etchings, Engravings and Sculpture of the Union League Club*. Chicago, 1907.

Martin, Edward M. *The Rôle of the Bar in Electing the Bench in Chicago*. Chicago, 1936.

Masters, Edgar Lee. *The Tale of Chicago*. New York, 1933.

Merriam, Charles Edward. *Chicago*. New York, 1929.

Milton, G. F. *Abraham Lincoln and the Fifth Column*. New York, 1942.

Moore, Edward. *Forty Years of Opera in Chicago*. New York, 1930.

Norton, Samuel Wilber. *Chicago Traction*. Chicago, 1907.

Otis, Philo A. *The Chicago Symphony Orchestra, 1891–1924*. Chicago, 1924.

Patterson, Joseph Medill. "Marshall Field's Will." *Collier's*, June 2, 1906.

Peterson, Virgil. *Barbarians in Our Midst*. Boston, 1952.

Poole, Ernest. *Giants Gone*. New York, 1943.

Randall, Frank A. *History of Chicago Buildings*. Urbana, Illinois, 1949.

Rhodes, James F. *History of the United States from the Compromise of 1850*. New York, 1895.

Scudder, Horace Elisha. *James Russell Lowell, A Biography*. New York, 1901.

Shackleton, Robert. *The Book of Chicago*. Philadelphia, 1920.

Simpson, Herbert D. *Tax Racket and Tax Reform in Chicago*. Chicago, 1930.

Spirit of the Union League Club, The. Chicago, 1926.

Stead, William T. *If Christ Came to Chicago*. Chicago, 1894.

Stidger, Felix G. *Treason History of the Order of Sons of Liberty*. Chicago, 1903.

Stone, Melville E. *Fifty Years A Journalist*. New York, 1923.

Sullivan, L. H. *Autobiography of an Idea*. American Institute of Architects, 1926.

Sutherland, Douglas. *Fifty Years on the Civic Front*. Chicago, 1943.

Tallmadge, Thomas. *A Story of Architecture in America*. New York, 1927.

Timmons, Bascom N. *Portrait of an American*. New York, 1953.

Union League of America—The True Designs of the Chicago Convention, or the Conspiracy of the Rebels and the Peace Democracy. New York, 1864.

Upton, George P. *Musical Memories*, Chicago, 1908.

Wendt, Lloyd and Kogan, Herman. *Give the Lady What She Wants*. Chicago, 1952.

——— *Big Bill of Chicago*, Indianapolis, 1953.

REPORTS

Adjutant General's Report. Springfield, Ill., 1898.

Fifty Years of Progress. Fiftieth Anniversary Issue of the Field Museum News. Chicago, 1943.

Social Evil In Chicago. Official Report of the Vice Commission of Chicago. Chicago, 1911.

The Negro in Chicago. Report of the Commission on Race Relations. Chicago, 1922.

Year Book of the Commercial Club. Chicago, 1939–40.

Year Books and Annual Reports of the Union League Club of Chicago. Chicago, 1880–1954.

MANUSCRIPTS

Boss, Henry B. *Secret Political Societies*, and other Mss regarding the history of the Union League of America in Chicago and the Midwest, including an unsigned Ms addressed to the Rev. William Barry; in the Chicago Historical Society, Autograph Letters, Vol. XXXIX, pp. 508–566.

Historical material on the Union League Club of Chicago compiled by J. Frank Aldrich.

Historical material on the Union League of America in the archives of the Union League Civic and Arts Foundation.

Minutes of the Union League Club of Chicago Board of Directors, Board of Managers, and Annual Meetings of the Club, complete from the day of founding, in the office of the Club Secretary.

Minutes of the Union League Club Auxiliary Association.

MAGAZINES

Architectural Reviewer, February, 1897. Burnham Library at the Chicago Art Institute.

Atlantic Monthly, July, 1865.

Graphic News (Chicago), June 12, 1886–March 22, 1890.

Review of Reviews, 1893.
Union League Club Bulletin.
Union League Men and Events.

NEWSPAPERS

Chicago American
Chicago Chronicle
Chicago Daily News
Chicago Dispatch
Chicago Evening Journal
Chicago Evening Mail
Chicago Evening Telegraph
Chicago Herald
Chicago Herald American
Chicago Herald Examiner
Chicago Inter Ocean
Chicago Post
Chicago Record
Chicago Record Herald
Chicago Times
Chicago Tribune

MISCELLANEOUS

Old Chicago city directories, scrapbooks on John Wentworth, Theodore Roosevelt, and others, as well as books of biographies of prominent Chicagoans consulted at the Chicago Historical Society. Miscellaneous material also included letters and statements from old members of the Union League Club, interviews, and tape recordings. Much material was obtained from the *Chicago American* newspaper morgue and the archives of the Chicago Crime Association.

INDEX

346

PRINTED IN U.S.A.